Pleasures of the Good Earth

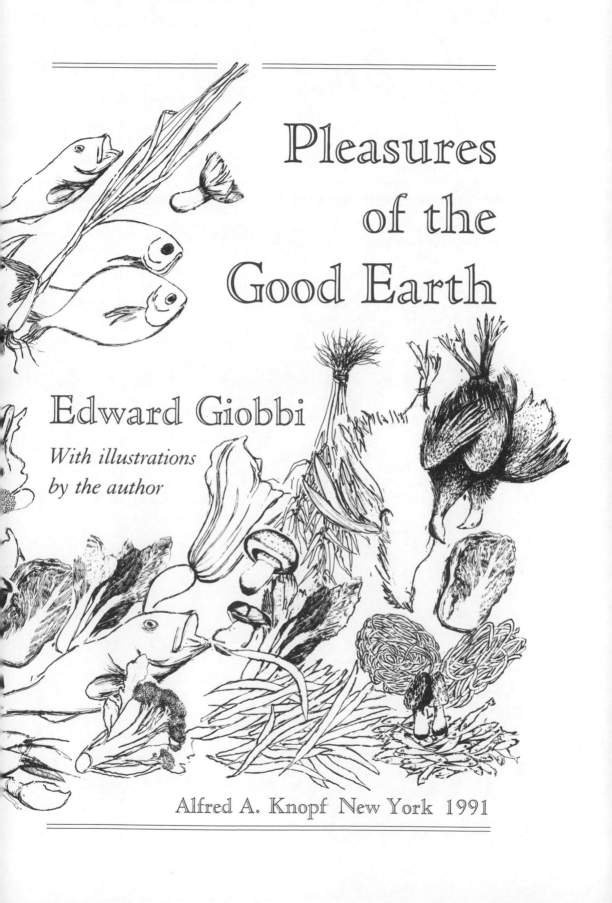

Pleasures
of the
Good Earth

Edward Giobbi

*With illustrations
by the author*

Alfred A. Knopf New York 1991

THIS IS A BORZOI BOOK
PUBLISHED BY ALFRED A. KNOPF, INC.

Library of Congress Cataloging-in-Publication Data
Giobbi, Edward.
   Pleasures of the good earth / by Edward Giobbi.—1st ed.
   (The Knopf cooks American series; 6)
      p.   cm.
   Includes index.
   ISBN 0-394-56130-9
   1. Cookery, Italian.   2. Gardening.   I. Title.   II. Series.
TX723.G483   1990
641.5945—dc20   90-4984
                                                       CIP

Manufactured in the United States of America
First Edition

To my father, Achille Giobbi

Contents

Foreword

I remember the first time I met Ed Giobbi. I liked him instantly. I think it must have been the earnest and sensual way he talked about food that made me feel in the presence of a kindred spirit. I felt like we had been friends forever. We started talking about what was then a new fascination of mine, but something he had eaten all his life: the deliciously bitter vegetable colza, or rape, or in Italian, *broccoletti di rape.* He gave me a recipe on the spot: cook some dry noodles the way you would cook a risotto by sautéing them in olive oil and lots of garlic, then slowly add liquid, and add chopped, cooked rape and Parmesan cheese at the end.

This appealing recipe is consistent with the approach to food and life that I find throughout Ed Giobbi's cooking and writing: directness (especially from garden to table) and instinctive healthy balance. In our modern American preoccupation with food, I fear that we get side-tracked seeking to make food that impresses rather than nourishes. What is so distinctive about the cooking in this book is that there is flavor and richness here that is the product not of manipulation, but of a profound respect for what comes from the earth and a true connection to nature and the cycle of the seasons. The chapter on chickens is particularly expressive of Ed Giobbi's determination to have tasty natural ingredients; and he doesn't gloss over the commitment required when he gives instructions on how to buy, raise, and butcher the birds.

Our connection to the food chain should not be a casual one, least of all to the cook. Ed Giobbi shows us how reckoning with this process awakens not just the mind, but the senses as well, and what a delicious and rewarding awakening that can be. Certainly in our naive way we have tried to follow the path of Chez Panisse, being convinced that healthy and responsibly produced food is also the most gratifying to the palate.

Wendell Berry writes rather poignantly in *The Unsettling of America* that "if you take away from food the wholeness of growing it or take away the joy and conviviality of preparing it in your own home, then I believe you are talking about a whole new definition of the human being." In the book you hold in your hands, Ed Giobbi's compelling words and tastes prove that there is still a human being by the old definition among us. May we go on hearing from him for some time to come.

—ALICE WATERS
December 1990

Vegetables
and
Wild Edibles

Spring   Summer

Mostly Fall and Winter

Wild Mushrooms

Vegetables

I think that no matter how old or infirm I may become, I will always plant a large garden in the spring. Who can resist the feelings of hope and joy that one gets from participating in nature's rebirth? I certainly can't. It is one of the most natural human instincts to want to make things grow, to nourish our own bodies and those of the ones we love. Such instincts are not satisfied by going to the supermarket and buying an uninspired plastic bag of vegetables. In fact, that is one of the quickest ways to squelch our natural impulses. But if you let the vegetables emerge, you will have not only the satisfaction of harvesting good things to eat but also the profound serenity that derives from a personal relationship with the earth.

I believe that most human unhappiness comes from alienation, from the feeling that one is not part of anything. But we all are part of the earth, and we need, particularly today, to reinstate our partnership with it. The gentle whiff of warm outdoor air after the many months of indoor living that winter imposes, the musky smell of freshly turned earth, the delicate sweetness of a spring rain—that is the beginning when we plant seeds in the ground. And the rest of the year we reap the rewards.

The rewards are what we eat, and cooking, to me, is part of this whole scheme. When I plant my garden, I put in only the vegetables and herbs and aromatics that I like, that I know I will use throughout the year. (I admit I always plant too much, but that is because I love to see things grow and I like to share my surplus.) I look forward to each crop and I anticipate with pleasure the seasonal accents that the garden

3

and the wild edibles on the land around us provide. There is a rhythm to the year and a wonderful variety to the dishes that come to our table.

I have structured this chapter in accordance with that rhythm, starting with the first spring crop, as well as the "found" vegetables (page 8) and the "wintered-over" vegetables (page 11) that nature provides each year. Then I move on to the summer and fall harvests and the vegetables that are sweetened by a touch of frost. Invariably, the vegetables, both cultivated and wild, that are harvested at the same time have a natural affinity, and I use them in seasonal combinations all through the year—in soups, in stews and mélanges, in sauces, in egg dishes, in mixed fries. So you will find an abundance of such recipes scattered throughout this chapter.

Finally, I end with one of nature's greatest gifts—wild mushrooms. I urge you to learn something about the mushrooms that grow in the country around you and to take advantage of the riches you may have been missing.

A Word to Beginning Gardeners

I think the most important piece of advice for a beginning gardener is to avoid starting with too large a garden. Plant a size you can manage without anger or frustration, and be sure you don't plant the entire garden in two weeks. It is better to plant your peas and lettuce early in the spring. Later, put in your tomatoes and peppers when the soil is warm and all danger of frost is gone. In late June plant your parsnips and a second planting of lettuce, rucola (arugula), green beans, savoy cabbage, and some tomatoes for a late-fall harvest. The idea is to stretch out your planting so that everything does not ripen at once.

Don't waste your time resenting the care your plants need by planting more than you can handle. Don't make a fetish of weeding. Get to know your soil and work with it rather than against it. Understand your climate. Garden at a comfortable pace; don't make it a penance. Productive gardens are synonymous with relaxed gardeners.

Gardening can be boiled down to a simple moral that should apply to all of man's different relationships to the earth: Don't fight nature, work with it.

SPRING

Asparagus

Early each spring, I continue to get asparagus from the bed I planted about 25 years ago. I put in 3-year-old roots and I refrained from harvesting the spears the first year (if I'd put in 1- or 2-year-old roots, I would have had to wait 2 or 3 years). I have never used sprays or pesticides on my asparagus, and to date I haven't had to worry about pests. When the stalks are ready—that is, when they're about 10 inches high, which usually occurs some time in early May—I cut them off with a sharp knife level to the ground.

I figure on enjoying 2 full months of homegrown asparagus—May and June. I stop cutting the first or second week of July to allow the roots of the plants to develop strength, which is necessary for next year's growth.

A final note about asparagus: the older the plants, the thicker the spears. Also, if cooked immediately after cutting, asparagus is as sweet as sugar, not unlike peas in that regard. And it is wonderful raw.

To cook asparagus, I steam, sauté, bake, or grill it. I never peel my garden asparagus; I just remove the tough ends.

To steam: Place the trimmed stalks in a colander set over boiling water and cook until tender but firm. A pound of average-thick spears should take about 6 minutes. Drain and dress with extra virgin olive oil, a little chopped flat-leaved parsley, fresh lemon juice, and salt and freshly ground black pepper to taste. (You can also add finely chopped garlic if you like.) Let stand 15 minutes before serving.

To sauté: Cut the stalks into 2-inch pieces. Cover the bottom of a skillet with olive oil, heat, then sauté the asparagus pieces until crisp-tender. I use sautéed asparagus as a bright, firm garnish for pasta and fish dishes (pages 91 and 151), and there is a natural affinity between eggs and asparagus (see page 44 for a frittata recipe).

To bake: Place whole stalks in one layer in an oiled baking tray, salt lightly, and sprinkle with olive oil. Bake uncovered in a preheated 400° oven for about 7 minutes.

To grill: Roll the asparagus stalks in olive oil and grill, turning often, over hot coals, about 5 to 6 minutes. May also be grilled under a hot broiler.

Asparagus with Pesto: Steam asparagus until tender and sauce with pesto (page 228) thinned with an equal amount of warm water. Season with salt and freshly ground black pepper to taste.

Asparagus and Mint with Potatoes

Here is a particularly appealing asparagus recipe that uses wild spearmint and scallions, which make their appearance at the same time as asparagus stalks.

Serves 4 as a vegetable course.

3 medium potatoes, unpeeled
2 tablespoons olive oil
1 medium onion, thinly sliced
3 cups chopped asparagus, cut
   into 1-inch pieces
3 tablespoons coarsely chopped
   fresh spearmint

1 cup sliced scallions
¼ cup chicken or beef broth,
   preferably homemade (for
   chicken broth, see page 194)
Salt and freshly ground black
   pepper to taste

In a pot of boiling water, boil the potatoes in their skins until cooked but firm. Be careful not to overcook them. Remove from the water and allow to cool.

Heat the oil in a medium skillet until hot. Add the onion, and when it begins to brown, add the asparagus pieces. Cook about 3 or 4 minutes, stirring.

Meanwhile, peel and slice the potatoes ¼ inch thick. Toss the potatoes in with the asparagus and add the spearmint, scallions, and broth. Cover and simmer for 5 minutes, tossing carefully to prevent the potato slices from breaking up. Season to taste with salt and pepper.

Asparagus with Shrimp

The colors are marvelous in this basic stir-fry. Early stalks are preferred, as they are thinner and cook more quickly.

Serves 4.

6 tablespoons olive oil
1 pound asparagus, preferably
    thin spears, cut into 1½-inch
    pieces

1 pound shrimp, shelled
Salt and freshly ground black
    pepper or hot pepper flakes
    to taste

2 fat cloves garlic, finely
    chopped
2 tablespoons finely chopped
    flat-leaved parsley

Heat 3 tablespoons of the oil in a medium skillet until hot. Add the asparagus pieces and sauté, uncovered, over moderate heat, tossing until tender but not overcooked. Remove the asparagus with a slotted spoon and set aside.

Heat the remaining 3 tablespoons of oil in the skillet until hot. Add the shrimp and salt and pepper or hot pepper flakes—I prefer the flakes—and cook briefly, uncovered, over high heat, tossing constantly, then add the garlic and parsley. When the shrimp are pink (about 1 to 2 minutes—be careful not to overcook them) return the asparagus to the skillet and cook together for about 30 seconds to 1 minute; adjust seasonings. Serve at once.

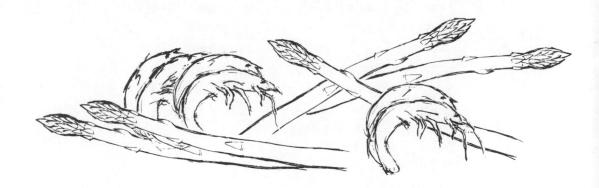

Found Vegetables of Spring

After a hard northeastern winter there is nothing more glorious than to see the first green that appears in my garden before it shows up anywhere else on our property. The crimson radicchio buds emerge in late February and early March, then in March and April the garden is speckled with fragile forms—from onions, garlic, turnip and parsnip greens to wintered-over leeks and the little cabbages that sprout from old stalks. The horseradish sends up shoots and the whole garden comes to life. Fiddlehead ferns appear in marshy spots, wild mint grows along the edge of the lawn, and dandelion greens add to the profusion. Of course, we never use pesticides of any kind, and in turn the land is good to us.

What is so wonderful to me is how well all these vegetables complement one another in flavor and texture when cooked together. This is my favorite vegetable dish—a stew of tender wild things and reborn vegetables cooked long and slow, with garlic, potatoes, and olive oil to bind the flavors. The taste is unique and I look forward to it each spring. You can use any combination of "found" vegetables and garden greens that come up in the spring in your area.

Stew of Found Vegetables

Serves 8.

About 2½ pounds found
   vegetables, coarsely
   chopped
4 cups diced potatoes
4 tablespoons olive oil
1½ to 2 tablespoons minced
   garlic

Hot pepper flakes to taste
   (optional)
Salt to taste
Garnish: Extra virgin olive oil

Put the vegetables and potatoes in a pot of boiling salted water and cook 4 minutes. Drain, reserving about 3 cups of the water. Heat the oil in a large skillet, add the garlic and optional hot pepper flakes, and cook until the garlic begins to take on color. Add the parboiled vegetables along with 1 cup of the reserved liquid and a little salt. Cover and simmer over low to medium heat, adding more water as needed. Stir occasionally, crushing the potatoes after they become soft. Cook about 1 hour. Garnish each serving with a little extra virgin olive oil, if desired.

Fiddlehead Ferns

Fiddlehead ferns are best cooked by themselves, not in combination. They have a unique flavor.

Serves 3.

½ pound fiddlehead ferns
2 tablespoons olive oil
1 clove garlic, finely chopped

Salt and freshly ground black
pepper to taste

Wash the ferns and steam them for 5 minutes.
In a medium skillet, heat the oil and sauté the ferns and garlic until the garlic begins to color. Add salt and pepper to taste. Serve hot.

Peas

By early to mid-May the peas that I planted in mid-March are ready. The pods are round and fully formed. Like corn, they are very sweet when newly picked, so pick them just before you are ready to use them and don't refrigerate them. If the peas are left to stand, the sugar in them turns to starch, at which point they become tough and not as sweet. I also put in edible pea pods (snow peas), which should be harvested when the pods are still relatively flat, and sugar snaps, which should be picked when the peas are fully formed.

I always cook peas in boiling, salted water to cover; they are tender in about 5 minutes. I use cooked peas when they are in season as a garnish for many kinds of pasta. When I cook them in mélanges of vegetables that are harvested at the same time—spinach, asparagus, and leeks—I blanch them first just until the water returns to a boil, then drain immediately. And I feature peas in spring soups.

I use edible pea pods Chinese style when I make a stir-fry with cut-up meat or fish, never in a dish cooked in liquid. Edible pea pods become inedible when stewed.

Sugar snaps I cook just a minute and use primarily as a garnish.

Peas with Prosciutto

My favorite way of serving fresh peas is with prosciutto as an accent or with tiny onions, as in the variation that follows.

Serves 4.

2 cups shelled peas
1½ tablespoons olive oil
1 medium onion, finely
  chopped
3 tablespoons coarsely chopped
  prosciutto (page 264)

1 tablespoon chopped flat-
  leaved parsley
¼ cup chicken broth, preferably homemade (page 194)
Salt and freshly ground black
  pepper to taste

Blanch the peas by plunging them into 4 cups boiling, salted water. Drain when the water returns to a boil.

In a skillet, heat the olive oil and sauté the onion and prosciutto until the onion turns translucent. Add the blanched peas, parsley, chicken broth, and salt and pepper. Simmer for 15 minutes.

VARIATION WITH TINY ONIONS AND MINT: Blanch as above **1 cup peas** along with **1½ cups small white onions,** peeled.* Drain and transfer to a small pan. Add **1 tablespoon chopped fresh mint or 1 teaspoon dried, salt** and **freshly ground black pepper** to taste, and **½ cup chicken or beef broth.** Cover and cook over moderate heat for 5 to 10 minutes, or until the peas are tender. Drizzle a little **olive oil** over each portion.

* To peel: Rub 2 or 3 little onions together in your hands, and the skins will come off.

Wintered-Over Vegetables— Leeks and Parsnips

Leeks: The leeks that appear in early spring are especially good, much better than the ones harvested in summer. The fact that they are the first vegetable to come up makes them all the more desirable, and they should be dug up quickly before they develop a woody center. I like them best braised. First I cut off the green ends, and then I make a slit in the white part so that I can wash each leek thoroughly. I arrange the leeks in a shallow baking dish with finely chopped onions and flat-leaved parsley sprinkled on top and about half an inch of broth poured around, then bake them, covered, in a 375° oven until they are tender and succulent. They'll taste as sweet as candy bars.

Parsnips: The parsnips that have been left in the garden for spring harvest are big and fat and full of sugar. Like leeks, they should be harvested rather quickly before the weather starts to warm up and they develop a tough core. As soon as the parsnip sends up a center shoot, then it's too late. I like parsnips braised in the same way I cook leeks, above. First scrape off the skin, then cut them lengthwise in threes.

Spinach

I thin my spinach, which I've planted in mid-March, by pulling up the young shoots, leaving a plant to develop every 10 inches or so. I use the young leaves in mixtures of found spring vegetable greens (page 8) and in soups. They are also good sautéed with peas when the garden yields just a handful of each.

Garden spinach does not need to be stemmed. There may be a few tougher end pieces that you'll want to discard, but generally the stems are tender.

Baked Spinach

My favorite way of preparing mature spinach is baking it with a little olive oil and garlic. The taste is intense and the color a brilliant, deep green.

Serves 4.

4 tablespoons olive oil
2 pounds spinach
2 cloves garlic, finely chopped

Salt and freshly ground black
   pepper to taste

Preheat oven to 400°.

Pour some of the olive oil into a large ovenproof casserole. Add the spinach and garlic and toss, then drizzle on the remaining olive oil. Salt lightly and grind fresh pepper over the spinach. Bake, covered, stirring occasionally. The spinach will be done in 15 to 20 minutes; don't over-cook it.

Spinach Sauce

This is a springtime green sauce or pesto for pasta, fish, or meat.

Serves 6 as a sauce for fish or meat, 4 as a sauce for 12 ounces of pasta.

1 pound spinach
2 tablespoons extra virgin olive
   oil
2 tablespoons flour, or 4
   tablespoons bread crumbs
½ cup chicken broth, preferably homemade (page 194)

Pinch of freshly grated nutmeg
2 tablespoons freshly grated
   Parmesan
Salt to taste
2 tablespoons pine nuts
   (optional)

Bring 2 to 3 cups of salted water to boil in a large pot, then add the spinach and cook, uncovered, for 2 to 5 minutes. Drain, let cool, and squeeze out all the moisture. Coarsely chop the spinach.

In a saucepan, heat the oil until hot. Toss in the flour or bread crumbs and, using a fork, mix completely with the oil. Add the broth, nutmeg, cheese, and salt to taste, stirring constantly; bring to a boil. Stir in the chopped spinach and pine nuts, if using. Transfer the mixture to a food processor and blend to a sauce, or grind in a mortar with a pestle.

Dandelion Greens and Other Wild Edibles

How can anyone object to a plant that is delicious to eat, does not require any care, is very nourishing, and produces beautiful yellow blossoms as well? And yet many people spend great sums of money on toxic chemicals to destroy their dandelions.

Dandelion greens appear every spring and are best to eat, either raw or cooked, in our northeastern region in early April before the blossoms develop. By mid-May the taste is stronger, but the leaves are still good in soups. Dandelions are one of the spring plants I look forward to, especially since they precede even my earliest lettuces. Aside from their good, slightly bitter taste, the greens are considered by Italians to be a tonic for the blood and the stomach.

A SIMPLE DANDELION SALAD: (Serves 4.) Wash and dry about **8 handfuls freshly picked dandelion greens.** Peel **2 small Kirby cucumbers** and cut them into chunks. Cut **2 tomatoes** into wedges. Now toss everything together and season to taste with **extra virgin olive oil, wine vinegar, salt, and freshly ground black pepper** to taste.

Other wild edibles that we enjoy are:

Purslane: A prolific weed that is found from the Atlantic to the Pacific. People used to tear it out of their gardens; now the seed for it is sold in garden catalogs. And no wonder—the fresh, succulent leaves are wonderful in salads. Moreover, according to the *New England Journal of Medicine,* purslane is the richest source of omega (the three fatty acids) of any vegetable yet examined. So eat purslane; it doesn't cost anything, it's tasty, and it's good for you.

PURSLANE SALAD: (Serves 2.) Wash and dry **2 cups purslane.** Slice **2 firm, not fully ripened tomatoes.** Toss in a salad bowl with **2 tablespoons wine vinegar, 2 tablespoons extra virgin olive oil,** and **salt and freshly ground black pepper** to taste.

Lamb's-quarter: A common weedy goosefoot with gracious foliage that is sometimes used as a potherb. It is best cooked in a vegetable stew or mélange.

Redroot: A weed that is distinguished by its red stem and leaves that resemble New Zealand spinach. I cook it as I would spinach or other greens.

Dandelion Greens with Broccoli and Potatoes

Serves 4 to 6.

10 cups freshly picked
   dandelion greens
2 medium potatoes, peeled
   and sliced
6 cups broccoli, cut into bite-
   sized pieces
Salt to taste

3 tablespoons olive oil
4 cloves garlic, or more to
   taste, coarsely chopped
Hot pepper flakes to taste
   (optional)
Garnish: Extra virgin olive oil
   (optional)

In a large pot of boiling water to cover, boil the dandelion greens and potatoes for 5 minutes. Add the broccoli and salt and cook for 2 minutes. Drain, reserving 1 cup of the water.

Heat the oil until hot in a shallow saucepan. Add the garlic and hot pepper flakes, if using, and cook, uncovered, until the garlic begins to color. Add the drained vegetables and the reserved cup of water, cover, and simmer for about 40 minutes. Halfway through the cooking time, check to see if more salt is needed. Garnish each portion with a teaspoon of extra virgin olive oil, if desired.

VARIATION WITH POTATOES AND ANCHOVIES: Boil **8 cups dandelion greens** with **4 medium potatoes, peeled and cut in quarters,** for 5 minutes. Sauté **4 cloves garlic, sliced,** in **3 tablespoons olive oil,** and when they begin to color, add **2 anchovy fillets, chopped.** Cook everything together with the reserved cooking water as above.

Dandelion Greens and Bean Soup

Serves 4 to 6.

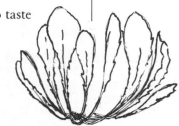

1 cup dried white beans (Great Northern or cannellini)
3 cups water
1 medium onion, coarsely chopped
2 whole cloves garlic
1 rib celery, finely chopped
Hot pepper flakes to taste (optional)
Salt to taste
8 cup freshly picked dandelion greens
⅓ cup rice
Garnish: Extra virgin olive oil

Soak the beans overnight in 4 cups water. Drain.

Combine the beans, the 3 cups of water, onion, garlic, celery, hot pepper flakes, if using, and salt in a medium pot. Cover and cook over low heat, just below the boiling point, for about 2 hours. Add the dandelion greens, cover, and cook for 1 hour. Add the rice and cook until tender, about 15 minutes. Serve in soup bowls and garnish each serving with olive oil.

Beans

As soon as the ground is warm, I plant a variety of beans to stimulate new and different recipes. Each variety has a distinctive taste that is brought out by the way you cook and season it. We have beans from mid-June until frost.

French beans: I do three plantings so that I will have them all summer. I simply steam the whole stemmed beans until just tender, then run them under cold water and dress them with lemon juice, chopped mint, chopped garlic, and a little extra virgin olive oil.

Italian pole beans: These are wide beans and I sometimes blanch them whole. But more often, I cut them in 2-inch sections and cook them in vegetable mélanges (potatoes and tomatoes make a favorite mix).

Asparagus beans: I harvest these long, thin beans in July. I usually cut them into 3-inch lengths and steam or simmer them with tomatoes. I use them primarily in salads.

Shell beans and cranberry beans: The beans have to be well developed in the pod before picking—about mid-August. Shell the beans, cook in water to cover 1 inch until tender—20–30 minutes. Drain and serve as a vegetable tossed with olive oil; they are also good in soups. They freeze well, and I usually package them along with the vegetables I would cook them with—stewed tomatoes and chopped celery seasoned with parsley and basil. They may also be dried (page 72).

Lima beans: I grow limas for soups and vegetable stews. They freeze well, too. I do not dry them.

Fava beans (broad beans): Still virtually unknown to most Americans, fava beans are adored by Italians and are best eaten raw, and the fresher, the better. I was first introduced to the classic combination of fresh fava beans with olive oil, fresh Pecorino cheese, and Italian bread by a marvelous old Italian, whom we met one day outside of Rome when I was there studying on a Guggenheim Fellowship. He was a harness maker and was sitting on his donkey cart when we started talking. He confessed that beyond all else fresh favas dipped in a little olive oil and eaten with fresh Pecorino cheese and a little good crusty bread were his favorite food.

Favas planted in March will be finished, gone, by the end of June. Pick the pods when they are full and round. To eat raw, first remove the bean from the pod, then remove the skin that covers the bean. I eat them like peanuts. They are also good in soup. As an added bonus, fava plants actually nourish the soil in which they are grown. For that reason, I always leave my fava plants in the ground over the winter.

Beans for drying: Simply leave the beans attached to plants until they are dried—harvest the pods, then shell them. Keep the shelled beans in a dry environment. Leave them in a paper bag.

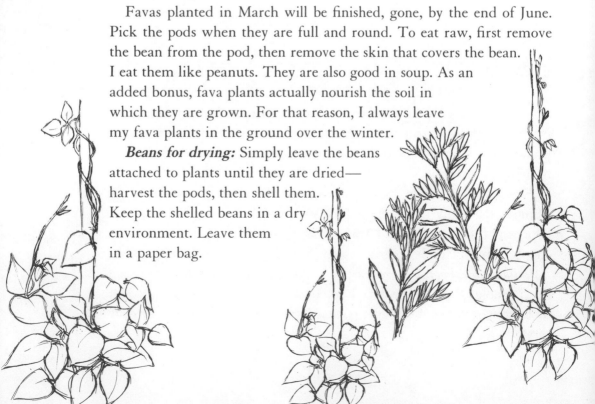

Green Beans and Potato Salad

Note the absence of any vinegar in this salad. The combination of oil and lemon juice seems to bring out the sweetness in the young beans. You can add a can of Italian-style tuna, drained, broken-up and folded into the salad, for a more substantial dish.

Serves 4.

½ pound tender green beans, ends snapped off

2 medium potatoes, boiled with their skins on and cooled

1 small onion, thinly sliced

3 tablespoons extra virgin olive oil

Juice of 1 lemon

2 tablespoons coarsely chopped fresh mint

Salt to taste

Cook the beans in boiling salted water, uncovered, until crisp-tender, but do not overcook. Drain and rinse in cold water.

Peel and cut the potatoes into ¼-inch-thick slices. Gently toss all the ingredients together in a bowl. Serve at room temperature, and do not refrigerate.

Green Beans and Rucola Salad

Serves 4.

1 pound green beans, broken into 1½-inch pieces

3 cups just-picked rucola (arugula), rinsed and patted dry

2 tablespoons extra virgin olive oil

2 tablespoons white or red good-quality wine vinegar

2 cloves garlic, finely chopped

Salt and freshly ground black pepper to taste

In a vegetable steamer over boiling water, steam the beans until tender, about 8 minutes. Rinse immediately in cold water and pat dry with paper towels.

In a salad bowl combine the beans with the remaining ingredients, toss gently, and serve.

Shell Beans Florentine Style

This dish is excellent with canned tuna or broiled meats and fish.

Serves 3.

2 cups shell beans, shelled (also known as cranberry beans)
2 cloves garlic, finely chopped
Salt and freshly ground black pepper to taste

2 tablespoons extra virgin olive oil
1 tablespoon chopped fresh sage, or 1 teaspoon dried
Garnish: Extra virgin olive oil

Put all of the ingredients in a small, heavy pot, preferably a terra-cotta pot. Cover the ingredients with about 1 inch of water. Cover tightly and cook over low heat for about 2½ hours, stirring occasionally.

Serve the beans hot or at room temperature. Garnish each portion with a little extra virgin olive oil.

Cranberry Beans and Tomato Salad

Cranberry beans are especially pretty, and in combination with tomatoes they make a very handsome dish. We often have this salad for a light lunch with quickly fried fish.

Serves 4.

2 cups cooked cranberry beans or other shell beans (page 16)
2 semiripe tomatoes, peeled and diced
1 small white onion, finely chopped
2 tablespoons coarsely chopped fresh basil

3 tablespoons extra virgin olive oil
3 tablespoons white wine vinegar or fresh lemon juice
Salt and freshly ground black pepper to taste

In a salad bowl combine all the ingredients and toss gently. Serve this salad at room temperature, and do not refrigerate.

Minestrone with Fava Beans

If you have planted fava beans, use some of them in this warming, light vegetable soup; otherwise, lima beans are very good.

Serves 4 to 6.

2 cups shelled fava beans
1 small onion, coarsely chopped
1 rib celery, coarsely chopped
2 tablespoons olive oil
1 tablespoon finely chopped
    flat-leaved parsley
1 carrot, coarsely chopped

1 cup coarsely chopped
    tomatoes
5 cups water
4 tablespoons rice
2 cups chopped spinach
Salt to taste

Cook the fava beans in a bot of boiling salted water for 2 minutes, drain, and rinse under cold running water. Remove the outer skins, discard, and reserve the beans.

In a soup pot, sauté the onion and celery in the olive oil, over moderate heat, until the onion begins to brown. Add the parsley, carrot, and tomatoes and cook, stirring, for several minutes. Add the water and beans, cover, and cook over low to moderate heat for about 50 minutes. Add the rice, cover, and cook for 10 minutes. Add the spinach, cover, and cook over low heat until the rice is tender, about 10 to 12 minutes. Add salt to taste and serve the soup hot.

Salad Greens

I get an early crop of salad greens by starting them in a cold frame. The next crop I plant in mid-May from seed, and after that I plant a mixture of the following seeds every 15 to 20 days until frost:

Royal oak leaf
Black-seeded Simpson
Bibb lettuce
Ruby
Romaine

I also plant:

Rucola (also known as arugula or rocket): This is best when the weather is cool. It gets stronger and more tough in summer, and the fall crop is good again. As well as in salads, it is good in soups and to make a pesto for pasta (see Summer Sauce, page 231).

Radicchio di Verona: I learned to grow radicchio by trial and error. My first growth was tall, green, and very bitter. Unimpressed, I let the plant die back and then the following February red heads peeked out of the snow, and when I harvested them, they were delicious. I have since learned—thanks to the deer who nibbled those green shoots down to the ground—that if I want fall radicchio, I cut back the greens in mid-September when they are about 3 feet high, and soon after the red heads will appear. So now I have it both ways: a crop for early spring and a crop for late fall.

Radicchio di Treviso: This is an elongated radicchio rather than the familiar round cabbagelike head. It is good for braising.

One of my favorite ways of using the first spring lettuces is to dress them with extra virgin olive oil, good wine vinegar or lemon juice, and a little salt and then mix them in with freshly cooked spaghettini.

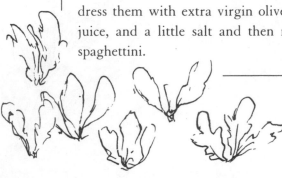

SUMMER

Summer Squash

Zucchini is my favorite summer squash.
As soon as the ground is warm, I plant just
one crop because it is so plentiful. I like
to harvest the zucchini when it is
no more than 5 inches long.
Small squash does not have
much moisture and has an
intense, delicate flavor. I cut it
up (unpeeled, of course) and sauté it
or mix it with other vegetables in a
stew or in a chicken dish.

When I do plant yellow squash, I pick it
when it is only 4 inches long—after that it gets
tough—and I sauté it with zucchini, both sliced
lengthwise, along with onions and tomatoes.

I love squash blossoms—fried, stuffed, pureed as
a sauce (see Pasta with Zucchini Blossom–Tomato Puree,
page 97). If you have your own garden, you can pick flowers
with the zucchini still attached when the fruit is 2 to 3 inches long.
Check the blossoms thoroughly for insects—in particular, bees—then
rinse, if necessary, and shake them dry. Sometimes insects become
trapped in the blossoms when they close, in which case make a vertical
slit through one side of each blossom with a small sharp knife and gently
shake. Dip the whole thing in batter or just in milk and then flour
and fry in vegetable oil for about 3 to 4 minutes. Delicious.

Fried Zucchini Blossoms

Serves 4.

20 zucchini or other squash
    blossoms, such as pumpkin
    or yellow squash
Flour for dredging
2 egg whites, lightly beaten
2 tablespoons finely chopped
    flat-leaved parsley

Corn oil or other vegetable oil
    for frying
Salt and freshly ground black
    pepper to taste

Dust the cleaned blossoms (page 21) with flour, dip them in the egg whites, and sprinkle each with some of the parsley. Dredge the blossoms in the flour one more time, covering them completely.

Heat about ¾ inch of oil in a large skillet until it is hot but not smoking. Add the blossoms, one at a time, until the skillet is loosely filled, and brown the blossoms lightly, turning them several times. Transfer the blossoms with tongs or a slotted spoon to paper towels to drain, and sprinkle them with salt and pepper. Serve at once. While the first batch is being eaten, fry up the second batch.

Mozzarella-Stuffed Zucchini Blossoms

Unlike simple fried zucchini blossoms that are rolled in flour and egg white, these cheese-filled ones are dipped in whole egg, which, being sturdier, helps maintain the shape of the flower as it cooks.

Serves 2.

½ cup chopped mozzarella
1 tablespoon finely chopped
    flat-leaved parsley
2 anchovy fillets, coarsely
    chopped
4 large zucchini blossoms, each
    about 4 inches long

Freshly ground black pepper to
    taste
Flour for dredging
1 egg, lightly beaten
Corn oil or other vegetable oil
    for frying

Combine the mozzarella, parsley, and anchovies and add pepper to taste. Carefully stuff the cleaned blossoms (page 21) with the filling and gently press the blossoms closed. Dust the stuffed blossoms with flour, dip them, one at a time, in the egg wash, and roll them in the flour, covering them completely. Fry the blossoms according to the directions on opposite page, blot them dry with paper towels, and serve while they are still hot and the cheese is runny.

Meat- and Zucchini-Stuffed Zucchini Blossoms Fried in Beer Batter

Here the blossoms are dipped in beer batter before frying. I chill the batter, not so much to relax the gluten in the flour (although, of course, it does do that), but to establish a real contrast in temperature between the batter and the hot frying oil, which creates a good crisp coating. You can achieve some of the same effect if you add an ice cube to the batter just before use.

Serves 4.

The beer batter:
1 cup all-purpose flour
1 egg white, lightly beaten
1 cup beer, regular or dark, but
    not flat, or dry white wine

Pinch of baking powder

The stuffing:
2 tablespoons olive oil
1 small onion, finely chopped
½ pound lean ground beef or
    pork
1½ pounds grated zucchini,
    drained in a colander for 20
    minutes and squeezed dry

1 tablespoon finely chopped
    flat-leaved parsley
1 egg white, lightly beaten
Pinch of freshly grated nutmeg
Salt and freshly ground black
    pepper to taste

12 large zucchini blossoms,
    each about 4 inches long

Vegetable oil for frying

*Meat- and
Zucchini-
Stuffed
Zucchini
Blossoms
(continued)*

Make the beer batter: Combine all of the batter ingredients in a bowl. Stir well and refrigerate for at least 1 hour.

Make the stuffing: Heat the olive oil in a medium skillet until hot, then add the onion, and cook over moderate heat, uncovered, stirring occasionally, until it turns translucent. Add the ground meat and cook until it begins to brown; stir in the zucchini, cover, and cook for 10 minutes. Transfer the meat mixture to a bowl and toss with the parsley, egg white, nutmeg, and salt and pepper to taste.

Inspect the blossoms for insects, especially bees. With a small sharp knife, slit the zucchini blossoms open and carefully pack each flower with some of the stuffing. Press each blossom gently closed. Heat about ¾ inch of vegetable oil in a skillet until hot. Remove the batter from the refrigerator and stir it well to mix. Dip the stuffed blossoms, one at a time, into the batter, then put them carefully, without crowding them, into the hot oil. Fry the blossoms, turning them with tongs, until nicely browned on all sides. Remove to paper towels to drain. Serve at once as an appetizer or light luncheon.

VARIATION WITH VEGETABLE-STUFFED ZUCCHINI BLOS-SOMS: Coarsely grate **2 zucchini, about 5 inches long,** and **2 medium potatoes, peeled.** Sauté **1 medium onion, finely chopped,** in **3 tablespoons olive oil** until soft; add the grated vegetables and cook over moderate heat, stirring often, until they are browned. Mix in **1 tablespoon finely chopped flat-leaved parsley, 4 tablespoons freshly grated Parmesan,** and **freshly ground black pepper** to taste. Stuff the blossoms, dip them in batter, and fry them as described above. Serve hot.

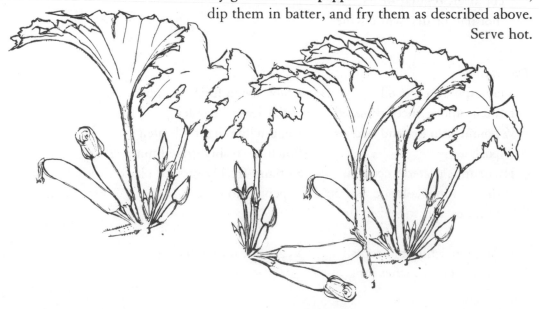

Grated Zucchini and Potatoes with Onions

Here is a loose variation on the grand standby hashed brown potatoes. This dish, which Ellie and I have frequently in the summer, is particularly fine with grilled fish or meats. By the way, while it is nicely brown on the top, this combination should not be pressed into a cake—like a Swiss potato cake, for example. The reason being, there is nothing to hold the ingredients together, no egg or binder, and all you would end up with is smashed grated zucchini and potatoes.

Serves 4.

2 medium zucchini	2 medium onions, finely
2 medium potatoes, peeled	chopped
3 tablespoons extra virgin olive	Salt and freshly ground black
oil	pepper to taste

Grate the zucchini on the coarse side of a cheese grater (you should have about 4 cups), and put in a colander. Salt lightly, and let the colander stand in the sink for about 20 minutes to drain. Grate the potatoes in the same way, then wrap in a piece of cheesecloth and squeeze out the excess moisture. Repeat with the zucchini. (This can also be done, but not as efficiently, with your hands.)

In an ovenproof, medium skillet, heat the oil over moderately high heat until hot. Add the onions and cook until they just begin to wilt. Add the potatoes and zucchini to the skillet and cook, stirring often with a metal spatula, for about 10 minutes. Season with salt and pepper to taste, cover, and lower the heat to moderate. Cook, stirring often to prevent the vegetables from sticking, for 10 minutes more.

While the mixture is cooking, preheat the broiler. Remove the skillet from the heat and place it under the broiler to lightly brown the top of the vegetables.

Herbs

These are the herbs that I use in cooking and want to have available fresh as long as they last. Many of them I dry for winter use. When substituting dried for fresh herbs, you want to use only about half the amount, but always taste to make sure. When I use herbs in cooking, I remember my father's advice that they should go in when you add the wine because the simmering wine is like an infusion and brings out the herb's bouquet. Often I will add a sprinkling of fresh herbs at the end of the cooking for their fragrance.

Basil: Annual. I plant two varieties: large-leaved sweet basil and small-leaved bush basil, known as ornamental, which I prefer for pesto. I use it both fresh and dried. I always put one or two plants in the garden in pots so that I can bring them in before the frost and have fresh basil until Christmastime.

Bay leaf: Perennial. I put a pot in the garden and bring it in for the winter. I use bay leaves both fresh and dried (it is much more pungent dried) in soups and stews. Remember to remove the leaves before serving.

Coriander (also known as cilantro or Chinese parsley): Annual; it reseeds to an extent, but the roots usually freeze. Most Americans in the past were familiar only with the seeds, used in pickling and baking. But it is the leaves that are so popular today with their pungent, earthy flavor. I plant coriander mostly because my wife, Ellie, likes it so much. She uses it on everything. Good only fresh.

Marjoram: Annual. I plant seeds each year and use the leaves, as needed, in stews. In the fall I bring in the whole plant to dry.

Oregano: Perennial. One plant will last for years. I use it in many, many dishes fresh in summer and dried in winter. Dried, it tends to be more pungent; fresh, it has a slightly minty taste.

Parsley: Annual; although it sometimes reseeds, the roots usually freeze. I plant only the flat-leaved Italian variety because it has more flavor than the more familiar curly variety, and I use it generously, always fresh. It's not good dried or frozen.

Rosemary: Perennial. In New England, except by the sea, rosemary can't survive the winter; I plant it in the garden in a pot so I can bring it in for the winter.

Sage: Perennial. A beautiful, hardy plant that spreads each year and is lovely in flower. I use sage leaves, both fresh and dried, in stews and on grilled meats.

Spearmint: Perennial. Another plant that lasts indefinitely. It is the first herb to appear in early spring and the last to go in the fall. I use it fresh in salads and fresh or dried in soups and stews and for tea. I find I use spearmint more and more in cooking.

Tarragon: Perennial that grows abundantly, particularly if you divide the roots every 3 or 4 years. It survives a northeast winter if there is enough snow. I find tarragon good, fresh or dried, with chicken and eggs particularly.

Thyme: Perennial. Another plant that lasts indefinitely and spreads. I use it both fresh and dried, often in place of oregano.

Drying herbs: I dry basil, mint, oregano, and thyme by cutting the branches close to the earth, then tying them together and hanging them. After the herbs are dry—about 6 weeks—I crumble the leaves with my hands and store them in containers. Save the seeds from the basil; you can plant them in the late spring.

Tomatoes

The most important vegetable in our large garden has always been— and still is—the tomato. We plant a great many tomatoes and serve them in a variety of ways when they are fresh. What we don't eat, we can, dry, or make into sauces.

Tomatoes are very satisfying to grow. I like the smell of tomatoes and I love the way the fruits look hanging on the plants, clustered closely together. They produce an abundant amount of fruit and need very little care; I rarely water the plants after they have sent up new shoots and never spray them with chemicals (if I see a tomato bug, I pick it off). All I do is stake and tie the plants and prune them as needed.

I plant five different kinds of tomatoes:

Plum tomatoes: Recently I have been putting in a variety from Italy that produces fruits about 3 inches long or more; San Marzano seed is generally available here and reliable. I use plum tomatoes for sauces and canning.

Orange tomatoes: I discovered these Burpee Jubilees several years ago, and although I was skeptical at first, the seeds produced the most magnificent number of firm, medium-sized bright orange tomatoes. Very meaty but with little juice, they are excellent raw in salads, perfect for making pasta sauce, and excellent when dried.

Medium-sized red tomatoes: I still plant a standard variety of these and use them in the same way I would the orange ones.

Giant tomatoes: I always plant some Big Boy or Big Girl seeds because the big slices look so pretty on a plate. I only use them raw.

Cherry tomatoes: I put in just a couple of plants. They are prolific and produce for a long time. In the fall, I bring some branches in, braid them, and hang them in a dry, airy place, then use them when they are semi-dry.

I rarely bother to peel tomatoes that I pick fresh from the garden.

To Can Tomatoes

There are many ways to can tomatoes. I usually stick to the recipe my mother used.

Drop the tomatoes into boiling water for a few seconds. Remove with a slotted spoon and let cool. Peel the tomatoes, cut them in half, pop out the seeds and remove excess juices by gently squeezing the tomato sections. Place the sections in sterilized jars; sterilize the jars by placing them in boiling water for several minutes. Sterilize the jar caps in the same way. Pack the tomatoes into the sterilized jars, being certain to force the tomatoes into the air spaces. I use the handle of a wooden spoon for this purpose. Put a fresh basil leaf or two in with the tomatoes and 1 teaspoon salt per pint (optional). Screw on the sterilized caps and place the jars, upright, in a canning kettle. Cover the jars with water so that the tops are submerged. Boil the pint jars for 15 minutes (30 minutes for quart jars), remove the jars from the water, and turn the jars upside down to see if the caps are sealed. If the seal is not perfect, air will bubble out. Screw the tops tight and store the jars in a cool place.

This is the method my mother taught me, and it has worked for me for years without the slightest problem; I have had tomatoes last more than 3 years canned in this fashion.*

Can Basic Tomato Sauce (below) in the same manner.

Basic Tomato Sauce

This is the sweetest tomato sauce you'll ever put in your mouth. I use it for innumerable pasta, polenta, fish, and meat dishes, and it is the basis for many kinds of meat sauces. I would probably put up the sauce, but the truth is, I enjoy making it fresh each time with my own canned tomatoes.

Makes 3 to 4 cups.

¼ cup olive oil
2 cups coarsely chopped onions
½ cup sliced carrots
2 cloves garlic, minced
4 cups canned Italian plum
  tomatoes, preferably home-
  canned

Salt and freshly ground black
  pepper to taste
2 tablespoons butter or extra
  virgin olive oil
1 teaspoon dried oregano
1 tablespoon chopped fresh
  basil, or 1 teaspoon dried

Heat the oil in a large skillet, add the onions, carrots, and garlic, and cook, stirring, until they are golden brown. Pour the tomatoes through a vegetable mill or sieve, mashing and pushing the pulp through with a wooden spoon. Discard the seeds. Add the pureed tomatoes to the skillet along with salt and pepper to taste. Simmer 15 minutes, partially covered. Put the sauce through the sieve or food mill, pushing the solids through, and return the strained sauce to the skillet. Add the butter or oil and herbs, partially cover, and simmer 30 minutes more.

---

* If you are overly cautious, you may want to follow the official guidelines in *Putting Food By*, by Greene, Hertzberg, and Vaughan. According to them, to be absolutely safe you should "fill clean scalded jars with boiling-hot tomatoes and their juice, leaving ½ inch of headroom. Add ¼ teaspoon crystalline citric acid (or 1 tablespoon lemon juice) to pints (or twice those amounts for quarts). Adjust lids and process in a boiling-water bath (212 degrees F/100 degrees C) for 35 minutes for pints, 45 minutes for quarts." (Janet Greene, Ruth Hertzberg, and Beatrice Vaughan. *Putting Food By*. 4th edition. Lexington, Massachusetts: The Stephen Greene Press, 1988.)

Red Tomato and Nut Sauce

This sauce or pesto is very fine on boiled or broiled meats or fish or with ricotta-stuffed veal breast (page 238).

Makes 2 cups, enough for 4 servings.

4 tablespoons walnut meats or
  pine nuts
1 tablespoon chopped flat-
  leaved parsley
3 tablespoons extra virgin olive
  oil

1 fat clove garlic, chopped
1½ cups fully ripened, peeled,
  seeded, and coarsely chopped
  tomatoes
1 tablespoon chopped fresh
  mint

Puree all the ingredients in a food processor, or pound them to a light paste in a mortar with a pestle.

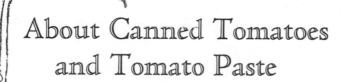

About Canned Tomatoes and Tomato Paste

If you use tomatoes a lot in cooking, it is important to can your own. Even if you don't have a garden, it is worth getting ripe tomatoes from a farmers' market to put them up. Today it is hard to know what you're getting when you buy canned tomatoes.

My observations after testing about a dozen or more different brands, some imported, most grown and packed in California, are as follows. With Italian brands now, it is hard to tell which have sauce added and which do not; most are sold packed in a thick sauce that will give you heartburn just looking at it, and the proportion is more sauce than whole tomatoes. I think this is a rip-off. Whole tomatoes have to be unblemished—one can

see if they are ripe and perfect—whereas tomato sauce can
be made from tomatoes in any condition and flavored to make
the taste acceptable. I do not trust what I cannot see when it comes
to food. American labels are explicit about whether the tomatoes
are packed in sauce, so I look at the fine print. However,
American brands seldom use plum tomatoes, and they are
the best for canning. What is irritating is that the taste of the
sauce is so artificial that it interferes with one's recipe. Furthermore,
you never know how thick it's going to be, and as a result, you aren't
in control.

So if you're going to cook well, make your own tomato sauce. Start
with whole tomatoes in their juice and cook them down to the
consistency and taste that you like. You may want to add tomato
paste, but a word about that.

Tomato paste is one of the most grossly abused products in this
country. It's what gave Italian-American cooking a bad name, and
personally I dislike the taste. In the Old Country, tomato paste was
prepared to use in the winter when fresh tomatoes were not available.
I remember when my relatives would cook down fresh tomatoes,
spread the sauce on wooden boards or terra-cotta tiles, and place
them on their roofs to dry in the hot sun. The dried sauce would be
peeled off the boards, packed into a crock, then covered with oil and
stored in a cool place. Their tomato paste was sweet and rich, and a
small amount would be used to make a delightful sauce. What we
get in little cans is not the same thing, and my advice is to avoid it.

I make homemade tomato paste by using dry plum tomatoes
cut in half and seeded in an electric food dryer until they are
semi-dry (300°F for about 3 hours). I then puree the semi-
dried tomatoes in a food processor with olive oil and
salt and pack the resulting paste in jars with
½ inch of olive oil on top, adding
4 to 5 basil leaves to the paste
as it's packed. Store in
a cool place.

Growing Tomatoes

My father loved to plant tomatoes, and he gave me many tips on how to grow them to large and juicy maturity. He used to talk about tomatoes like they were people, saying that the plants don't like cold water on their leaves, that wet leaves on a tomato plant will encourage insects, so when I do water, I always water my plants as he did, at the roots.

Whenever my father had a few extra tomato plants he couldn't fit into his own garden, he would sneak them among my mother's flowers. This used to infuriate her because she wouldn't discover them until they were bearing fruit, and, being an Italian, my mother would never pull up a productive plant.

Like my parents, I always can my own tomatoes and use them throughout the year. I usually put up about 100 quarts of tomatoes, which is plenty. Also, like my parents, my wife and I seldom eat fresh tomatoes out of season. The Italians have great respect for natural, fresh foods, and often very little respect for those who do not share their feelings.

I remember one visit to Italy in the mid-sixties when we were warned to be very careful selecting fresh tomatoes too early in the season at the markets, because many of the tomato flowers had been injected with hormones in order to force the fruit's maturity weeks sooner than was natural. The Italians called them *pomodore alla pompetta,* which translates as "injected tomatoes." Knowledgeable natives tested the tomato by slicing it open; if there were seeds, then it hadn't been injected. A terrible commentary on a country that has taken such pride in its fresh, natural produce.

Tomato Soup with Broccoli, Corn, and Swiss Chard

This summer combination can be increased by the addition of a half cup or so of small cut pasta half an hour before the end of the cooking time.

Serves 6.

2 tablespoons olive oil
1 medium onion, coarsely
chopped
1½ cups seeded and chopped
fully ripened tomatoes
2 tablespoons coarsely chopped
fresh basil
2 cups corn kernels (cut from
the ears with a sharp knife)

4 cups water
1 rib celery, coarsely chopped
1 cup coarsely chopped Swiss
chard
2 cups chopped broccoli
1 medium carrot, coarsely
chopped
Salt to taste

Heat the olive oil in a medium soup pot and sauté the onion over moderate heat until it just begins to wilt. Add the remaining ingredients, stir, and bring to a boil. Cover and simmer gently, stirring occasionally, for 1½ hours.

Drying Tomatoes—Red or Orange

I am hooked on orange tomatoes, and I like to dry them as well as red ones. The jarred, dried tomatoes will last at least a year and are excellent as a garnish for broiled or boiled meats and fish.

Makes 1 pint.

6 large ripe tomatoes, red or
orange
Salt to taste

2 whole fresh basil leaves
1 clove garlic, sliced (optional)
Extra-virgin olive oil

Cut the tomatoes into approximately 1¼-inch-thick slices. Remove the seeds and dry the tomato slices on an electric dryer. It will take about 3½ hours for the tomatoes to dry out. Be sure to turn the tomatoes over after the first 1½ hours. Once dry, salt the tomatoes and place them in a widemouthed pint jar. Add the basil and garlic slices, if using, and add olive oil to cover until it rises ½ inch above the tomatoes. Cover and refrigerate the jar.

Dried Tomato Sauce

This is particularly good with a thin pasta like spaghettini or linguine. If you cook the pasta in the sauce for the last few minutes of its cooking, the sauce thickens a little and the pasta absorbs the flavor of the tomatoes, making it more tasty. An ideal winter dish when you crave the intense flavor of tomatoes.

Makes enough sauce for ¾ pound of pasta to serve 2 or 3.

3 tablespoons olive oil
1 small onion, finely chopped
¼ cup finely chopped celery
1 tablespoon finely chopped
  flat-leaved parsley
2 cloves garlic, finely chopped
19 dried tomatoes packed in
  olive oil, finely chopped

2 cups chicken broth,
  preferably homemade (page
  194)
Salt and freshly ground black
  pepper or hot pepper flakes
  to taste (I prefer hot pepper)

Heat the oil in a medium skillet, add the onion, celery, and parsley, and cook over moderate heat until the onion becomes translucent. Add the garlic and dried tomatoes and cook until the garlic begins to color. Stir in the broth and season to taste with salt and pepper or hot pepper flakes. Cook over medium to low heat for 15 minutes.

Remembering My Grandfather

When I used to visit my grandfather during the summer on his farm in Centobuchi in the Italian Marches, he would often be sitting on an old wooden chair near a row of tomato plants. Sitting there, he would use the point of a hoe to open small dirt dikes, and allow water to flow into narrow irrigation ditches that surrounded his rows of tomato plants. It would take about 15 minutes to water each row. He would than block up the dike, and move his chair to the next row.

I would often take a chair to the field with me, along with a bottle of wine that had been cooling in the well and two glasses. Then I would ask my grandfather questions about his life and about growing things. He would talk, and we would sip, changing our positions every 15 minutes. I often think of how tranquil, how harmonious, it was to be near those growing plants and flowing water with my grandfather.

My editor suggested I make a drawing of my grandfather sitting on a chair tending to the irrigation of the crops. I thought about it but I could not visualize drawing a portrait from memory of my grandfather that did my memory of him justice.

In 1959, while visiting my grandfather in Italy with my wife, I was admiring a chair my grandfather made. My wife suggested that I ask him for it. I loved it because it reminded me of him. He happily agreed to give it to me and I bought him a large rocking chair. We brought the chair back to America and I sit in it every time we sit down to eat. The chair is a symbol of my grandfather: it is sturdy, honest, practical, and has great dignity—it is a perfect portrait of my grandfather.

Stuffed Tomatoes

There are stuffed tomato recipes and there are stuffed tomato recipes. In most cases the tomatoes have no flavor and all you taste is the stuffing.

What happens is that baking steams the tomato until it becomes soft and loses its fresh taste. I prefer to brown stuffed tomatoes close to the heat under a hot broiler so that the flame chars the top of the tomato half with the stuffing, and the tomato shell remains firm with a distinct broiled tomato accent.

In my opinion the best stuffed tomatoes are made with hard, firm, semiripe tomatoes stuffed with garlic slivers, topped with rosemary (or bread crumbs can be used), and laced with extra virgin olive oil. Served this way at room temperature, they are divine. If I do use a stuffing, I prefer the base to be cooked rice or polenta, which keeps the integrity of the tomato intact.

Garden Tomatoes Stuffed with Polenta

Serves 6.

6 medium semiripe tomatoes

The polenta:

Approximately 1 cup water	Salt to taste
¾ cup fine cornmeal	
2 tablespoons finely chopped flat-leaved parsley	Freshly ground black pepper to taste
3 tablespoons freshly grated Parmesan	Extra virgin olive oil

Slice off the tops of the tomatoes and scoop out the pulp and seeds. Discard the seeds and set the tomatoes aside.

For the polenta: Make polenta with the water, cornmeal, and salt to taste according to the instructions on page 141. Stir the parsley, cheese, and pepper to taste into the polenta.

Preheat the broiler.

Stuff the tomatoes with the polenta filling and place them in a lightly oiled baking pan. Drizzle each tomato with a little olive oil and broil close to the heat until the polenta turns a golden brown.

VARIATION WITH RICE STUFFING: Sauté ⅔ **cup rice** with **1 onion, chopped,** in **2 tablespoons olive oil,** then cook with **1⅓ cups water,** following directions on page 129. Toss the cooked rice with **2 to 3 tablespoons chopped fresh basil,** ¼ **cup freshly grated Parmesan, salt** and **freshly ground black pepper** to taste, then fill the 6 tomato shells. Drizzle a little **extra virgin olive oil** on top and broil as above.

Tomato, Onion, and Pepper Salad

Like other Italians, I rarely use ripe tomatoes in salads. We prefer tomatoes that are half-green, with just a blush of red—unripe-looking ones, in fact. The reason for this is that tomatoes at this stage do not disintegrate when they are tossed, and their slight tartness, as compared with the glorious sweetness of a fully ripened fruit, complements the acid of any vinegar or lemon juice in the salad dressing. Don't be alarmed. A greenish tomato on the outside is pink within; tomatoes ripen from the inside out.

A very nice addition to this salad is 1 cup of purslane leaves. (For more about purslane, see page 13.) It also goes without saying that a handful or two of just-picked lettuce leaves, particulary rucola, add a marvelous bite.

Serves 4.

3 almost-ripe homegrown tomatoes, quartered or sliced

1 medium red onion, thinly sliced

2 thin-skinned frying peppers, cut into ½-inch slices

2 tablespoons chopped fresh basil

3 tablespoons extra virgin olive oil

2 tablespoons wine vinegar

Salt to taste

Toss the tomatoes, onion, and peppers in a salad bowl. Sprinkle the basil over the top and drizzle the oil and vinegar over all the ingredients. Toss gently and add salt.

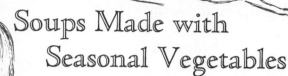

Soups Made with Seasonal Vegetables

Soup is beyond a doubt the most important food in our diet. I serve soup more than anything else, because I find that a warm soup soothes my innards; for me it is like a tranquilizer. I must admit, I have a prejudice—I do not cook nor do I eat soup with cream in it. It's not for dietary reasons, but cream soups were never served in our home, and I never got used to the taste. Soups are rarely made with cream in Italy. Often when an Italian soup is called creamed, the recipe does not contain cream but the "creamed" vegetables are simply pureed. Be it cauliflower, asparagus, or beans, that is the way I prepare my "creamed" soups.

I have seasonal favorites that I prepare only during the season of a particular vegetable. Here is one for each season, and you'll find other soups throughout this chapter under different vegetables. (Check under Soup in the index.)

Spring Vegetable Soup

Serves 4.

1 cup finely chopped celery
1 cup finely chopped carrots
1 cup finely chopped leeks
  (page 59)
½ pound chicken parts (I use
  the leg and thigh)

Salt to taste
6 cups water
1 cup peas
¼ cup rice
6 cups loosely packed spinach
  leaves

In a soup pot, combine the celery, carrots, leeks, chicken, salt, and water. Bring to a boil, skim, then cover and boil gently for 2 hours. Remove the chicken and take the meat off the bones. Return the meat to the broth, add the peas and rice, and cover, then boil gently for 5 minutes. And the spinach, cover, and boil until the rice is cooked, about 10 minutes.

Early Summer Soup

Serves 6.

½ cup coarsely chopped
   celery
2 cups coarsely chopped Swiss
   chard (page 78)
2 cups chopped greens, such
   as spinach or turnip greens
1 medium onion, finely chopped
5 cups water
Salt to taste
2 medium potatoes, peeled
   and diced

½ cup peas
2 cups bite-sized pieces of
   broccoli
2 small zucchini, diced
½ cup small cut pasta, such as
   shells or elbows
¼ cup fresh basil leaves
3 fat cloves garlic, peeled
3 tablespoons oil
3 tablespoons freshly grated
   Parmesan

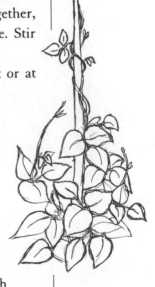

In a medium soup pot, combine the celery, Swiss chard, greens, onion, water, and salt. Cover, bring to a boil, lower the heat and simmer for 1 hour. Add the potatoes, peas, broccoli, and zucchini and cook for 15 minutes. Add the pasta and adjust the salt, then stir, cover, and boil, stirring gently and often until the pasta is al dente.

While the soup is cooking, finely chop the basil and garlic together, then combine the basil-garlic mixture with the oil and cheese. Stir into the soup.

Let the soup stand at least 5 to 10 minutes, then serve hot or at room temperature.

Fall Soup with Wild Mushrooms and Cranberry Beans

Serves 4.

2 tablespoons olive oil
¼ cup chopped prosciutto,
   preferably homemade
   (page 264)
1 medium onion, finely
   chopped

1 cup chopped tomatoes
2 tablespoons chopped fresh
   basil, or 1 tablespoon
   dried
1 cup fresh cranberry beans
   (shell beans)

3 cups sliced wild mushrooms
    (such as plurettes or oyster)
    or cultivated mushrooms
5 cups water
1½-inch piece of Parmesan
    rind (optional)

Salt to taste
1 medium potato, peeled and
    diced
2 cups cauliflower flowerets,
    cut into bite-sized pieces

Heat the oil in a medium soup pot and sauté the prosciutto for 3 to 5 minutes, then add the onion and sauté until it becomes translucent. Stir in the tomatoes and basil and continue cooking for about 5 minutes. Add the beans, mushrooms, water, cheese rind, if using, and salt; cover and boil gently for 1½ hours. Add the potato and cauliflower and cook an additional 30 minutes.

Winter Bean and Pasta Soup

Serves 6.

2 tablespoons olive oil
1 medium onion, finely chopped
1½ cups dried cannellini or
    Great Northern beans,
    soaked overnight in water
    to cover
3 cups cold water
2 cups chopped tomatoes
1 fresh pig's foot, split
    lengthwise

1 tablespoon dried basil
2 carrots, finely chopped
1 rib celery, finely chopped
Salt and freshly ground black
    pepper to taste
1 cup small cut pasta, such as
    small shells or tubettini
Garnish: Extra virgin olive oil
    (optional)

Heat the oil in a soup pot, preferably a terra-cotta pot. When the oil is hot, add the onion and cook it uncovered over moderate heat until it is lightly browned. Add the remaining ingredients except for the pasta, cover, and boil gently over a low heat, stirring from the bottom of the pot occasionally. Cook until the beans are tender, about 2½ hours.

Cook the pasta in a small pot of rapidly boiling salted water until it is al dente. Drain and mix in with the bean soup. Serve with a teaspoon of extra virgin olive oil drizzled over each portion, if desired.

Corn

I have had bad luck in growing corn on occasion. This is because the coons will ravage the field right before the corn is ready to be picked. The coons know when it's ripe by the smell of it, which is very sweet. I know that corn is ready for picking when the silk just begins to brown, or dry out. I am testing this theory—unless the coons beat me to it.

Remember to plant corn in a box pattern—that is, in a number of rows—so that the plants can pollinate. Or have a beehive nearby; the bees will do the job.

Despite numerous theories on how to boil corn, I seldom do it that way. I prefer it baked or roasted.

To roast: Leave the husks on and simply put the ears over very hot coals for about 5 minutes per side, then remove the charred leaves and silk and serve. Butter isn't even necessary, although sometimes a little extra virgin olive oil and salt and pepper enhance the exceptionally fresh flavor of the corn.

To bake: Leave husks on and bake, uncovered, in a 440° oven for 15 to 20 minutes, depending upon the size of the ears. Remove husks and lace with extra virgin olive oil.

Eggplant

I grow eggplant every year with mixed results. Sometimes I get an abundant harvest and sometimes a meager one. I don't know why it is the one vegetable crop I can't count on, particularly when we enjoy it so much and its freshness is so important.

What turns eggplant bitter is simply age. When it is fresh, there is no need to salt it to draw out the juices before cooking. Nor is there any need to peel eggplant when it is young and tender.

To bake: Deep-fried, batter-dipped eggplant slices used in eggplant lasagna and parmigiana have always disturbed me because of the excessive amount of oil absorbed by the eggplant. I have developed instead a way of preparing the slices so that they are sweet and delicious and absorb little oil. Simply place eggplant slices on an oiled baking tray, drizzling a little olive oil on top, and bake them in a preheated 500° oven until they are lightly browned. They will taste good as is and make a much lighter and tastier lasagna (page 125), parmigiana, or anything else that calls for fried eggplant.

Baked Eggplant

Serves 3 to 6.

1 tablespoon olive oil
1 medium onion, finely
  chopped
3 small eggplants, unpeeled, 6
  to 8 inches long
6 tablespoons fresh bread
  crumbs

1 tablespoon finely chopped
  flat-leaved parsley
Salt and freshly ground black
  pepper to taste
Sliced fresh tomatoes
Garnish: Extra virgin olive oil

Preheat oven to 450°.

Heat the oil in a small skillet, add the onion, and sauté until it is translucent. Cut the eggplants in half, lengthwise. With a sharp knife, cut a crosshatch pattern approximately ⅛ inch deep on each eggplant's surface. Mix the bread crumbs and parsley with the onion and add the salt and pepper. Place the eggplant on a baking tray. Spread the bread crumb mixture over the cut surface of the eggplant; cover each half with the sliced tomatoes. Bake, uncovered, for 30 minutes. Serve hot or at room temperature and sprinkle with a little extra virgin olive oil before serving.

Celery

I plant celery every year, starting it in flats and transplanting the seedlings in late spring. The celery I grow is not as thick and tender as the celery sold in food markets, but it is much tastier, with a wonderful perfume. I use celery more as an herb or aromatic than as a vegetable, and the common garden variety that I grow functions perfectly in that role. I never blanch my celery plants because I prefer the more intense flavor of the green heads, but if I keep some plants into the winter I cover them with leaves. That way I can have celery from August to January.

Carrots

I plant seeds in mid-March and expect to be eating the carrots by mid-July. I use carrots primarily as an aromatic vegetable in soups and stews.

Beets

I confess to liking the look of beets more than their taste, but I always plant them, if only for the following salad and for the greens that are good in soups or in a stew of found vegetables (page 8). Plant them in mid-March, the same as carrots. Use the thinnings as beet greens. As the beets grow, bank the dirt around the plants.

Beet Salad

Any time I cook beets, I leave at least ½ inch of the stem attached to the beet so it will not "bleed" into the water, thus losing its color and flavor.

Serves 6.

3 medium potatoes, unpeeled
4 medium beets, with at least ½ inch of the stem attached
1 white onion, thinly sliced
1 tablespoon chopped fresh mint

3 to 4 tablespoons extra virgin olive oil
3 tablespoons good homemade wine vinegar (page 314)
Salt and freshly ground black pepper to taste

Boil the potatoes until tender in lightly salted water to cover; peel and dice. Wash the beets gently, and cover them with cold water. Boil (separately from the potatoes) until tender when pierced with a knife; drain and cool. Rub off the skins and slice. Toss them with the rest of the ingredients. Serve at room temperature.

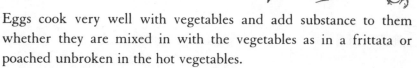

Eggs and Vegetables

Eggs cook very well with vegetables and add substance to them whether they are mixed in with the vegetables as in a frittata or poached unbroken in the hot vegetables.

Here is a basic frittata, or open-faced omelet, with several variations. It can be made with almost any cooked vegetables that are compatible—spinach, asparagus, peas, potatoes, broccoli, eggplant, mushrooms, peppers. You will need about 4 cups cooked chopped vegetables for 6 eggs, which will serve 4 people for a lunch accompanied with a green salad and crusty French or Italian bread. A wedge of frittata makes a good appetizer and is fine picnic fare.

Rape Frittata

Serves 4.

6 cups rape, cut into pieces	6 eggs, lightly beaten
3 tablespoons olive oil	Salt and freshly ground black
1 medium onion, thinly sliced	pepper to taste

Blanch the rape in salted, boiling water for 3 minutes, then drain and set aside. Heat the oil in a medium skillet, add the onion, cover, and cook until it begins to brown. Add the rape and pour the beaten eggs on top. Season to taste with salt and pepper, cover, and cook over a very low heat for 20 to 25 minutes, until cooked through—the eggs on top will be set. Do not stir while cooking. Let the frittata sit for 5 minutes before serving, then cut into wedges. Can also be served at room temperature.

VARIATION:
Asparagus and Leek Frittata

This is a particularly delightful combination in spring. The leeks are sweet and succulent, having rested in the earth all winter, the asparagus is ready for cutting, the mint is young and mild, and the chickens contribute by happily laying eggs.

Serves 6.

2 medium-thick leeks, or
   4 small leeks, trimmed to
   include 1 inch of green
1 cup chicken broth,
   preferably homemade (page
   194)
6 tablespoons olive oil
2 medium onions, sliced

1 pound medium-thick
   asparagus spears, cut into
   2-inch pieces
8 eggs, beaten
2 tablespoons coarsely
   chopped fresh mint
Salt and freshly ground black
   pepper to taste

Split the leeks lengthwise and, after washing them, put them in a small skillet with the broth, cover, and cook gently until tender—about 30 minutes. Heat 3 tablespoons of the oil in a medium skillet, then sauté the onions until they begin to brown. Remove the onions with a slotted spoon to a plate. Heat the remaining oil and cook the asparagus, tossing occasionally, until it begins to brown. Now add the cooked onions and leeks along with about 2 tablespoons of the cooking broth. Pour in the eggs and mint and cook as above.

VARIATION:

Onion, Pepper, and Potato Frittata

Serves 4.

4 tablespoons olive oil
1½ cups sliced onions (about
   2 medium onions)
3 cups sliced bell peppers,
   preferably red
2 small potatoes, parboiled for
   about 15 minutes, then
   peeled and sliced ¼ inch
   thick

6 eggs, beaten
Salt and freshly ground black
   pepper to taste

Heat the olive oil in a heavy medium skillet, then sauté the onions and peppers, uncovered, over medium heat until the onions begin to brown. Add the potatoes and cook several minutes longer. Add the eggs and cook as above.

Poached Eggs in Vegetables

Sauté in **olive oil** whatever vegetables you choose, cooking them until they are just tender. **Asparagus, spinach, tomatoes** with **peppers, eggplant, peas** are all good. You can also use leftover vegetables. You will need about ¾ **cup for each egg.** Make an indentation in the vegetables and drop the egg in (you can do as many as the pan will hold). Season with **salt** and **freshly ground black pepper to taste,** cover, and cook over medium heat until the egg whites are cooked.

Peppers

I plant a lot of *bell peppers.* Some of them I'll pick green and some I let ripen on the vine until they turn red or yellow. The yellow variety are called California Wonders.

I also put in Italian *frying peppers.* I like them because they cook quickly and the skins are tender.

Recently, I have been planting *Hungarian wax peppers* that ripen from yellow to red. This is a thick, long pepper that is mildly hot. It is prolific and looks lovely.

For *hot peppers,* I plant a long, thin Italian variety, which I use for hot relishes and which I also dry. Use these judiciously, particularly when they are green, because then they are full of oil and are more volatile. When they turn red, they start to dry out. Don't plant hot peppers alongside the sweet, because through cross-pollination your sweet peppers may become hot.

I always manage to plant more peppers than I need despite the fact that I use them so much in cooking, as well as raw in salads. I love to see their bright colors on the plants.

To Dry Hot Peppers

I dry my hot peppers by pulling up the plants when the peppers are red —in late September or early October. I scrape off the roots, then hang the plants upside down in a sheltered place with good air circulation. An ideal location would be an open, sheltered area. Ventilation is essential. Peppers should dry in about 1½ months, depending on the size of the peppers. Or dry them in an electric dryer (you must use the long, narrow variety of pepper for this) for about 4 hours.

The peppers can be used directly from the branch or they can also be stored in airtight containers.

Peppers cannot be frozen successfully.

Red and Yellow Peppers

Red and yellow peppers are simply ripe peppers. Green peppers are unripened, and you are apt to see them more in the supermarkets because they have a longer shelf life. (They can be harvested weeks before they ripen.) All peppers turn color (red or yellow—even orange or purple) when allowed to ripen on the vine.

Until recently, red and yellow peppers were available only during the late summer and fall, but now you can get them year-round, mostly from Holland.

We know that the harsh Dutch climate precludes the growing of peppers in quantity outdoors, so imported Dutch peppers must be grown in greenhouses, and I have some reservations about them. They can't possibly have the same shelf life as green peppers. I do not know how the peppers are grown, and I am suspicious of what chemicals may have been used to make them hold up. They look unnatural and are ridiculously expensive. So my advice is to use red and yellow peppers during their season and stay away from the tasteless, expensive imported peppers.

Food for thought: In 1986, the FDA was faulted by the General Accounting Office for inspecting less than 1 percent of the annually imported fruits and vegetables for pesticides and other chemicals that are barred for domestic use because of safety concerns.

48

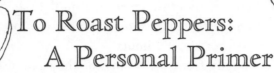

To Roast Peppers:
A Personal Primer

Roasted bell peppers have become very popular over the last decade or so, as well they should—they are delicious. I marvel at the number of ways suggested to roast them. To roast, it would seem, is not to roast but to grill. Having watched my mother make them as far back as I can remember, and then having prepared them innumerable times myself, I present here my thoughts:

- The best peppers to roast are ripe, thick-skinned red and yellow ones, although green ones can also be used.

Roasted Peppers and Broiled Tomatoes

This is an incomparable combination.

Ripe (but not soft)
  unrefrigerated, homegrown
  tomatoes (1 per person)
Garlic, cut into slivers
Fresh rosemary

Salt and freshly ground black
  pepper to taste
Extra virgin olive oil
Roasted peppers, 1 per person
  as needed (see box)

Preheat broiler.

Halve the tomatoes. Stuff about 4 slivers of garlic into each tomato half and place the halves, flesh side up, in a baking pan. Sprinkle with rosemary, salt and pepper, and olive oil. Broil close to the heat until the edges of the tomatoes begin to char. Remove from the broiler and discard the garlic slivers. Let the tomatoes cool. Serve with sliced roasted peppers and Bruschetta (page 294). A piece of cheese—fresh Pecorino-Romano or a good imported provolone—is also very nice with this combination.

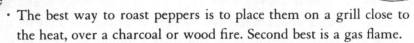

- The best way to roast peppers is to place them on a grill close to the heat, over a charcoal or wood fire. Second best is a gas flame.
- Do not puncture the peppers with a fork; if you do, the steam that builds up in the pepper as it cooks escapes, and the pepper collapses.
- Roast the peppers, turning them, until the skins blister, but not so long that the flesh burns. When blistered all over, remove the peppers from the heat and let cool. At this point, they will (and should) collapse. (*Do not put peppers in a paper bag to ease the removal of the skin, as many cooks recommend.* That way the peppers continue to cook and, in fact, overcook in their own heat.)
- Remove the charred skin from the peppers, pinching it off with your fingers. Split the peppers, remove the seedpods and seeds, and slice the flesh lengthwise into ½-inch-wide strips.
- Do not wash peppers after they are peeled.

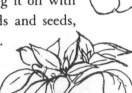

Basic Stuffed Bell Peppers

Serves 4.

4 bell peppers, preferably red or yellow	2 cups chopped tomatoes
1 onion, finely chopped	1 tablespoon minced fresh basil
1 tablespoon extra virgin olive oil plus additional for drizzling	1 cup cooked rice
	Salt and freshly ground black pepper to taste

Preheat the oven to 450°.

If desired, char the peppers over a high flame and let them cool. Peel off the charred skin. Cut off the top inch of each pepper (charred or not). Remove the seeds and ribs. Reserve the pepper tops.

In a skillet, sauté the onion in the oil until it begins to brown. Add the tomatoes and basil and simmer, covered, for 5 minutes. Add the rice, salt, and pepper and simmer, covered, stirring, for 10 minutes.

Stuff the peppers with the rice mixture and arrange snugly in a baking dish. Replace the tops on the peppers and drizzle with additional oil. Bake the peppers for 20 minutes. Serve the peppers hot or at room temperature.

VARIATION WITH SWISS CHARD: Prepare the peppers as above. In a skillet, sauté **1 onion, finely chopped,** in **1 tablespoon olive oil** until it begins to brown. Add **2 medium tomatoes, chopped,** and **1 tablespoon dried oregano** and simmer, covered, for 5 minutes. Add **3 cups coarsely chopped and blanched Swiss chard,** and **salt** and **freshly ground black pepper to taste,** and cook for 5 minutes. Mix in **¾ cup cooked rice** and stuff the peppers. Bake as above.

Meat-Stuffed Frying Peppers

Frying peppers make a more delicate stuffed pepper because the skins are less coarse.

Serves 3 to 6.

6 large frying peppers, each
    about 6 inches long
1 onion, finely chopped
1 tablespoon extra virgin olive
    oil plus additional for
    drizzling
¼ pound ground pork
¼ pound ground beef
Salt and freshly ground black
    pepper to taste

⅓ cup dry white wine
1 tablespoon chopped fresh
    basil, or 1 teaspoon dried
1 tablespoon minced flat-leaved
    parsley
1 cup cooked rice
2 egg whites, lightly beaten

Preheat the oven to 475°.

Prepare the peppers as in the basic recipe, preceding. In a skillet, sauté the onion in the oil until it begins to brown. Add the pork, beef, salt, and pepper, and continue to sauté over moderately high heat until the meat begins to brown. Add the wine and basil and simmer, covered, until the wine is evaporated. Transfer the mixture to a bowl and stir in the parsley, rice, and egg whites. Stuff the peppers and bake for 25 minutes.

Hot Peppers Stuffed with Anchovies

This is a wonderful garnish for broiled or fried fish.

Serves 4 as a garnish.

4 long hot peppers*
4 anchovy fillets, salted or
    packed in oil (if salted, use
    cleaning instructions below)

Garnish:
Finely chopped garlic
Salt to taste
Extra virgin olive oil

Broil the peppers until they are lightly charred. Peel off the charred skins; make a slit down one side and carefully remove the seeds and veins. Slip an anchovy fillet into each pepper. (If anchovies are salted, pull the fillets off the bone and, discarding the bone, wash the fillets in cold water. Salted anchovies are more delicate if canned.) Garnish with garlic, salt, and oil.

   *I like to use a mild hot pepper like Hungarian wax.

Hot Oil

Use this oil on prepared foods that you might like to spice. It is especially good on fried and broiled foods.

Makes 1 pint.

1 cup dried whole hot peppers
    (page 46)

4 cloves garlic, crushed
Olive oil

Finely chop the dried peppers or use a food processor. Put the chopped peppers into a pint mason jar. Add the garlic and fill the jar with a good-quality olive oil. Store the jar in a cool place and allow the mixture to sit for several weeks before you use it. Add more hot peppers if the oil is not hot enough to suit your taste.

Hot Pepper Relish

I make several types of hot pepper relish that we enjoy all year. One is a chunky hot pepper relish, which I like to use as a garnish, especially with dried fish, and one is a hot pepper sauce.

3 tablespoons olive oil
2 cups chopped hot red peppers (cayenne, jalapeño, Japanese)*
1 medium onion, chopped
2 cups diced zucchini, cut in ½-inch cubes
2½ cups coarsely chopped ripe tomatoes
2 or 3 cloves garlic, finely chopped
Salt to taste

Heat the oil in a medium skillet, add the peppers, onion, and zucchini. Cook over medium heat until the onion becomes translucent. Add the tomatoes, garlic, and salt. Cover and simmer for about 20 minutes.

Note: The sauce can be frozen or canned in jars; I prefer to can it.

To can: Sterilize ½-pint jars in boiling water for several minutes. Remove and fill with simmering sauce. Screw on lids. Place in a canning kettle, and cover with water 1 inch above the tops of the jars. Boil for 15 minutes. Remove the jars from the water, tighten the lids, and store in a cool place.

* Adjust the spiciness of the relish by substituting sweet peppers for some of the hot ones.

Hot Pepper Sauce

This is my favorite hot pepper sauce; it's especially good served with fried, broiled, or boiled foods.

Makes about 2 cups.

8 to 10 cups hot red peppers, cored and cut into 2-inch pieces*
½ cup olive or vegetable oil
1 tablespoon chopped garlic (optional)
Salt to taste

Dry the peppers in an electric dryer for about 3 hours (soft dry). They can also be dried in the sun or in a greenhouse but should be soft dried no matter the method. It will take several days in a greenhouse.

Put the dried peppers in a food processor with the remaining ingredients and blend until smooth. Pack the puree into jars, pressing down on the puree so that there are no air bubbles. Cover with ½ inch of olive or vegetable oil. Keep the jars in a cool place or refrigerate. Replace the oil as the relish is used. If refrigerated, the sauce will last most of the winter.

* The degree of hotness depends upon the types of peppers used. You can also regulate the hotness by combining sweet red peppers with the hot peppers.

Horseradish

This wonderful plant is perennial and it grows bigger each year even if you harvest the roots (there's always a residue of the root system that comes back). The plant needs no care, no pesticides, and fresh horseradish is always available. A word of caution though: Plant the horseradish in a far corner of your garden or it will take up more space than you want. Harvest in the fall by digging up with a pitchfork or shovel; the roots run deep. Just cut off a portion of the thick root as needed.

I prefer horseradish pureed with tomatoes as a sauce.

Tomato Horseradish Sauce

Makes 2 cups.

2 tablespoons olive oil
1 small onion, coarsely chopped
2 fat cloves garlic, coarsely
    chopped
1½ cups chopped tomatoes

Salt and freshly ground black
    pepper to taste
½ cup cubed peeled
    horseradish, or 1 cup grated
    horseradish

Heat the oil in a small saucepan and add the onion. Cook uncovered until translucent. Add the garlic and continue cooking until the garlic takes on color. Add the tomatoes and salt and pepper, cover, and simmer for about 10 minutes. Put the horseradish cubes in a food processor and chop fine. Add tomato sauce to the processor and blend. Serve at room temperature with fried or boiled foods.

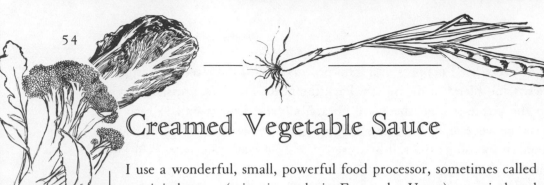

Creamed Vegetable Sauce

I use a wonderful, small, powerful food processor, sometimes called a mini-chopper (mine is made in France by Varco), to grind and puree small amounts of vegetables, herbs, and aromatics. For instance, I'll combine garlic, scallions, mint, parsley, fresh tomatoes, rucola, olive oil, with maybe white wine, broth, lemon juice, or soy sauce, and puree everything to the consistency of heavy or light cream in a matter of seconds. No one can believe there isn't cream in these sauces, they are so creamy and smooth. You can create just the right combination to suit the needs of your dinner—fresh mint, garlic, lemon juice, scallions, and olive oil, for example, make a perfect foil for broiled fish (see below). You can also make a lovely creamy sauce with cooked vegetables, thinned with stock, or try canned Italian-style tuna creamed with broth, parsley, olive oil, and onions. Once you have pureed the sauce, taste it, and then add salt and pepper as needed and adjust other seasonings; if there's too much mint, balance it with some fresh tomatoes; if the puree is bland, you might want to add a few drops of soy sauce.

It's easy, it's healthy, and it's a tasty way to make a sauce.

Here are some combinations that have worked well for me:

For broiled fish:
- ⅓ cup fresh mint leaves
- ⅓ cup scallions
- 1 clove garlic
- 1 teaspoon fresh lemon juice
- Salt and freshly ground black pepper to taste

For fish and boiled meats:
- ½ cup tomatoes
- ⅓ cup scallions
- ¼ cup fresh basil leaves
- 1 clove garlic
- About 8 sprigs flat-leaved parsley
- ¼ cup olive oil
- ½ teaspoon prepared mustard (if using as sauce for meat)
- Salt and freshly ground black pepper to taste

Potatoes

Sometimes I grow potatoes, but more often I rely on the variety that farmers' markets give us today. I like the big California thin-skinned potatoes and the yellow potatoes (Golden Yukon) one finds in the fall and wintertime.

I use potatoes constantly in vegetable mélanges (page 56). Here are several dishes that feature the potato in traditional ways, but note that they are seasoned with olive oil rather than butter and cream. Olive oil brings out the natural flavor of the potato.

Potatoes Stuffed with Tomatoes, Parmesan, and Fresh Herbs

Serves 8.

4 baking potatoes, unpeeled
1 cup diced tomatoes
1 tablespoon finely chopped
   flat-leaved parsley
¼ cup thinly sliced scallions
1 tablespoon finely chopped
   fresh mint

4 tablespoons freshly grated
   Parmesan (optional)
Salt and freshly ground black
   pepper to taste
Garnish: Extra virgin olive oil

Preheat the oven to 400°.

Bake the potatoes until done—when a fork goes easily through the skin and into the flesh, about 45 minutes.

Preheat the broiler or preheat the oven to 500°.

Carefully halve the potatoes lengthwise and scoop out the insides, guarding against splitting the potato shells. Combine the potato pulp and the remaining ingredients, except the olive oil. Fill the potato skins with the potato pulp mixture, drizzle the olive oil over them, and brown the tops under the preheated broiler or in the preheated oven until they are lightly colored.

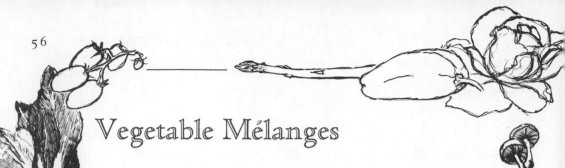

Vegetable Mélanges

I adore a mélange of vegetables. The possible combinations are end-less, but I prefer to match vegetables that are harvested at the same time because they seem to go well together. Often the garden will yield just a handful of this or that, so it is natural to cook together what is at hand to make a satisfying dish—one that is, incidentally, very healthy because of the absence of saturated fat and because of the freshness and nutritional value of the vegetables. One essential ingredient is potatoes, because they thicken the moisture that is re-leased by the vegetables and act as a binder.

Vegetable mélanges make a perfect lunch served hot or at room temperature with crusty or toasted bread. They can also serve as a base for other dishes: You can poach a piece of fish or shrimp right in a sauté of, say, celery, potatoes, tomatoes, and onions, or you can combine the mélange with chicken parts, sautéed separately.

Actually, I have two ways of cooking vegetables together. One is to let all the ingredients simmer slowly for a long time until the cut-up potatoes turn to mush so that they function as a sauce, the way

Boiled Potatoes with Oil and Parsley

Serves 3 or 4.

4 large potatoes, unpeeled
3 tablespoons extra virgin olive oil
2 tablespoons finely chopped
   flat-leaved parsley

Salt and freshly ground black
   pepper to taste

Boil the potatoes with their skins on—20 to 30 minutes. Check their doneness by piercing the potatoes with a fork. Peel the cooked potatoes and slice them into ¼-inch rounds. Mix the potatoes with the olive oil and parsley, then season to taste with salt and pepper. Serve hot or warm.

cream would. The delicious stew made up of found spring vegetables on page 8 is an example of this kind of soupy mélange.

My other technique is to sauté all the vegetables and aromatics together in olive oil until they are just tender. Coarser vegetables, such as cabbage, Swiss chard, and root vegetables, need to be parboiled several minutes before sautéing. The cabbage family—broccoli, cauliflower, brussels sprouts—should be just blanched, "washed in boiling water," as my mother used to say; this seems to tenderize them and set the color. In both instances the potatoes should be prepared in the same pot with the other vegetables—whether parboiling or blanching is used. The more tender, delicate summer vegetables—tomatoes, peppers, zucchini, asparagus, eggplant—don't require preliminary cooking in this way, and the potatoes in a mélange with these are sliced thin so everything is done together, in about 10 minutes.

Chopped onions cooked in olive oil invariably form the base for a vegetable mélange, and garlic is frequently added, particularly with the more tender, fast-cooking vegetables. But it is all a question of individual taste, and as you take to cooking your garden vegetables this way, you'll work out your own combinations.

You will find all kinds of vegetable mélanges throughout this chapter—check the index for vegetables mélanges.

Potatoes Roasted with Rosemary

Serves 8.

Olive oil as needed
5 baking potatoes, peeled and halved lengthwise
3 tablespoons dried rosemary
Salt and freshly ground black pepper to taste

Preheat the oven to 400°.
Rub the bottom of an ovenproof pan with oil and arrange the potatoes in the pan. Sprinkle the potatoes with the rosemary and salt and pepper and bake, turning occasionally, about 20 minutes, until tender when tested with a fork.

Mashed Potatoes My Way

Serves 4.

3 large potatoes, unpeeled
2 to 3 tablespoons extra virgin
  olive oil

Salt and freshly ground black
  pepper to taste

Boil potatoes for 20 to 30 minutes. Check their doneness by piercing the potatoes with a fork. Peel, and then put them through a potato ricer. Mix in the oil and season to taste with salt and pepper. Serve immediately.

VARIATION WITH TOMATOES: After putting the potatoes through the ricer, mix in **2½ cups chopped and drained tomatoes, 1½ tablespoons finely chopped fresh basil, and 2 to 3 tablespoons extra virgin olive oil.** Serve hot or at room temperature, garnished with cubed tomatoes.

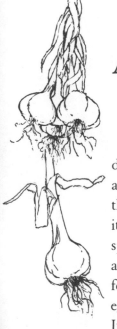

About Garlic, Onions, Leeks, and Scallions

Garlic: Very easy to grow, garlic is, in fact, ready to use when you dig it up. It does not have to be dried, but I do hang the bulbs to air for about 2 weeks. There is no comparison between homegrown garlic and those sad, wizened, papery heads in the markets. It is so much sweeter; it's simply fresher. Plant garlic bulbs in the late fall. The garlic will sprout in early spring. The leaves have a wonderful, light garlic flavor and are excellent cut up and served in spring salads and in a stew of found vegetables (page 8). Do not pick the central leaf (the leader). In early June, step on the plants to crush the greens. Dig garlic up in early July.

Braid the garlic leaves and hang to dry. Garlic will last all year. Elephant garlic, a milder garlic, is grown the same way.

Onions: My favorite is the white onion, and I plant white onion sets every spring. I harvest most of the onions when they are about 1½ inches in diameter; they are exceptionally sweet with succulent greens. I leave some of the onions in the ground and dig them up after the greens turn brown. These onions grow to about 3 inches in diameter, and I find them more delicate than the yellow or red onions. The easiest way to peel small white onions is to rub 2 or 3 of them together in the palms of your hands until the papery skin flakes off.

Leeks: In May I transplant to the garden the leeks I have started from seed in flats, and they are ready to harvest in the fall, although they can also be left to winter over (page 11). Leeks require very little care; just mound dirt around them about every 3 weeks so that when you harvest the plant there is plenty of sweet white flesh, which is the tender part of the leek. I use leeks a lot in vegetable combinations and in soups. Be sure to clean them well, first trimming away the tough green leaves, then making a slit or two down to the white part and letting water run through to remove all the dirt.

Scallions: These grow best when the seeds are planted as soon as the ground can be worked. The seeds soften, and when the earth warms, they shoot right up.

Sweet and Sour Onions

Serves 4.

3 tablespoons olive oil
3 tablespoons good white wine
    vinegar
1 tablespoon sugar
½ cup chopped tomatoes, or
    1 tablespoon tomato paste
    (page 31)

Salt and freshly ground black
    pepper
1 pound small white onions,
    peeled (see above)

In a saucepan, cook the olive oil, vinegar, sugar, tomatoes, and a pinch of salt and pepper over moderate heat until the sauce begins to thicken, about 5 minutes. Add the onions, cover, and cook over low heat for about 45 minutes. Add more vinegar, if desired, and cook until the onions begin to brown, about 15 minutes more. Taste and adjust seasonings.

MOSTLY
= FALL AND WINTER =

About the Cabbage Family

Summer cabbage: I plant a Dutch variety of summer cabbage, starting it in the greenhouse so I can put in seedlings in late spring for harvesting in midsummer. I use it primarily for vegetable soups and stews and for making sauerkraut.

Savoy cabbage: I prefer this type of cabbage because it is so much tastier. It is best harvested after a hard frost, so I put the cabbage seeds directly into the garden in July and harvest heads in November. I use savoy in many dishes—soups, stews, and pasta—and the tender leaves are good for stuffing. Occasionally I plant Napa or Chinese cabbage, but it is more for looks than for taste.

Broccoli: This is such a versatile vegetable that I sometimes plant two crops, putting in the first seedlings in the spring. Home-grown broccoli is so much more sweet and sugary; sitting around in the market gives it a heavy taste. I peel the stems and use them along with the flowerets in myriad ways—stewed with garlic and potatoes and other vegetables, baked with black olives, as a garnish for pasta and main course dishes.

Romanesque broccoli: A Roman member of the broccoli family that I have come to love. It is one of the most beautiful vegetables I have seen and one of the tastiest. A winter vegetable, it has a head the size of a large cauliflower with tightly packed flowerets that come to a point and are a brilliant pea green. And it tastes divine—sweeter and more delicate than broccoli and more distinctive than cauliflower. Plant it like broccoli, and after the head starts to form in the center, remove the first two tiers of bottom leaves so that the nutrients go to the head. To cook, blanch it and then sauté with oil and garlic. I predict that one day this wonderful vegetable will be raised by truck farmers here.

Rape: Known in Italy as *broccoletti di rape* and *cime di rape,* and in America as broccoli rab, rape is actually a member of the turnip family, but not to be confused with turnip greens or mustard greens. It has been crossed with broccoli to develop the bud. I plant from seed in August so I can harvest it in November after the frost. A broccoli-like bud will appear in the center—pick before the bud flowers. Remember rape is a winter vegetable; don't try to grow it in the heat or it will bolt. It is a great vegetable with a slightly bitter edge that makes a fine accent in stews and soups, with beans and pasta, and with fish. I peel the stems, roughly chop, and blanch (cooking just until the water returns to a boil) the rape before incorporating it in a dish.

Cauliflower: I put seeds in the ground in July so I can harvest my cauliflower in the fall, when it tastes best, after a frost has sweetened it. I don't blanch the plants by tying them; in my opinion a little greenish tinge gives cauliflower more flavor. I always separate the flowerets and blanch them in boiling water before sautéing them in olive oil with other aromatic vegetables. It's a vegetable that goes particularly well with pork or sausages.

Brussels sprouts: I plant sprouts the same way I do summer cabbage, but they should be harvested after a frost for good flavor. I like them best blanched and then simmered until tender-crisp with garlic and oil, a little water, and a touch of hot pepper flakes. They are also good combined with other cabbage family vegetables. The first time I planted brussels sprouts, I got mostly large leafy plants, but very small sprouts. Then I noticed that a few plants had had their tops nibbled off by rabbits, and they were full of large sprouts. After that, I cut the tops off the plants when they were about 2 feet high, and sure enough, this pruning made all the sprouts grow large—another example of how you can learn from nature just by observing it.

Stuffed Savoy Cabbage Rolls in Light Tomato Sauce

Serves 5 or 6.

1 medium savoy cabbage

The stuffing:

½ pound ground pork
½ pound ground veal
2 teaspoons minced garlic
2 tablespoons golden raisins
2 tablespoons pine nuts
1 cup fresh bread crumbs
2 egg whites, lightly beaten
2 tablespoons finely chopped
   flat-leaved parsley

Salt and freshly ground black
   pepper to taste
2 tablespoons finely chopped
   fresh basil
2 tablespoons freshly grated
   Parmesan

The sauce:

3 tablespoons olive oil
1 medium onion, finely
   chopped
1 cup peeled, seeded, and
   coarsely chopped tomatoes

1 cup chicken broth, preferably
   homemade (page 194)

Garnish: Finely chopped flat-
   leaved parsley

Carefully remove the leaves from the cabbage head. In a large pot of boiling water, blanch them, drain immediately, and let cool. (If the head is very tight and the leaves are difficult to remove, plunge the whole head into the boiling water first and boil for about 5 minutes. Drain, then remove the leaves.)

Make the stuffing: Combine all of the stuffing ingredients in a bowl and set aside.

Make the sauce: In a medium skillet, heat the olive oil until hot, add the onion, and when it begins to color, add the tomatoes. Cover and simmer for about 5 minutes. Stir in the broth and cook several minutes to combine the flavors.

Preheat the oven to 450°.

Spread the cabbage leaves out on the counter. For each leaf, make a ball of stuffing about the size of a golf ball. Flatten each ball slightly and put it in the middle of the leaf. Fold the stem end of the leaf over the stuffing, tucking in the sides, and roll the leaf up. Continue in the same manner with the remaining leaves and stuffing, placing the rolls snugly in a medium baking pan as they are made. Pour the tomato sauce over the cabbage rolls, cover the pan with foil, and bake for 30 minutes. Garnish with parsley.

Cabbage and Spinach Soup with Leeks and Croutons

Makes 4 large portions.

6 cups water
2 cups coarsely chopped green summer cabbage
2 medium leeks, cut into ¼-inch rounds
Salt and freshly ground black pepper to taste
1 large potato, peeled and cut into 1-inch pieces

½ cup small cut pasta, such as tubettini, or 6 tablespoons rice
½ pound spinach, chopped
Garnish:
Homemade croutons*
Extra virgin olive oil

Put the water, cabbage, leeks, and salt and pepper in a medium soup pot. Cover, bring to a boil, and boil gently for 1¾ hours. Add the potato and cook 10 minutes. Add the pasta or rice and cook for 5 minutes. Add the spinach, cover, and cook until the pasta is done al dente. Taste, and correct the seasonings.

Divide the soup among soup bowls, garnish each serving with some croutons, and drizzle a little extra virgin olive oil over the top. Serve immediately.

* To make croutons, heat 3 tablespoons olive oil until hot in a medium skillet. Cut 6 slices of bread into ½-inch cubes and sauté, stirring often, until golden brown.

Savoy Cabbage with Cranberry Beans

Serves 4.

2 tablespoons olive oil
1 medium onion, finely
 chopped
2 cloves garlic, finely chopped
2 pounds fresh cranberry beans
 or other shell beans (about
 2 cups shelled)
4 cups tightly packed 1-inch-
 wide pieces savoy cabbage

3 cups chicken broth or water
Hot pepper flakes to taste
 (optional)
2 tablespoons chopped fresh
 sage
Salt to taste
2 medium potatoes, peeled and
 cut into quarters

In a medium soup pot heat the oil and sauté the onion until brown. Add the garlic and cook for another minute. Add the beans along with the cabbage, broth, hot pepper flakes (if using), sage, and salt to taste. Cover and cook over a moderate heat for 1 hour. Add the potatoes and continue cooking for an additional 20 minutes, until the potatoes are done.

Sauerkraut

Not too many years ago, I had an extraordinary crop of summer cabbage, fifty pounds of it. Sauerkraut seemed to be the logical way of preserving it. So I bought a large crock, and following directions, I chopped up the heads, transferred the cabbage to the crock, salted it, covered it, and then left it in our pantry. To my utter dismay, our entire kitchen was soon smelling like a skid row latrine. Nothing unusual had taken place. The cabbage was doing what it was meant to do—ferment. It tasted wonderful; you just couldn't get near it!

What follows is a recipe for sauerkraut that has an enticing aroma and that I can personally recommend for its delicate flavor. The directions came to me by way of an elderly German woman, a simple hausfrau. You can increase the amount according to how much cabbage you want to preserve.

Makes 1 quart.

¾ pound summer cabbage   1 teaspoon granulated sugar
1 teaspoon kosher salt

Cut the cabbage in half and core it. Slice the cabbage thinly, wash, and drain.

Sterilize the canning jar and its lid by submerging them in boiling water to cover for several minutes. Remove the jar from the water, and while it is still hot, pack it with the raw cabbage, to about 1 inch from the top of the jar. Add the salt and the sugar. Fill the jar with boiling water and seal with the lid. Let the sauerkraut stand for about 5 weeks in a cool place before using. Store in a cool place for up to a year. To use, drain, but do not rinse.

Rape and Lentil Soup

Serves 4.

1 medium onion, finely
    chopped
½ cup finely chopped carrots
½ cup finely chopped celery
⅓ cup lentils
5 cups water
1 teaspoon dried basil
Salt and freshly ground black
    pepper or hot pepper flakes
    to taste

8 cups rape, stems peeled, cut
    into chunks
½ cup rice
Garnish: Extra virgin olive oil
    (optional)

Put all of the ingredients except the rape, rice, and oil into a medium soup pot. As the Italians would say, cover and boil this mixture *dolce-mente,* or sweetly (gently), for one hour.

Add the rape and cook, covered, for 20 minutes more.

In the meantime, cook the rice in 1 cup water (page 129).

Spoon some of the rice onto the bottom of each soup plate and ladle the soup over the rice. Garnish each portion with a teaspoon of extra virgin olive oil, if desired.

VARIATION: **Spinach, turnip greens, escarole,** or any leafy green can be used in the soup, but I prefer rape.

Broccoli Bari Style

Serves 4.

1 bunch broccoli, broken into
  flowerets, with stems peeled
  and cut up (7 to 8 cups)
½ cup water
2 cloves garlic, coarsely chopped
Salt to taste

Hot pepper flakes to taste
  (optional)
3 tablespoons good wine
  vinegar
2 tablespoons extra virgin olive
  oil

Put all of the ingredients except the vinegar and olive oil into a
medium skillet or shallow pot. Cover the pot and bring the water to a
boil. Lower the heat and simmer for approximately 5 minutes. Add the
wine vinegar, cover, and cook the broccoli for an additional 5 minutes.
At this point, all of the moisture should have evaporated from the pot.
Add the olive oil and toss to coat the broccoli. Serve hot.

Broccoli with Tomatoes and Anchovies

Serves 4.

3 tablespoons olive oil
1 medium onion, thinly sliced
Hot pepper flakes to taste
4 canned anchovies, chopped
¾ cup chopped tomatoes

1 teaspoon oregano
1 bunch broccoli, broken into
  flowerets, with stems peeled
  and cut up (7–8 cups)

Heat the oil in a wide skillet. Add the onion, and when it begins to
brown, add the hot pepper flakes and anchovies. Cook this mixture for
a moment; add the tomatoes and oregano. Cover the skillet, lower the
heat, and simmer for 10 minutes.

Meanwhile, blanch the broccoli in salted boiling water just until it
turns bright green. Drain the broccoli, reserving 1 cup of the water.

Add the broccoli to the tomato sauce along with some of the reserved
water if it is needed. Cover and simmer this mixture for approximately
5 minutes.

Romanesque Broccoli Dressed with Olive Oil, Lemon, and Anchovies

Serves 3.

4 cups cut-up Romanesque
broccoli (or regular broccoli)
2 tablespoons extra virgin olive
oil
Juice of ½ lemon
2 anchovy fillets, finely
chopped

Freshly ground black pepper
or hot pepper flakes to taste
1 clove garlic (or more), finely
chopped

Steam the broccoli until it is tender. Be sure not to overcook.

Mix all of the remaining ingredients together and pour over the cooked broccoli. Serve hot or at room temperature.

VARIATION: This may be made with **broccoli** flowerets and peeled stems.

Broccoli with Rape

Serves 6.

2 pounds rape
1 head broccoli
4 tablespoons olive oil

4 cloves garlic, finely chopped
Hot pepper flakes to taste
Salt to taste

Wash the rape, peel the stems, and cut into chunks. Peel the stem of the broccoli, and cut it into quarters. Cut off the flowerets. You should have about 6 to 7 cups of stems and flowerets.

Blanch the broccoli and rape in salted, boiling water. Drain as soon as the water returns to a boil, and reserve ½ cup of the cooking water.

Heat the oil in a large skillet. Add the garlic and hot pepper flakes, and as soon as the garlic begins to brown, add the broccoli and rape, salt, and reserved water. Cover and simmer for 15 minutes.

Cauliflower with Beans

This dish is good with broiled meats and fish.

Serves 4 as a vegetable course.

3 tablespoons olive oil
1 medium onion, finely chopped
1 small cauliflower, cut into
   flowerets, blanched, and
   drained
2 cups cooked cannellini or
   Great Northern beans (page
   73)

Salt and freshly ground black
   pepper or hot pepper flakes
   to taste
2 teaspoons chopped fresh
   oregano, or 1 teaspoon dried
1 tablespoon chopped flat-
   leaved parsley
Broth or water if needed

Heat the oil in a medium shallow saucepan, then add the onion and sauté until translucent. Add the cauliflower flowerets, cover, and simmer for 5 minutes, stirring often. Add the beans along with the salt and pepper or hot pepper flakes, oregano, and parsley; cover, lower the heat, and simmer for 15 minutes. If moisture is needed, add some broth or water.

Cauliflower with Onions and Tomatoes

I have never had this recipe anywhere except our home and in the area in Italy my parents came from, which was known for the excellent cauliflower grown there. I remember well how beautiful the fields looked in the winter in a sea of white and green. One tablespoon of tomato paste diluted with a little water can be used instead of chopped tomatoes.

Serves 6.

1 cauliflower, cut into flowerets
5 tablespoons olive oil
1 medium onion, coarsely
   chopped
3 to 4 tablespoons white wine
   vinegar

1 cup coarsely chopped
   tomatoes
Salt and freshly ground pepper
   or hot pepper flakes to taste

Blanch the cauliflower flowerets in boiling water; drain. Heat the oil in a medium skillet, and sauté the onion, uncovered, over medium heat, stirring often, until translucent. Then add the cauliflower and continue to sauté, stirring often, being careful not to break up the flowerets. When the onion and cauliflower begin to brown and stick a little, add the vinegar, cover, and cook, stirring, until the vinegar cooks off. Stir in the tomatoes, salt, and pepper or hot pepper flakes and simmer, covered, until the cauliflower is tender, about 5 to 10 minutes. Do not overcook.

Rice and Cauliflower Soup

Serves 3 or 4.

4 cups beef or chicken broth, preferably homemade (for chicken broth, see page 194)

½ cup rice
3 cups cauliflower flowerets
Salt to taste

Bring the broth to a boil and add the rice, mix, cover, and lower the heat. Simmer the rice until it is almost done, then add the cauliflower and boil gently, covered, for 3 to 4 minutes. Add salt to taste and serve immediately.

VARIATION: **Broccoli** flowerets can be substituted for cauliflower.

Fried Cauliflower Balls

We enjoy this recipe made with cauliflower, but broccoli can be used instead.

Makes 8 balls, serving 2.

2 cups cauliflower flowerets
1 egg white, lightly beaten
1 tablespoon bread crumbs
1 tablespoon freshly grated Pecorino Romano
Dash of freshly grated nutmeg

Salt and freshly ground black pepper to taste
Bread crumbs for coating
Vegetable oil
Garnish: Lemon wedges

Boil the cauliflower in salted water until tender, about 4 minutes, then drain, chop coarsely, and put into a small mixing bowl. Mix in the egg white, 1 tablespoon bread crumbs, cheese, nutmeg, and salt and pepper. Form balls about 1½ inches in diameter and roll in bread crumbs. Heat about 1 inch of oil in a small skillet, and when the oil is hot, gently place the balls in the oil—do not crowd—and fry to a golden brown. Blot with paper towels and serve immediately with lemon wedges.

Cauliflower and Broccoli Salad

Serves 3 or 4.

3 cups cauliflower flowerets
3 cups broccoli flowerets
2 cups coarsely chopped ripe
   tomatoes at room
   temperature
2 tablespoons extra virgin olive
   oil

2 cloves garlic, finely chopped
2 or more tablespoons vinegar
3 tablespoons finely chopped
   flat-leaved parsley
Salt and freshly ground black
   pepper to taste.

Boil the cauliflower and broccoli flowerets in salted water, uncovered, for about 5 minutes. Rinse in cold water, drain, and put them in a serving bowl. Put the tomatoes, oil, garlic, vinegar, parsley, salt, and pepper into a food processor and blend. Taste; you may need more vinegar. Pour the sauce over the cauliflower and broccoli and mix. Do not refrigerate this dish. Serve it at room temperature.

Baked Cauliflower, Potatoes, and Leeks

Serves 3 or 4.

2 large potatoes
2 thick leeks, washed and cut
   into 3-inch lengths
3 cups cauliflower flowerets
3 tablespoons olive oil

1 tablespoon finely chopped
   flat-leaved parsley
Salt and freshly ground black
   pepper to taste
2 tablespoons grated Parmesan

Preheat the oven to 450°.

Peel the potatoes and boil them with the leeks for 10 minutes, then add the cauliflower and cook for several minutes more. Drain, reserving ½ cup cooking liquid. Slice the potatoes ¼-inch thick and place in a shallow baking dish, along with the leeks, cauliflower, and the reserved liquid. Sprinkle oil, parsley, salt and pepper, and cheese over all. Cover and bake for 20 minutes.

Brussels Sprouts with Potatoes and Tomatoes

Serves 4.

3 potatoes, peeled and cut into
   1-inch sections
3 cups brussels sprouts
2 tablespoons olive oil
1 medium onion, coarsely
   chopped
1 cup seeded and chopped
   tomatoes

1 teaspoon dried basil
Hot pepper flakes to taste
   (optional)
Salt to taste
Garnish: Extra virgin olive oil
   (optional)

Boil the potatoes and brussels sprouts in rapidly boiling, salted water for 10 minutes. In the meantime, heat the oil in a medium skillet. When the oil is hot, add the onion and sauté over moderate heat until it begins to brown. Add the tomatoes, basil, and hot pepper flakes, if using; cover, and simmer over a low heat for 10 minutes.

Drain the brussels sprouts and potatoes, reserving 3 tablespoons of the cooking water. Add the vegetables and the reserved liquid to the tomato mixture, and salt to taste. Cover and simmer over low heat for about 8 minutes.

If you desire, sprinkle each portion with a little extra virgin olive oil.

Dried Beans

You can find dried beans in all sizes and all colors. The beans used most in Italian cooking are the large, meaty cannellini beans. Fresh cranberry beans are very popular, and kidney beans are often used. A not-so-common white bean about the size of our Great Northern white bean is grown in Sarano in Tuscany and is called fagioli di Sarano. It is the bean that is used in what I consider the best bean dish ever created: Fagioli al Fiasco (page 74). Since fagioli di Sarano are not available in America, I bought the seeds in Florence and planted them in my garden in Katonah. They did very well. (Maybe with some prodding a seed company will make them available here.)

My problem with many dried beans is that often the outer skin remains tough even after the bean is cooked. I buy the best-quality imported cannellini beans I can find, and the results are always the same—tough outer skins. However, the skins of the fagioli di Sarano are thin and cook before the beans are overcooked. I have the same good results with beans I grow for drying. I find the Great Northern bean (I get the seeds from Burpee) cooks evenly and has a wonderful texture.

As with all beans that I plan to dry, I leave the fully developed beans on the plant until late fall, allowing the pod to shrivel, then I pick it and shell it. It needs no further drying.

I happen to think that dried beans cooked properly are just about the best food you can eat. I always cook them in a terra-cotta soup pot because it provides a slow, even heat.

It is interesting to note that cooked dried beans served with meat and fish (which is very popular in Italy) is becoming very popular in the better restaurants in New York City.

Preparation of Dried Beans

Makes 3 cups.

1 cup dried beans, either Great
    Northern, cannellini, kidney,
    or beans you have dried
3 cups cold water
2 cloves garlic, finely chopped
Salt and freshly ground black
    pepper to taste

1 teaspoon crushed dried
    rosemary
1 small onion, finely chopped
1 rib celery, finely chopped
1 bay leaf
2 teaspoons chopped fresh sage
    leaves

Soak the beans in water overnight, drain, and put all the ingredients, including the 3 cups of water, in a medium soup pot, preferably terracotta. Cover and simmer over low heat for about 2 hours, until the beans are tender but not overcooked. Do not boil; the heat should be constant but not boiling. Cooked this way the beans will remain intact.

The beans are now ready for recipes that include cooked dried beans. Beans can be cooked and refrigerated for later use. They will keep in the refrigerator for a week, and boiling them after that time will make them last a few days longer.

Dried Beans and Pasta

Serves 6.

1 cup dried beans (I use Great
    Northern), soaked overnight
    in 3 cups water
Salt to taste
2 tablespoons olive oil
1 medium onion, finely
    chopped
1 rib celery, finely chopped

1 medium carrot, finely
    chopped
Hot pepper flakes to taste
1 cup chopped tomatoes
½ cup small cut pasta, such as
    tubettini or small elbows
Freshly grated Pecorino
    Romano

Put the soaked beans and their water in a heavy soup pot, add 1 more cup of water and salt, cover, and bring to a slow boil.

Meanwhile, heat the oil in a medium skillet, add the onion, celery, and carrot and sauté, uncovered, over moderate heat until the onion begins to brown. Add the hot pepper flakes and tomatoes, cover, lower the heat, and simmer for 10 minutes. Add the beans, mix in well, and lower the heat so that the beans simmer gently but do not boil. Cook for about 3 hours, until the beans are tender. Cooking time for beans can vary from 2 to 3 hours—it depends on many factors, including how old the beans are, and how much water is used. Add the pasta and continue cooking until the pasta is cooked. Serve immediately, with grated cheese.

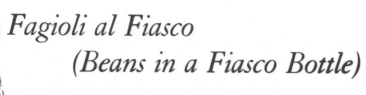

Fagioli al Fiasco (Beans in a Fiasco Bottle)

The original recipe calls for sage, but I like rosemary with beans. The challenge is to cook the beans in a bottle in embers in a fireplace. It's a little tricky but worth trying. I have had a disaster or two, but it does work when done properly. The bottle should be thicker than a standard bottle, and it should be warmed before being placed on the embers. The beans are divine with broiled meats or fish, and especially good with a fine-quality canned tuna (Ventresca) that has been packed in olive oil.

Makes 6 cups.

3 cups dried beans, preferably fagioli di Sarano, but Great Northern will do, soaked overnight in 6 cups water
1 teaspoon freshly ground black pepper
1 tablespoon chopped fresh or dried rosemary

1 tablespoon fresh sage, or 2 teaspoons dried
2 teaspoons finely chopped garlic
4 tablespoons extra virgin olive oil
½ teaspoon salt (I use kosher)

Make your fire first: You need enough hot wood ash to build a mound around the bottle up to the beans (a little bit higher than the beans is better). In order to have enough ash I light the fire in the fireplace in the morning—then let it die down.

Drain the soaked beans and put them into a half-gallon wine bottle, preferably a Chianti bottle with the straw base removed, although any bottle will do. Add remaining ingredients. Shake well, then add water so that the water level is about ½ inch above the beans—lightly stuff the bottle opening with gauze or cotton so steam can escape.

Warm the bottle with the beans and place it on the hot ashes. Mound more hot ash around the bottle—if the ash is too hot (red wood embers against the bottle), the bottle will crack. If the ash is too cold, the beans will not cook. The beans have to simmer in the liquid, not boil. It will take 3 to 4 hours to cook. When cooked, the beans should have absorbed all the liquid. Allow the bottle to cool slowly, then shake out the beans into a serving bowl.

Chickpeas with Fennel

I have never tried growing chickpeas, so I rely on Italian or Greek markets that make a point of putting out fresh sacks of dried beans every year. Be wary of packaged supermarket beans; you never know how old they are.

Serves 4.

2 tablespoons olive oil
1 medium onion, finely
  chopped
2 cups chopped tomatoes
2 teaspoons chopped fresh
  basil, or 1 teaspoon dried
2 bulbs fennel, sliced
  (about 4 cups)

2 cups cooked chickpeas,
  drained
½ cup water
Salt and freshly ground black
  pepper to taste

Heat the oil in a medium skillet or pot and sauté the onion until it begins to take on color. Add the tomatoes and basil, cover, and simmer for 10 minutes. Add the fennel, cover, and continue cooking over a moderate to low heat for approximately 20 minutes. Add the chickpeas, water, salt, and pepper, cover, and cook over a low heat for approximately 20 minutes more.

Mixed-Vegetable Fry

We usually eat very little fried food, but one dish we love is a mixed fry of vegetables, which are dipped in a batter before frying. My favorite batter is the one my mother used to make with flour, white wine, baking powder, and egg whites; it is so light that it does not interfere with the delicate flavor of the fresh vegetables. I like to use seasonal vegetables from the garden that seem to complement one another so well—combinations like zucchini flowers with small zucchini still attached, white onions, cauliflower flowerets, onion blossoms, green tomato slices. I always serve fried vegetables with a hot pepper relish (page 52) and lemon wedges, crusty Italian bread, and homemade white wine.

Mixed-Vegetable Fry

Before I fry the vegetables, I test to see if the oil is the right temperature by dropping a small dollop of batter into the hot oil. The oil should sizzle vigorously, but the dollop should not burn immediately.

Serves 4.

The batter:

2 cups flour
A pinch of baking powder
3 egg whites, lightly beaten

1½ cups dry white wine or beer
Salt and freshly ground black pepper to taste

Corn oil for frying

The vegetables:

½ cauliflower, cut into flowerets and blanched for 3 minutes
½ bunch broccoli, cut into flowerets and blanched for 3 minutes

12 medium mushrooms
½ pound asparagus, cut into 1½-inch sections and blanched

Flour for dredging

Mix together all of the ingredients for the batter. Refrigerate for at least 1 hour.

Heat approximately ¾ inch of corn oil in a medium skillet. Remove the batter from the refrigerator and add an ice cube or two to it. Dust the vegetables with flour, dip into the batter, and carefully drop them into the hot (but not smoking) oil. Do not crowd the pan.

When the vegetables are golden brown, remove them from the oil with a slotted spoon. Place them on a paper towel to absorb the excess oil. Serve immediately.

Fennel

My grandfather planted great quantities of fennel (also known as finocchio and, incorrectly, as anise). In most of Italy, fennel is planted in the early fall and harvested during the winter months. Like broccoli, fennel prefers cold weather, so I used to plant fennel seedlings in July and harvest in the fall. For a long time the fennel bulbs I produced were small and narrow with an intense taste, so I used it only as an herb in fish soups and stews. But last year I planted the end of April (they will take a light frost) and I got really large bulbs by mid-summer, which I used in salads. If you don't have the same luck, buy the plump bulbs in the market that come from California.

Fennel and Orange Salad

Serves 4.

2 cups thinly sliced fennel
2 oranges with rind still on, cut into ¼-inch-thick rounds
10 black olives, pitted and sliced

Juice from ½ lemon
2 tablespoons extra virgin olive oil
Salt and freshly ground black pepper to taste

Mix all of the ingredients together in a salad bowl.

VARIATION WITH FENNEL AND RUCOLA: Instead of the 2 oranges, use 2 cups **rugola.** Omit the black olives, and toss with **vinegar** (instead of lemon), **olive oil,** and the **salt and pepper to taste.**

Jerusalem Artichokes

Plant Jerusalem artichokes (or sunchokes) in a far corner of your garden that you don't intend to use for another purpose. After you put in the potatolike tubers, they multiply and send up tall shoots. They need no care and just keep spreading. To harvest, dig up the tubers as wanted, after the first year. I like them best raw, peeled and cut into strips in salad. To cook, peel and boil in salted water, then drain and toss with olive oil and salt and pepper.

Swiss Chard

Swiss chard was served often in our home when I was a child. My mother insisted that my father plant plenty of it. She adored Swiss chard and used it in just about everything. She cooked it with rice; she used it in summer vegetable soups; she cooked it with potatoes and by itself. She stuffed things with it, and when we complained of her constant use of the vegetable, she insisted it "freshened the stomach." I have grown so fond of it that I look forward to it in the summer and fall. I might add that it's a very beautiful plant with its big, bright green leaves, and when it's at its healthy peak in September and October, it certainly adds to the visual delights of the garden. I grow the green Swiss chard with the white rib, not the red variety, and I plant in the spring so that it is well established when warm weather comes. A vegetable garden can be as beautiful as a flower garden if tended with the same love.

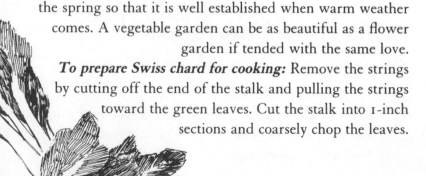

To prepare Swiss chard for cooking: Remove the strings by cutting off the end of the stalk and pulling the strings toward the green leaves. Cut the stalk into 1-inch sections and coarsely chop the leaves.

Braised Swiss Chard

Serves 4.

3 tablespoons olive oil
2 cloves garlic, finely chopped
1 medium onion, coarsely
  chopped
1 pound Swiss chard, prepared
  as described on opposite
  page

1 cup water
1 medium potato, peeled and
  cut into 1-inch cubes
Salt to taste

Heat the oil in a shallow, medium saucepan, add the garlic and onion, and cook uncovered until the garlic begins to take on color. Add the remaining ingredients, cover, and cook over a moderate heat for 45 minutes.

Swiss Chard with Tomatoes and Parsnips

Swiss chard is usually healthy and tender at the same time as the parsnips are plump and sweet—a lovely combination.

Serves 4 to 6.

3 tablespoons olive oil
1 medium onion, coarsely
  chopped
2 cups coarsely chopped
  tomatoes
10 cups Swiss chard, prepared
  as described on opposite
  page

4 cups chopped parsnips,
  scraped, halved lengthwise,
  and cut crosswise into
  1½-inch pieces
Salt to taste

In a medium saucepan heat the olive oil until hot, then add the onion and tomatoes. Sauté, covered, for 5 minutes. Add the Swiss chard and parsnips with salt to taste and cook, covered, over moderate heat for 30 minutes.

Swiss Chard and Rice Stew

I like to serve this dish with crusty bread and a garden salad.

Serves 3 as a main course.

1 medium onion, coarsely chopped

¼ cup coarsely chopped celery

3 tablespoons coarsely chopped fresh basil

2 tablespoons olive oil

Hot pepper flakes to taste (optional)

1 cup coarsely chopped tomatoes

1 medium potato, peeled and diced

2 cups water

6 cups coarsely chopped Swiss chard, prepared as described on p. 78

1 cup peas

Salt to taste

¼ cup good-quality rice

Sauté the onion, celery, and basil in the olive oil in a medium saucepan, uncovered, over moderate heat until the onion is translucent. Add the hot pepper flakes (if using), the tomatoes, and potato and cook, covered, stirring occasionally, for 5 minutes. Add the water, Swiss chard, peas, and salt to taste, bring to a boil, and simmer gently, covered, for about 15 to 20 minutes. Add the rice and cook, covered, over low heat until done. Ladle into soup bowls and serve at room temperature drizzled with a little extra virgin olive oil over the top. Do not refrigerate.

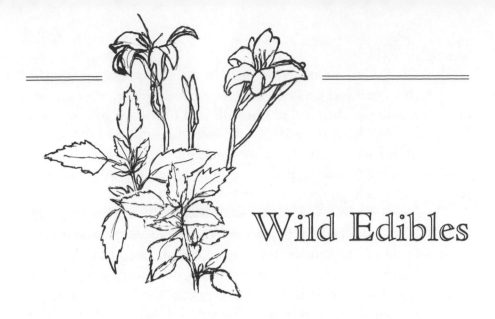

Wild Edibles

About Wild Mushrooms

Among my fondest childhood memories are the mushroom hunts with my father in late September and October in the Connecticut country-side. We would walk about 5 miles to the cow pastures that were studded with tree stumps, and there we gathered the mushrooms. My father always brought along a bottle of his own wine to give the farmer for permission to hunt mushrooms in his fields. The best time to look for mushrooms was the day after a rainfall, and I remember those clear, beautiful days that were alive with the calling of crows and the wonderful variety of fall smells. I would carry a basket with a clothesline tied across it, and my father carried a long, low, 2-bushel basket. I was always so excited that I couldn't wait to get to the fields. Once there, I was left to wander around on my own (with my father always in sight), and immediately I would make wonderful discoveries: a bird's nest, an animal burrow, and, of course, mushrooms. I would be close to the earth, as only a child can be, and I discovered that the closer I got to the earth, the easier it was to find mushrooms. If I saw a mushroom, I would get on my knees almost breathless with anticipation and gently brush the leaves aside, and more often than not, it would turn out to be a large clump or clumps of mushrooms pushing their way through the sod. The smells were so strong—of the earth, of the decaying vegetation, of the leaves, the grass, and, most of all, the mushrooms—it was intoxicating.

When I had filled my basket, my father would go through the

mushrooms and, to my disappointment, usually discard about 75 percent of what I had picked; often the prettiest mushrooms were thrown out. He would put the good mushrooms into his basket, and I would try to remember what the edible ones looked like and then go eagerly off to look for more. Afterward we would sit under a tree or in the sunshine, eat the lunches that my mother had prepared, and then continue our task until our baskets were full.

When we got home, my mother would wash the mushrooms, pick them over, and can them for future use. We ate some of the mushrooms fresh, some in salads, some in stews, some broiled, and others sautéed.

I remember a small orange mushroom that was especially prized for its flavor, and it grew in large clusters around chestnut tree stumps. The mushroom would be blanched, drained, and then tossed with olive oil, vinegar, salt, and pepper and served at room temperature as an appetizer. Unfortunately, the chestnut tree trunks where we now live are too old to bear mushrooms, so I have not found any more of that variety since my childhood.

Most people are frightened to death of wild mushrooms, and the danger of eating a toxic one is not to be ignored. But there are many edible, choice mushrooms, and the joy of gathering them certainly justifies the effort it takes to learn to identify the most reliable species. In fact, there are mycological societies that take people into the countryside to gather wild mushrooms and teach them how to distinguish the edible mushrooms from the others.

You should remember that most toxic mushrooms are not fatal, and that many inedible mushrooms are not toxic. But there are some lethal mushrooms, and you should avoid anything that resembles them.

There are many ways to learn to distinguish the toxic and inedible mushrooms from the edible. Everyone has his own system, and I shall talk about my way, which may not be the best way, but it works for me.

Whenever I find a mushroom that interests me, I first look it up in my books. I have four that I am especially fond of: *One Thousand American Fungi* by Charles McIlvaine and Robert K. MacAdam, *The Mushroom Hunter's Field Guide* by Alexander H. Smith, *The Audubon Society Field Guide to North American Mushrooms,* and an Italian book entitled *Funghi dal Vero* by Bruno Cetto.

I first identify the group that the mushroom belongs to; the *Boletus* group, for instance. I then check out all of the toxic mushrooms in that group and compare them with the mushroom I am investigating (the color photographs are very useful). Once I am certain that the mushroom I am trying to identify is not one of the toxic species, I try to identify it as one of the mushrooms in that group that is edible. I am now ready for the next test: to see if it is in fact edible. I sauté the mushroom in a little oil with no salt, pepper, or herbs and taste a small portion. If the texture and taste are good, then I eat a little more the next day, and if I have no reaction, I am convinced that the mushroom is good. I always test a new mushroom in the morning so that I have a full day to recuperate in case I have a bad reaction—stomach cramps, vomiting, etc. After I am satisfied that the mushroom is good, and after I have eaten it, then I serve it to my family.

A standing rule: The beginner should never pick a white mushroom until he can positively identify the deadly *Amanita verna* (destroying angel). One should avoid the entire *Amanita* group. Once I identify a mushroom, I do not forget it. If there is a mushroom in the group that resembles the deadly amanita, I avoid it.

In my mushroom guidebooks, out of 165 best-known mushrooms, I have found 2 deadly types, 113 edible, 12 toxic, and 3 toxic to some people. I might add that although there are inedible species of mushrooms that grow on trees, there are none that are toxic, as far as I know.

The features most commonly used in identifying mushrooms are the following: (1) the bulb at the base of the stalk or the stalk itself; (2) the ring around the top of the stalk; (3) the gills; (4) the cap; (5) the color. But this does not apply to all mushrooms: Some do not have stalks (puffballs, for instance), and some do not have gills (again, puffballs). Most mushrooms, though, have both.

By the way, do not attempt to memorize too many species in one season. I only try to master a few a year.

The following are the mushrooms I find most frequently within 1 mile of our home in Katonah:

Oyster mushrooms (**Pleurotus ostreatus**): Resembling oyster shells, they are a dull, creamy gray with smooth tops and gills underneath. They generally grow in great clumps on tree stumps and should be picked soon after they appear, since they become woody as they age. Last October, I was driving down a dirt road in a torrential rain with heavy winds when I saw a huge clump of oyster mushrooms about 30 feet up an almost-dead tree.

I rushed home and got a ladder to help me reach the first branches. Though the tree was swaying back and forth in the hurricanelike winds, I climbed up to the mushrooms, and by wrapping my legs around the tree and tying myself to the trunk to free my hands, I managed to cut off about 30 pounds of mushrooms. I blanched and froze them as soon as I got home and am still eating that treasure.

Morels **(Morchella esculenta):** Morels appear in April and May, depending on the weather, and are very easy to distinguish. They are cone-shaped (1 inch to occasionally 5 inches high) with a surface like a brain and hollow inside. They are hard to find and very fickle, since they don't come back in the same place each year. Morels are the most desirable mushroom, because they are so delicious.

Puffballs **(Lycoperdales):** A family of mushrooms that comes in many sizes and types, from quarter-sized *Lycoperdum pyriforme* to basketball-sized *Calvatia gigantea*. Great caution should be taken gathering the small puffballs because white amanita caps have been mistaken for them. Puffballs should be white when cut in half; discard those that are not.

Hen-of-the-woods **(Polypilus fondosus):** An easy wild mushroom to identify—it's vibrant orange and grows on trees, unlike other wild mushrooms. When cut into, it reveals the most magnificent tone of pale-pink granite or travertine marble. Hen-of-the-woods resembles coral, in fact, and has branches and thick stubby stems. It looks almost as if it should be growing in the sea.

Pig's ears **(Cantharelius clavatus):** Mushrooms you'll find growing on stumps close to the ground in clusters. They are shaped like a pig's ears, and like all stump mushrooms, they must be picked soon after they appear or they will be woody.

Shaggymane **(Coprinus comatus):** Shaggymane is an elongated mushroom, off-white with dark gills. As it matures, it is not as good; it gets inkier and becomes soft, so pick it young.

Fairy rings **(Marasmius oreades):** The small white fairy rings grow in a ring. I tend to avoid them, because there could be some deadly amanitas among them, which are hard to spot.

Cepes or porcini **(Boletus edulis):** Here are the most prized of the boletus mushrooms. All boletus mushrooms are easy to identify because of the thick stem and rounded cap that is spongy underneath with no gills. In these species there are a number of edible and choice mushrooms; a couple are toxic, but not deadly.

Honey mushrooms (**Armillaria mellea**): A special treat, honey mushrooms are usually found in large quantities. My mother used to can them to use throughout the year. The texture and taste are excellent, and honey mushrooms always graced her sauces. I had forgotten what they looked like, and I discovered, to my dismay, that after the death of my father in 1966, I could no longer identify them. Then several years ago, I noticed a profusion of mushrooms on my neighbor's lawn; they were honey colored with firm caps and gills—height, fully grown, about 3 inches. They grew in large clusters under trees and out in the open. I took the usual precautions and tested a few. To my delight, I discovered that they were the mushrooms that I had been looking for all those years. I know of two spots within a half mile of our house where they grow in great profusion, so our freezer is full of honey mushrooms year-round.

Wild Mushrooms: Cleaning, Freezing, Drying, and Canning

To Clean Mushrooms: Carefully wash the mushrooms, then, with a sharp knife, cut off the ends of the stalks. If the stalk is white and solid with no worm holes, that indicates that the mushroom cap is clean and you can leave it intact. If there are worm holes in the stalk, cut the cap in half to inspect; if there are worm holes in the cap, discard the mushroom.

Mushrooms get wormy very quickly. The worms are harmless, but still it is better to use only healthy mushrooms.

To Freeze Mushrooms: I find freezing to be the easiest way to preserve mushrooms, and there is no spoilage. Wash the mushrooms carefully, then blanch them in boiling water. Drain the mushrooms and put them into freezer bags. You can combine several types; label and date the bags. (I keep them as long as 3 or 4 years.) Defrost the mushrooms in the refrigerator or plunge them into boiling water and drain before using.

To Dry Mushrooms: Remove the stems and wash the caps. Pat the caps dry and place them in an electric dryer at 350° for approximately 3 hours. To dry mushrooms without an electric dryer, gently wash the mushrooms and leave the stems on, but cut off the lower part. Tie the mushrooms by their stems on to a string and hang them in a dry area. Some people dry their mushrooms near their furnaces.

About Canning Mushrooms: My mother used to can mushrooms, but I find it easier and safer to freeze them. I also think mushrooms that have been frozen taste better.

To Substitute for Wild Mushrooms: Soak one 2-ounce package boletus dried mushrooms in warm water to cover for a half hour. Strain through several layers of cheesecloth if you want to use the soaking liquid. Sauté the drained mushrooms with 4 cups sliced cultivated mushrooms into 2 to 3 tablespoons olive oil.

Puffballs with Eggs

We gather a variety of puffballs on our property. My favorite is the smaller tan-to-brown–skinned Lycoperdum umbrinum, *but I do enjoy gathering the giant puffballs as well. Our children used to squeal with joy when they found a basketball-sized giant puffball. The following is my favorite puffball recipe.*

Serves 4.

3 tablespoons olive oil	1 tablespoon finely chopped
1 to 2 cups puffballs, sliced into	flat-leaved parsley
½-inch sections	½ cup dry white wine
Salt and freshly ground black	6 large eggs
pepper to taste	⅔ cup milk

Heat the oil in a medium skillet, add puffball slices, and cook, uncovered, over moderate heat for about 10 minutes, stirring often. Add salt and pepper to taste, parsley, and wine. Cover and lower heat. Cook until wine evaporates.

Meanwhile, whisk the eggs and milk together thoroughly and season with salt and pepper. Add the eggs to the puffball slices, stir to mix. Cover and cook over low to moderate heat, stirring often, until the eggs are cooked. Serve with crusty bread or Bruschetta (page 294).

Wild Mushrooms with Marsala

This simple combination is good with broiled meats and especially pleasing with fried chicken breasts.

Serves 4.

3 tablespoons extra virgin olive
oil
1 small onion, finely chopped
6 cups wild mushrooms, such
as *Clavaria cinerea,* morels,
or boletus, cut into bite-sized
pieces

¼ cup Marsala or sherry
Salt and freshly ground black
pepper to taste

Heat the oil in a medium skillet and sauté onion over moderate heat until it turns translucent, then add the mushrooms and cook over moderately high heat, stirring often, until they just begin to stick to the bottom of the pan. Pour in the Marsala or sherry, add salt and pepper to taste, and lower the heat to moderate. Cover and cook until the Marsala and moisture in the mushrooms cook out.

Honey Mushrooms with Tomatoes

Serve with broiled or roasted meats, game, and pasta.

Serves 6.

3 tablespoons olive oil
1 medium onion, finely
chopped
3 cloves garlic, finely chopped
2 tablespoons finely chopped
flat-leaved parsley
2 cups coarsely chopped
tomatoes

8 cups honey mushrooms or
other wild mushrooms, such
as boletus, oyster, and the
like (cut the large mushroom
caps in half)
Salt to taste

Heat the oil in a skillet or medium saucepan, add the onion, and cook, uncovered, until translucent. Toss in the garlic and parsley, and cook for 1 minute, then add the tomatoes and cook, over moderate heat, covered, for 5 minutes. Add the mushrooms and cook, covered, for another 5 minutes, salt to taste, and continue to cook the mixture for 5 minutes more.

Hen-of-the-Woods with Oil and Garlic

Hen-of-the-woods, as many as
    you are lucky enough to find
Extra virgin olive oil
Finely chopped garlic, to taste

Salt and freshly ground black
    pepper to taste

Wash the mushrooms well, pat dry, and cut into large pieces. Cut off and discard the tough part of the stems, then slice the stems lengthwise into 1-inch strips. Heat the oil and sauté the mushrooms over moderate heat, stirring often, for about 20 minutes. Add the garlic and salt and pepper to taste, and cook, stirring from time to time, for 10 minutes. The mushrooms should be well cooked and pliable when done.

Mushrooms and Parmesan Salad

This recipe calls for fresh boletus mushrooms, preferably small, firm ones. But I have made it with large firm cultivated mushrooms, and it tasted fine.

Serves 4.

7 medium firm boletus or
    cultivated white mushrooms,
    sliced paper-thin
20 thin slices soft parmigiano
    or other grainy mild cheese*
    (use a cheese shaver to cut
    the slices)

Juice from 1 lemon
Salt and freshly ground black
    pepper
Garnish: Extra virgin olive oil

Combine all of the ingredients and mix gently. Serve at room temperature as a first course.

* Grana parmigiano is a Parmesan that has been aged not more than a year and is used for eating rather than for grating.

Pasta, Rice,
and
Polenta

Pasta

About pasta

If you think about it, there's hardly a pasta sauce that doesn't contain a vegetable or combinations thereof. Pastas in their various shapes are great carriers for almost anything you grow in your garden. Too many Americans, I'm afraid, still consider pasta to be something swimming in some kind of tomato sauce. I hope I can convince you how many other vegetables there are that make a delicious and colorful sauce base— sweet ripe peppers for a red or yellow puree, asparagus, spinach, broccoli for a bright-green puree, as well as many of the pesto sauces (page 228), zucchini blossoms, horseradish, and more, all giving their own colors and accents. But a pasta does not necessarily have to be dressed in a pureed sauce; rough-textured sauces consisting of chopped vegetables cooked in a little broth and/or wine make excellent dressings (sometimes the vegetables are left whole or in chunks). In addition, whole or chopped vegetables like peas, cut asparagus, or broccoli and cauliflower flowerets can be added as garnishes, and sausage slices and succulent chunks of seafood or meat give added flavor and substance.

I prepare pasta dishes in basically four ways, and I have grouped the recipes that follow under these different techniques.

1. The pasta is cooked and dressed in a pureed sauce served with or without garnishes. Some sauces are uncooked, some lightly cooked, whereas others are cooked quite a long time.

2. The pasta is cooked and tossed with a rough-textured sauce of

cooked chopped vegetables; sometimes ground meats are cooked in with the vegetables, sometimes garnishes are added. Often fish and seafood are cooked in with these rough-textured sauces or used as a garnish.

3. The pasta is partially cooked, then finishes its cooking in the sauce, usually a thin sauce or broth (see the box on pasta, opposite page, for an explanation of the rationale behind this technique).

4. The pasta is cooked and then baked in a sauce with vegetables, cheese, and perhaps meat.

Tubetini

Rigatoni

Rotelli

Shells

Pappadelle

Farfalle

Penne

Canelloni

Fettucine

Pasta Shapes and Dried versus Fresh Pasta

Although there are always exceptions to the rule that certain types of pasta require certain sauces, the marriage should be one in which the pasta complements the sauce and the sauce does not overwhelm the pasta. For example, linguine is considered the right thing for a white clam sauce because its thin, flat shape enables it to absorb more of the liquid in that particular sauce than a thicker pasta would. But should you want to use a cut pasta like a farfalle with a thin sauce, a good solution is to cook the pasta until it is almost done and then finish cooking it with the clam sauce (without the clams in it and adding a little more liquid, such as white wine); that way the pasta will become saturated with the sauce and you have solved the problem.

The general rules are thin pasta with fish and seafood sauces, cut pasta with meats and vegetables, egg pasta with meat sauces and with cream sauces. But be flexible and use the rules only as a guide.

Perhaps the biggest rip-off in the food industry today is what is touted as "fresh" pasta. It's impossible to cook it properly because it has not been allowed to dry as it should and the result is a tangled, gluey mess. When homemade pasta is prepared it should be dried at least an hour before it is cut and at least another hour before it is cooked; actually the longer the pasta dries, the better it will cook. Soft pasta will not separate properly in the boiling water and it cannot be cooked al dente because it cooks unevenly and too quickly.

So why is the pasta not properly dried? The answer is obviously economic: Drying requires space and additional labor. If you have any doubts on the subject, buy a package of dried fettuccine (egg noodles) imported from Italy. Cook them according to instructions and at the same time cook "fresh" fettuccine, and then compare. Anyone who has a taste for pasta will agree that this is one of the rare instances when fresh is not best.

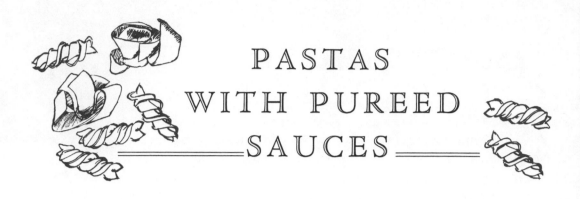

PASTAS WITH PUREED SAUCES

Spaghettini or Capellini with Pesto My Way

For other pesto sauces to serve with pasta, see page 228.

Serves 3.

2 to 3 cups beef or chicken broth, preferably homemade (for chicken broth, see page 194)

¾ pound spaghettini or capellini

1 cup coarsely chopped fresh basil leaves

1 or 2 cloves garlic, coarsely chopped

¼ cup extra virgin olive oil

3 tablespoons pine nuts

1 tablespoon chopped flat-leaved parsley

Salt and freshly ground black pepper to taste

Garnish: ¼ cup freshly grated Parmesan or Pecorino Romano

Bring 2 cups of the broth to a boil in a medium soup pot, add the pasta, and cook, stirring often, until it is done al dente. All of the broth should be absorbed by the pasta. If the broth is absorbed but the pasta is not done, add more broth.

Meanwhile, put the basil, garlic, oil, pine nuts, parsley, salt, and pepper into a food processor and blend. Add enough broth to the pesto to make it the consistency of light cream. (It must not be thick!)

Add the pesto to the pasta and gently toss. Serve immediately with a dusting of grated cheese on each portion.

Pasta with Black Olive Pesto

Occasionally the ingredients for a pesto are lightly cooked before they are blended to a paste as here.

Serves 3.

2 tablespoons extra virgin olive oil
1 fat clove garlic, finely chopped
4 anchovies, finely chopped
24 dried black olives, pitted and chopped
2 teaspoons chopped fresh oregano, or 1 teaspoon dried
Hot pepper flakes to taste
¾ cup beef or chicken broth, preferably homemade (for chicken broth, see page 194)
2 tablespoons pine nuts
¾ pound linguine or spaghetti
Garnish: Chopped flat-leaved parsley

Heat the olive oil and sauté the garlic and anchovies. When the garlic begins to take on color, add the chopped olives along with the oregano, hot pepper flakes to taste, and the broth. Cover and cook over low heat for 4 to 5 minutes. Pour the mixture into a food processor along with the pine nuts and blend smooth.

In a large pot of rapidly boiling salted water, cook the linguine or spaghetti until done al dente. Toss with the sauce and garnish each portion with chopped parsley.

Pasta with Horseradish-Tomato Puree

In this and the following two recipes the sauce ingredients are lightly cooked and then pureed. Horseradish sauce is especially good in the fall when fresh horseradish is available.

Serves 4.

2 tablespoons olive oil

1 medium onion, coarsely chopped

3 cups peeled, seeded, and chopped tomatoes

2 teaspoons chopped fresh oregano, or 1 teaspoon dried

Salt and freshly ground black pepper to taste

½ cup chopped horseradish

1 tablespoon chopped flat-leaved parsley

2 cloves garlic, chopped

1 pound cut pasta, such as penne or farfalle

Garnish: Extra virgin olive oil

Heat the olive oil and sauté the onion until it begins to brown. Then add the tomatoes along with the oregano and salt and pepper to taste. Cover, lower the heat, and simmer for 15 minutes. Pour the tomato sauce into a food processor along with the horseradish, parsley, and garlic; blend to a creamy consistency.

Meanwhile cook the pasta in a large pot of rapidly boiling salted water until done al dente. Toss with the sauce and serve garnished with a little extra virgin olive oil.

VARIATION:

Pasta with Red Pepper Puree

Serves 4.

3 tablespoons olive oil

4 cups sliced onions

3 large red or yellow bell peppers, sliced about ½ inch thick

2 cups chicken broth, preferably homemade (page 194)

Salt and freshly ground black pepper to taste

⅓ cup light cream

1 pound cut pasta, such as farfalle or penne

Garnish: Freshly grated
  Parmesan or finely chopped
  flat-leaved parsley

Heat the oil until hot and sauté the onions and peppers until the onions begin to brown, about 20 minutes. Add the broth and salt and pepper to taste and simmer, covered, for about 5 minutes. Put the onion-pepper mixture along with the cream into a food processor and blend until smooth.

Meanwhile, cook the pasta in a large pot of rapidly boiling salted water and toss with the warm puree. Serve immediately on heated plates. Garnish with grated cheese or finely chopped flat-leaved parsley.

VARIATION:
Pasta with Zucchini Blossom-Tomato Puree

Serves 4.

¼ cup olive oil
1¼ medium onions, chopped
2 cups peeled, seeded, and
  chopped ripe tomatoes
5 fresh basil leaves
32 large zucchini blossoms or
  other squash blossoms, such
  as pumpkin or yellow squash,
  inspected for insects and sliced
  crosswise ¼ inch thick

Salt and freshly ground black
  pepper to taste
1 pound spaghettini
Garnish: Freshly grated
  Parmesan or extra virgin
  olive oil

Heat the olive oil and sauté the onions until translucent, then add the tomatoes and basil leaves and cook, covered, over moderate heat for 5 minutes. Add the zucchini or other squash blossoms and season with salt and pepper to taste. Simmer, covered, for 15 minutes. Pour the mixture into a food processor and puree until smooth.

Meanwhile, cook the pasta in a large pot of rapidly boiling salted water until done al dente, and toss with the warm sauce. Garnish with Parmesan or olive oil.

Cut Pasta with Primavera Sauce and Tuna

Serves 4.

4 cups seeded and roughly
chopped ripe tomatoes
¼ cup pine nuts
2 fat cloves garlic, coarsely
chopped
¼ cup coarsely chopped fresh
basil
2 tablespoons coarsely chopped
flat-leaved parsley

¼ cup extra virgin olive oil
Salt and freshly ground black
pepper to taste
7 ounces canned Italian-style
tuna (in olive oil), preferably
home-canned (page 268)
1 pound cut pasta (I prefer
penne or farfalle)

In the bowl of a food processor, place the tomatoes, pine nuts, garlic, basil, parsley, olive oil, and salt and pepper to taste. Process to a creamy consistency. Add tuna to the primavera sauce in the processor and blend until smooth.

In a large pot of rapidly boiling water, cook the pasta until done al dente; drain. Toss with the sauce and serve immediately.

Rigatoni Salad with Broccoli and Tuna Sauce

This is a wonderful late-summer or early-fall combination when your broccoli is up and ready and your tuna, canned from last year, is just begging to be opened.

Serves 6 to 8.

1 pound rigatoni or other cut pasta, such as penne or farfalle

1 bunch broccoli, stems peeled and cut into 1-inch pieces, flowerets cut into bite-sized pieces

6 tablespoons extra virgin olive oil

Salt and freshly ground black pepper to taste

4 cloves garlic, finely chopped

2 tablespoons finely chopped flat-leaved parsley

¼ cup coarsely chopped fresh mint

Hot pepper flakes to taste

1 6-ounce can Italian-style tuna (in olive oil), preferably home-canned (page 268), drained

1½ cups thinly sliced scallions

Cook the rigatoni or other pasta in a large pot of rapidly boiling salted water for 5 minutes. Add the broccoli stems and flowerets and cook until the pasta is done al dente. Drain the pasta and broccoli, reserving 1 cup of the water, and transfer the pasta and broccoli to a shallow serving dish. Let cool slightly, then toss with 3 tablespoons of the olive oil and salt and pepper to taste.

In a food processor blend together the garlic, parsley, mint, remaining 3 tablespoons of oil, and hot pepper flakes. Add the tuna and the reserved cooking water and process to a creamy consistency.

Pour the sauce over the pasta and broccoli, add the scallions, and toss gently. Serve at room temperature.

Pasta with Asparagus Sauce and Sweet Sausage Garnish

Serves 4 to 6.

3 tablespoons olive oil
1 medium onion, coarsely
  chopped
1 pound medium-thick
  asparagus, cut into 1-inch
  lengths
Salt and freshly ground black
  pepper to taste
¾ pound Italian-style sweet
  sausage, preferably
  homemade (page 270)
About 2 cups chicken broth,
  preferably homemade (page
  194)

1 tablespoon finely chopped
  flat-leaved parsley
1 pound cut pasta, such as
  penne, ziti, rigatoni, or
  farfalle
Garnish: Freshly grated
  Pecorino Romano or
  Parmesan, or extra virgin
  olive oil

In a medium skillet or shallow saucepan, heat the oil until hot and
sauté the onion until it begins to wilt. Add the asparagus and salt and
pepper and continue to sauté until the asparagus is tender. Remove the
asparagus-onion mixture with a slotted spoon and set aside.

Prick the sausage, put it in the pan, and brown over moderate to low
heat, turning occasionally until done through. Remove the sausage from
the pan, cut in half lengthwise, and slice thin. Discard the fat from the
pan.

Put the sautéed asparagus-onion mixture and 1½ cups of the chicken
broth into a food processor and blend until smooth. Return this sauce
to the saucepan and bring it to a gentle boil, then add the parsley and
taste for salt and pepper. The consistency of the sauce should be like
light cream; add more broth if needed.

Cook the pasta in a large pot of boiling salted water until done al
dente, drain, and toss with the sauce. Add the sausage slices and serve
on heated plates garnished with freshly grated cheese or extra virgin
olive oil.

Pasta with Broccoli and Sausage

The base of the sauce here is a tomato puree that is cooked with wild mushrooms and sausage. The broccoli serves as a garnish.

Serves 6 to 8.

5 tablespoons olive oil
1 pound sweet Italian-style
  sausage, preferably
  homemade (see page 270)
4 cups wild or cultivated
  mushrooms (I use oyster
  mushrooms)
Salt and freshly ground black
  pepper to taste
1 large onion, coarsely chopped
1 large carrot, thinly sliced

3 cloves garlic
4 cups chopped tomatoes
1 cup chicken or beef broth,
  preferably homemade (for
  chicken broth, see page 194)
2 tablespoons chopped fresh
  basil, or 1 tablespoon dried
1½ pounds cut pasta, such as
  penne or farfalle
4 cups broccoli flowerets

Heat 2 tablespoons of the oil in a medium skillet, prick the sausages, and brown them lightly over moderate heat, turning occasionally. Discard all of the fat and oil, add the mushrooms, and continue cooking the sausages, uncovered, over a moderate heat, stirring often until the mushrooms begin to brown. Add salt and pepper to taste and remove the sausages and mushrooms from heat and set aside.

Meanwhile, heat the remaining 3 tablespoons of olive oil in a medium saucepan that is wide rather than deep. Add the onion and carrot and sauté them uncovered over a moderate heat until they begin to brown. Add the garlic and continue sautéing for several minutes, then add the tomatoes along with the broth and basil. Cover and boil gently for 15 minutes. Pour into a food processor and blend. Return the sauce to the pot and add the sausages and mushrooms. Taste for salt and pepper, cover, and simmer this mixture for 1 hour, stirring occasionally.

Cook the pasta in rapidly boiling salted water for 5 minutes and then add the broccoli. Cook until the pasta is done al dente and then drain the pasta and broccoli. Remove the sausages from the sauce and cut them into bite-sized pieces. Toss them with the pasta, broccoli, and sauce. Serve immediately.

Pappardelle with Venison Sausage

This popular sauce from Tuscany, which is made with pureed tomatoes and aromatics that are cooked a long time with the sausages, is served with pappardelle (an egg pasta about ½ inch wide available in Italian shops); a wide flat dried fettuccine can be used instead.

5 tablespoons olive oil
1 pound venison sausage, preferably homemade (page 271)
1 medium onion, coarsely chopped
1 carrot, coarsely chopped
1 rib celery, coarsely chopped
4 cups canned plum Italian tomatoes with their liquid, preferably home-canned (page 28)

2 teaspoons chopped fresh basil, or 1 teaspoon dried
1 pound pappardelle
Garnish: Freshly grated Parmesan

Heat 2 tablespoons of the olive oil in a medium skillet and brown the sausage.

Meanwhile, heat the remaining 3 tablespoons olive oil in a medium saucepan and sauté the onion, carrot, and celery until the onion begins to brown. Add the tomatoes along with the basil and simmer, covered, for 15 minutes. Put the tomato mixture into a food processor and blend. Return the sauce to the pan, add the sausages, and continue cooking for about 2 hours. Remove the sausages and slice them thin.

Cook the pasta in a large pot of boiling salted water until done al dente; drain. Toss with the sauce and garnish with the sliced sausage and freshly grated Parmesan.

PASTAS WITH ROUGH‑TEXTURED SAUCES

Pasta with Tomato and Celery Sauce

Serves 4.

- 3 tablespoons olive oil
- 2 tablespoons finely chopped flat-leaved parsley
- 2 cloves garlic, finely chopped
- 1 medium onion, finely chopped
- 2 cups coarsely chopped tomatoes
- 2 ribs celery, cut in ¼-inch slices
- 1 teaspoon butter (optional)
- Salt and freshly ground black pepper to taste
- ¾ pound cut pasta, such as rigatoni, penne, or farfalle
- *Garnish:* Finely chopped flat-leaved parsley or freshly grated Parmesan

Heat the oil in a medium shallow saucepan. Add the parsley, garlic, and onion and sauté, uncovered, over moderate heat until the onion wilts. Add the tomatoes along with the celery, butter (if using), salt and pepper; cover and simmer for 15 minutes.

Meanwhile, cook the pasta in a large pot of rapidly boiling salted water until done al dente. Drain and toss with the sauce. Garnish each portion with parsley or Parmesan.

VARIATION:

Pasta with Green and Red Tomato Sauce

This is an unusual combination—the tartness of the green tomatoes complements the sweetness of the red.

Serves 4.

2 medium onions, finely
    chopped
4 tablespoons olive oil
6 cups sliced green tomatoes
2 cups chopped red tomatoes

Salt and freshly ground black
    pepper to taste
1 pound cut pasta
Garnish: Chopped flat-leaved
    parsley

Sauté the onions in olive oil until golden, then add the tomatoes, season with salt and pepper to taste and simmer, covered, for 20 minutes. Meanwhile, cook the pasta in a large pot of rapidly boiling salted water until done al dente, drain, and toss with the sauce. Garnish each serving with chopped parsley.

VARIATION:

Pasta with Green Tomato Sauce

Serves 4.

Sauce:

1 medium onion, finely
    chopped
3 tablespoons olive oil
2 cloves garlic, finely chopped
3 cups sliced green tomatoes
1½ cups chicken broth,
    preferably homemade
    (page 194)
1 tablespoon chopped fresh
    basil, or 1 teaspoon dried

Salt and freshly ground black
    pepper to taste
2 tablespoons freshly grated
    Pecorino Romano

1 pound pasta (any type can be
    used here)
Garnish: Pecorino Romano or
    extra virgin olive oil

Sauté the onion in the oil until translucent, add the garlic, and cook a few minutes. Add the tomatoes, chicken broth, and basil. Season with salt and pepper to taste and simmer, covered, 10 minutes. Add 1 table-spoon of Pecorino cheese and cook 10 minutes more. Add another tablespoon of cheese and continue cooking, stirring occasionally for an additional 10 to 15 minutes. Meanwhile, cook the pasta until al dente in rapidly boiling salted water, drain, toss with the sauce, and garnish each serving with Pecorino Romano or a little extra virgin olive oil.

VARIATION:

Pasta with Rape and Tomatoes

Serves 4.

12 cups rape, stems peeled
2 cloves garlic, finely chopped
6 tablespoons olive oil
Salt and hot pepper flakes to
　taste
1 small onion, finely chopped

2 cups chopped tomatoes
2 teaspoons chopped fresh
　oregano, or 1 teaspoon dried
1 pound cut pasta, such as
　penne or farfalle

Blanch the rape for 1 minute in a large pot of boiling salted water, then drain.

In a large skillet or saucepan, sauté the garlic in 3 tablespoons of the olive oil for a few seconds, then add the blanched rape and season with salt and hot pepper flakes to taste. Cover and cook over low heat for about 20 minutes, stirring occasionally.

Meanwhile, heat the remaining 3 tablespoons of olive oil and sauté the onion until translucent. Then add the tomatoes and oregano and simmer, covered, for 20 minutes; add rape and cook, covered, for several more minutes.

While the sauce is cooking, cook the pasta in a large pot of rapidly boiling salted water until done al dente. Drain, toss with the sauce, and serve immediately.

VARIATION:

Pasta with Broccoli and Anchovies

Serves 4.

5 cups broccoli flowerets
4 cloves garlic, finely chopped
4 tablespoons olive oil
Hot pepper flakes to taste
2 teaspoons chopped fresh
  oregano, or 1 teaspoon dried

1 ounce can anchovy fillets,
  drained and coarsely
  chopped
1 pound spaghettini or spaghetti
Garnish: Finely chopped flat-
  leaved parsley

Blanch the broccoli for 1 minute in boiling salted water, then drain.

Sauté half the chopped garlic in 2 tablespoons of the olive oil until it begins to color, then add hot pepper flakes to taste and the drained broccoli. Cook, uncovered, adding a little water if necessary, for about 5 minutes.

In another skillet, heat the remaining 2 tablespoons of olive oil and sauté the rest of the chopped garlic along with the oregano and anchovies, stirring frequently, until the garlic begins to color.

Cook the pasta in a large pot of rapidly boiling salted water, drain, and toss with the garlic and anchovy mixture; add the broccoli and garlic mixture and toss again. Garnish each portion with chopped parsley.

VARIATION:

Pasta with Rape and Ground Pork

Serves 4.

¾ pound coarsely ground lean
  pork
Salt and freshly ground black
  pepper to taste
Hot pepper flakes to taste
  (optional)
12 cups rape, stems peeled

3 tablespoons olive oil
Water or broth if needed
¾ pound cut pasta, such as
  penne or farfalle
Garnish: Extra virgin olive oil
  (optional)

Put the pork in a medium skillet, season to taste with salt, pepper, and hot pepper flakes, if desired, and cook until lightly browned. Drain off and discard all fat.

Meanwhile, blanch the rape in boiling salted water to cover, then drain. Add the rape to the pork, sprinkle with the olive oil, cover, and cook on low to medium heat, stirring occasionally, for 20 minutes. Add a little water or broth if dry.

While the rape and pork are cooking, cook the pasta in a large pot of rapidly boiling salted water until al dente. Drain and combine with the rape and pork. Serve immediately on heated plates. Garnish with extra virgin olive oil, if desired.

Pasta with Meat Sauce

This meat sauce is such a useful sauce to have on hand that I always make extra to put by. You will only use half of the sauce for 1 pound of spaghetti.

Serves 4 to 6.

For the meat sauce:

2 tablespoons olive or vegetable oil
½ pound lean ground beef or veal
½ pound lean ground pork
1 medium onion, finely chopped
1 medium carrot, finely chopped
Salt and freshly ground black pepper to taste

⅓ cup dry Marsala
2 tablespoons chopped fresh basil, or 1 tablespoon dried
1 ounce dried Italian mushrooms, covered with warm water and soaked for 15 minutes
6 cups seeded and chopped tomatoes

1 pound spaghetti or other pasta

Heat the oil in a medium saucepan that is wider than it is deep. Add the beef or veal and pork and cook, uncovered, over a moderate heat, breaking the meat up with a fork. When the meat loses its color, add the onion, carrot, and salt and pepper to taste. Continue cooking, uncovered, over a moderate heat, stirring often until the meat begins to brown. Drain off and discard the fat. Add the Marsala and basil, cover, and lower the heat. Simmer, stirring often, until the wine cooks out. Remove the mushrooms from the soaking liquid, strain the liquid, and add both the mushrooms and the liquid to the meat mixture along with the tomatoes. Cover and boil gently for about 1½ hours.

Cook spaghetti or other pasta in a large pot of rapidly boiling salted water until done al dente. Drain and mix with about half the sauce.

Pasta Sauce Made with Goat Meat

Once I asked an old gentleman from Calabria what his favorite pasta was, and without hesitation he said pasta served with goat meat sauce. He gave me the recipe, and the following is my slightly modified version, which I like very much.

Serves 6 to 8.

½ cup diced salt pork
1 medium onion, peeled and
  left whole
1 medium carrot
2 pounds goat meat, including
  the bones
½ pig's foot, split lengthwise,
  or a piece of pork with the
  bone
Salt and freshly ground black
  pepper to taste
½ rib celery
1 cup dry white wine

4 cups peeled and seeded tomatoes, put through a food mill
2 tablespoons tomato paste, preferably homemade (page 31)
1 cup warm water
3 cloves garlic, with the skins
  on
2 tablespoons chopped fresh
  basil, or 1 tablespoon dried
1½ pounds pasta, such as
  fettuccine (dried, imported)
Freshly grated Pecorino
  Romano

Heat the blade of a heavy knife over an open flame for about 30 seconds. Place the salt pork on a chopping board and chop it with the hot knife until it becomes a paste. Put the paste in a large saucepan and slowly cook over moderate heat until it melts. Turn the heat to medium, add the onion along with the carrot, goat meat, pig's foot or other pork, and salt and pepper to taste and cook, stirring often, until the meat is golden brown. Add the celery and wine, cover, lower the heat, and simmer gently until the wine cooks out. Then add the tomatoes, tomato paste, water, garlic, and basil, cover, and boil gently for 2½ hours. Remove the meat and vegetables with a slotted spoon and keep them warm; discard the bones. The cook may eat the garlic cloves spread on a piece of bread, or squeeze them back into the sauce.

Cook the pasta in rapidly boiling salted water until done al dente. Drain well, and in a large, wide serving bowl toss it with the sauce and sprinkle with the grated Pecorino Romano. You may serve the meat and vegetables along with the pasta or as a second course.

Pasta with Tomatoes, Wild Mushrooms, and Fried Eggplant

This pasta is tossed with a rough-textured sauce and then garnished with fried eggplant. It is best made with cut pasta such as penne or farfalle.

Serves 4 to 6.

2 tablespoons olive oil

2 medium onions, finely chopped

3 cups sliced wild or cultivated mushrooms (I use oyster mushrooms)

2 cups seeded and chopped tomatoes

2 tablespoons chopped fresh basil, or 1 tablespoon dried

½ cup chicken broth, preferably homemade (page 194)

Salt and freshly ground black pepper to taste

1 medium eggplant, cut into ¼-inch slices

Flour for dredging

Vegetable oil for frying

1 pound cut pasta, such as penne or farfalle

4 to 6 tablespoons freshly grated Pecorino Romano

In a medium skillet or saucepan, heat the olive oil until hot, then sauté the onions, uncovered, over moderate heat until they begin to brown. Add the mushrooms and cook for 5 minutes. Add the tomatoes, basil, and chicken broth along with salt and pepper to taste, cover, and simmer the sauce for 45 minutes, stirring occasionally.

Meanwhile, dust the eggplant with flour and shake off all the excess. In a small skillet, heat ¾ inch of oil until hot and fry the eggplant slices, a few at a time, until brown on both sides. Remove and blot with paper towels. Slice into ½-inch-wide strips and set aside.

Cook the pasta in a large pot of rapidly boiling salted water until done al dente, drain, and add to the sauce. Toss with the Pecorino Romano (1 tablespoon per person). Serve immediately with each portion garnished with strips of eggplant.

Pasta with Cauliflower

This recipe was given to me by a young Sicilian who worked on a cruise ship. I met him in Manganaros, the famous Italian food store in New York City. It is an unusual recipe because it uses egg white as part of the dressing.

Serves 6.

1 medium cauliflower, cut into flowerets (about 6 cups)
¾ pound cut pasta, such as farfalle or penne
¼ cup olive oil
1 large onion, finely chopped
Hot pepper flakes or freshly ground black pepper to taste
2 tablespoons finely chopped flat-leaved parsley

2 teaspoons chopped fresh oregano, or 1 teaspoon dried
Salt to taste
6 egg whites, lightly beaten
Garnish: Freshly ground Pecorino Romano or finely chopped flat-leaved parsley

Boil the cauliflower flowerets in salted water for 5 minutes. Drain, cool, and chop coarsely. Put the pasta in a large pot of boiling salted water. As the pasta is cooking, heat the oil in a medium skillet and sauté the onion, hot pepper flakes or ground pepper, parsley, and oregano until the onion begins to brown. Add the cauliflower and salt to taste. When the pasta is cooked al dente, drain it, leaving a little moisture still on the pasta. Toss it in a serving bowl with the egg whites for approximately 30 seconds. Add the cauliflower and onion mixture and toss. Serve immediately with a garnish of Parmesan or parsley.

Spaghetti with Garlic Greens and Anchovies

I like to make this recipe in early spring when the garlic leaves, or greens, are young and tender. Do not pick the leaders (central stalks). Wild garlic— domestic garlic that has gone to seed—can also be used. The garlic greens serve as a garnish and the spaghetti here is just coated with a barely cooked mixture of oil, chopped garlic, and anchovies.

Serves 4 to 6.

1 pound spaghetti
¼ cup olive oil
1 tablespoon finely chopped
garlic, or more, if you like
8 anchovy fillets, either packed
in oil or salted, coarsely
chopped
Hot pepper flakes or freshly
ground black pepper to taste

2 tablespoons finely chopped
flat-leaved parsley
2 teaspoons chopped fresh
oregano, or 1 teaspoon dried
Salt to taste
Garnish:
6 tablespoons finely chopped
garlic greens
2 tablespoons extra virgin olive oil

In a large pot of rapidly boiling salted water, cook the pasta until done al dente. While it is cooking, heat the olive oil in a large skillet until hot, add the garlic, anchovy fillets, hot pepper flakes or black pepper, parsley, and oregano and sauté for a few seconds, uncovered, over moderate heat until the garlic begins to color. Add about ¼ cup of the hot water in which the pasta is cooking and cook for about 1 minute. Remove from the heat.

When the pasta is cooked, drain and add it to the skillet. Turn up the heat, add salt to taste, and toss for about 30 seconds. Garnish each portion with the fresh chopped garlic greens and a little extra virgin olive oil.

Spaghettini with Fresh Sardines

In this recipe and the variations that follow, the seafood is cooked in with the vegetables that dress the pasta.

Serves 6.

1 pound fresh sardines
3 tablespoons olive oil
3 cloves garlic, finely chopped
1½ tablespoons finely chopped
flat-leaved parsley
Hot pepper flakes to taste
(optional)
2 cups peeled, seeded, and
chopped tomatoes

1 tablespoon tomato paste,
preferably homemade (page
31), diluted in 1 cup hot
water
2 teaspoons chopped fresh
oregano, or 1 teaspoon dried
1 pound spaghettini

Prepare the sardines: Remove the heads. Cut open the belly and remove the entrails, then pull out the spine with your thumb and forefinger.

Heat the olive oil and sauté the garlic, parsley, and hot pepper flakes, if using, until the garlic begins to color. Add the sardines and cook until they fall apart, then add the tomatoes along with the diluted tomato paste and oregano. Simmer gently, stirring often, for 30 minutes.

Meanwhile, cook the pasta in a large pot of rapidly boiling salted water until done al dente, drain, toss with the sauce, and serve immediately.

VARIATION:

Pasta with Cod, Tomatoes, and Mint

In this recipe you can use any firm-fleshed fish, such as scrod, catfish, or bass.

Serves 6.

3 tablespoons extra virgin olive
   oil
3 cloves garlic, finely chopped
A healthy number of hot
   pepper flakes (depending on
   your taste)
3 tablespoons finely chopped
   flat-leaved parsley
3 tablespoons finely chopped
   fresh mint

1½ pounds Italian plum
   tomatoes, peeled, seeded,
   and cut into wedges
1 pound fresh cod fillets, cut
   into 1-inch-wide strips
1 pound cut pasta, such as
   farfalle or penne

Heat the olive oil and add the garlic, hot pepper flakes, parsley, and mint, and sauté until the garlic just begins to color. Then add the tomatoes, cover, and cook about 10 minutes, stirring often to break up the tomatoes. Add the fish pieces to the sauce, cover, and simmer for about 5 minutes, occasionally turning the sauce over gently, in a rolling motion, so as not to break up the fish. Meanwhile, cook the pasta in a large pot of rapidly boiling salted water until al dente. Drain and toss with the sauce.

VARIATION:

Spaghettini with Whiting and Spring Lettuce or Rucola

Serves 6.

3 tablespoons olive oil

4 cloves garlic, finely chopped

Hot pepper flakes to taste

2 tablespoons finely chopped
    flat-leaved parsley

3 tablespoons coarsely chopped
    fresh mint

1 cup peeled, seeded, and
    chopped tomatoes

½ cup dry white wine

2 medium whitings (about
    1 pound each), gutted, gilled,
    and scaled, but with heads
    left on

¾ pound spaghettini

¼ pound spring (baby) lettuce
    or rucola (arugula), cut into
    strips

Heat the olive oil, add the garlic and hot pepper flakes to taste, and sauté until the garlic begins to take on color. Toss in the parsley, mint, and tomatoes, cover, and cook over moderate heat for about 5 minutes. Then pour in the wine and continue to cook, covered, for about 6 to 8 minutes more. Add the fish, cover, and simmer until it is cooked, about 6 to 8 minutes.

Gently remove the fish with a spatula, remove and discard the skin and bones, and set the flesh aside.

Meanwhile, cook the pasta in a large pot of rapidly boiling salted water until al dente and combine with the sauce. Turn up the heat and cook, tossing constantly, for about 30 seconds. Transfer to a serving bowl and toss with the fish and lettuce or rucola. Serve immediately.

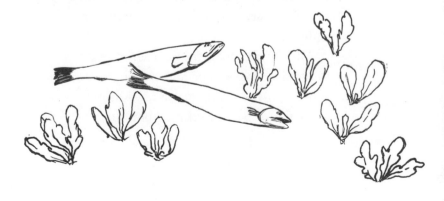

Butterfly Pasta with Smoked Salmon and Wild Mushrooms

Any place that sells smoked salmon is bound to have some end pieces or trimmings, so ask for them and make this unusual pasta dish.

Serves 6.

2 tablespoons butter and
  2 tablespoons olive oil or
  4 tablespoons olive oil
1 medium onion, finely
  chopped
4 cups sliced wild or cultivated
  mushrooms, or 1 ounce
  dried Italian mushrooms,
  soaked for 15 minutes in
  tepid water
½ pound smoked salmon ends,
  thinly sliced, or smoked
  salmon shreds

3 tablespoons brandy
6 tablespoons chicken broth,
  preferably homemade (page
  194)
Freshly ground black pepper to
  taste
1 pound farfalle or similar cut
  pasta
Garnish: 2 tablespoons finely
  chopped flat-leaved parsley

Heat the butter and oil in a wide skillet and sauté the onion and mushrooms, uncovered, until the liquid from the mushrooms cooks out. If dried mushrooms are used, strain and reserve the liquid, cook the mushrooms for about 5 minutes, then add the reserved liquid and cook until it cooks out. Add the salmon and cook for several minutes, then add the brandy and cook until the brandy cooks out. Pour in the broth and season with black pepper and simmer for approximately 5 minutes.

Meanwhile, cook the pasta in rapidly boiling salted water until it is done al dente. Drain and add it to the skillet with the salmon and mushrooms. Toss the pasta for a minute or so. Serve immediately with a garnish of parsley on each portion.

Pasta with Grilled Scallops

Here the grilled scallops serve as a garnish for the cut pasta, which is tossed in a sauce of mushrooms, celery, and tomatoes. For this recipe, I prefer to use Long Island scallops.

Serves 4.

2 tablespoons olive oil plus a
little additional for scallops
1 small onion, finely chopped
1½ cups thinly sliced
mushrooms
1 tablespoon finely chopped
shallots
1 cup finely chopped celery
2 cups peeled, seeded, and
chopped tomatoes
1 tablespoon finely chopped
flat-leaved parsley

Hot pepper flakes to taste
(optional)
¾ pound cut pasta, such as
penne or farfalle
2 tablespoons brandy
¾ pound sea or bay scallops
1 fat clove garlic, finely
chopped
Salt and freshly ground black
pepper to taste

In a medium skillet, heat 2 tablespoons olive oil until hot and sauté the onion and mushrooms over medium heat until the onion begins to take on color. Add the shallots and celery and continue to sauté for several minutes. Add the tomatoes, parsley, and hot pepper flakes, if using, cover, and simmer for 20 minutes.

While the sauce is cooking, cook the pasta in a large pot of rapidly boiling salted water until done al dente, drain, add to the sauce and stir in the brandy. Toss the pasta in the sauce over high heat for about 1 minute.

Meanwhile, combine the scallops in a bowl with the garlic, a little olive oil, and salt and pepper. Place the scallops in a basket grill or thread onto skewers and grill over hot coals for about 1 minute on each side for bay scallops and a minute or two longer for sea scallops. Serve the pasta in warm bowls—each serving topped with some of the grilled scallops.

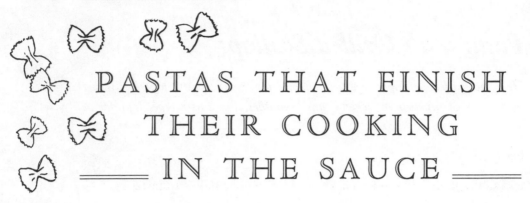

PASTAS THAT FINISH THEIR COOKING IN THE SAUCE

Pasta with Clams, Broccoli, and Brandy

Serves 6.

1 bunch broccoli, with
   flowerets and peeled stems
   cut into bite-sized pieces
3 tablespoons olive oil
Hot pepper flakes to taste
   (I like to use a generous
   amount)
2 large cloves garlic, finely
   chopped
2 tablespoons chopped fresh
   basil

2 cups plum tomatoes, peeled,
   seeded, and sliced
1 dozen medium clams, sliced,
   broth strained and reserved
1 pound flat pasta, such as
   farfalle
¼ cup brandy
Salt to taste
Garnish: Finely chopped
   flat-leaved parsley

Boil the broccoli in a large pot of salted water for 2 minutes. Drain. Heat the oil in a medium skillet and sauté the hot pepper flakes, garlic, and basil until the garlic begins to take on color. Add the tomatoes and simmer, covered, for 10 minutes. Add the broccoli and cook for 5 minutes more, then pour in the clam broth, bring the sauce to a boil, and add the sliced clams.

Meanwhile, cook the pasta in rapidly boiling salted water until about 2 minutes before it is done al dente. Drain the pasta and add it to the broccoli and clam sauce along with the brandy. Cook the pasta and sauce for about 2 minutes, stirring often. Add salt to taste. Serve immediately with a garnish of chopped parsley on each portion.

VARIATION:
Pasta with Shrimp, Peas, and Tomatoes

Serves 6.

3 tablespoons olive oil
3 cloves garlic, finely chopped
3 tablespoons finely chopped
   flat-leaved parsley
2 cups fresh peas
2 cups peeled, seeded, and
   chopped tomatoes
2 tablespoons chopped fresh
   basil, or 1 tablespoon dried

Salt and hot pepper flakes to
   taste
1 pound shrimp, shelled
1 pound cut pasta, such as
   penne or farfalle
2 tablespoons brandy
Garnish: Finely chopped flat-
   leaved parsley

In a large skillet heat the oil until hot and sauté the garlic and parsley over moderate heat, uncovered, stirring often, until the garlic begins to take on color. Add the peas, along with the tomatoes, basil, and salt and hot pepper flakes. Lower the heat, cover, and simmer for about 20 minutes.

Meanwhile, cook the pasta in a large pot of rapidly boiling salted water until done nearly al dente, then drain.

Add the shrimp to the tomato-pea mixture and cook for 1 minute. Then add the hot pasta and brandy and cook, stirring constantly, for 1 to 2 minutes or just until the shrimp are pink. Be careful not to over-cook the shrimp.

Garnish with parsley and serve at once.

VARIATION:
Cut Pasta with Clams, Shrimp, and Rape

Serves 6.

1 pound cut pasta, such as
   penne or farfalle
8 cups rape, stems peeled
8 cherrystone clams, chopped,
   juice strained and reserved
¼ cup olive oil

4 cloves garlic, finely chopped
Hot pepper flakes or freshly
   ground black pepper to taste
⅔ pound shrimp, shelled
Garnish: Extra virgin olive oil

Cook the pasta in rapidly boiling salted water for 5 minutes, then add the rape, and continue to cook until a few minutes before the pasta is done al dente.

Next, open the clams, chop and reserve the flesh and strain and reserve the juice. Set aside.

Heat the olive oil in a large skillet, add the garlic and hot pepper flakes or ground black pepper to taste and sauté until the garlic begins to take on color. Add the strained clam juice. When the pasta is almost done al dente, drain it and the rape. Toss both into the skillet with the garlic and clam juice. Turn up the heat and cook, uncovered, mixing constantly for about a half minute, until the clam juice is absorbed by the pasta. Add the shrimp and continue cooking, covered, stirring often, until the shrimp turns pink, about 2 minutes. Add the chopped clams and mix with the pasta for about 15 seconds. Serve on hot plates garnished with a little extra virgin olive oil.

Pasta and Clams My Way

Serves 4 to 6.

The fish stock:

4 cups water
1 rib celery, cut in half
1 carrot, cut into 2-inch chunks
1 small onion, chopped
1 teaspoon dried basil
1 tablespoon coarsely chopped
  flat-leaved parsley

2 pounds fish heads and bones,
  preferably from whitefish,
  rinsed of all blood, and gills
  removed
Salt and freshly ground black
  pepper to taste

12 cups spinach
Salt and freshly ground black
  pepper to taste
8 cherrystone clams,
  or 12 littleneck
  clams
3 tablespoons olive oil

3 or 4 fat cloves garlic, finely
  chopped
Hot pepper flakes to taste
  (optional)
2 tablespoons finely chopped
  flat-leaved parsley
1 pound linguine or spaghetti

Make the fish stock: In a stockpot combine all the stock ingredients, bring the liquid to a boil over moderate heat, and boil it gently—a simmer, really—for 45 minutes. Strain the stock into a bowl. You should have about 1 cup. If you have more than that, return the stock to the pot and reduce it over high heat.

While the stock is simmering, cook the spinach, uncovered, in a large pot of boiling salted water for 5 minutes. Drain and when it is cool squeeze out as much of the water as possible. Chop the spinach. In a food processor puree the spinach with the stock and salt and pepper to taste.

With a very sharp knife, open the clams carefully, reserving the clam juice in a small bowl. Chop the clams.

In a large skillet heat the oil over moderate heat until hot and add the garlic and pepper flakes, if using. When the garlic just begins to turn color—don't let it brown—add the reserved clam juice and 2 tablespoons parsley and cook, stirring occasionally, for 5 minutes.

Meanwhile, bring a large pot of salted water to a boil and in it cook the pasta until amost al dente. Drain the pasta and toss it into the skillet. Increase the heat to high and stir constantly until all of the clam juice is absorbed by the pasta. Add the chopped clams and spinach puree and heat, stirring, for about 30 seconds. Serve on heated plates at once.

Linguine and Skate

Serves 6.

3 tablespoons olive oil
1 onion, finely chopped
2 cloves garlic, finely chopped
1 tablespoon chopped flat-leaved parsley
2 cups peeled, seeded, and chopped ripe tomatoes
2 tablespoons chopped fresh basil

Salt and freshly ground black pepper to taste
2 tablespoons brandy
2 pounds skate wing, skinned on both sides (bones intact) and cut into 3 pieces
1 pound linguine
Garnish: Chopped flat-leaved parsley

In a medium skillet, heat the olive oil and sauté the onion until it begins to brown. Add the garlic and parsley and continue to sauté until the garlic begins to color. Then add the tomatoes along with the basil and salt and pepper to taste. Cover and simmer over low heat for 15 minutes. Add the brandy and skate wing pieces and simmer, covered, for 20 minutes more. With a fork, flake the skate off the bones into the sauce; discard bones.

Meanwhile, cook the pasta in a large pot of rapidly boiling salted water until done nearly al dente, drain, and add it to the skate mixture. Cook, uncovered, 1 minute more and serve at once, garnished with chopped parsley.

Rigatoni with Fish Balls

Serves 6.

2 large whitings (about 2¾ pounds of fish), or the equivalent of cod, red snapper, or other white-fleshed fish, with heads on
¼ cup olive oil
2 cloves garlic, finely chopped
Hot pepper flakes to taste
1 bell pepper, preferably red, finely chopped
2 tablespoons finely chopped flat-leaved parsley
4 cups chopped, seeded tomatoes

Salt and freshly ground black pepper to taste
2 teaspoons chopped fresh oregano, or 1 teaspoon dried
¼ cup pesto (page 228)
2 egg whites, lightly beaten
¼ cup freshly grated Parmesan (optional)
1 pound rigatoni or similar cut pasta, such as penne
¼ cup brandy
Garnish: Finely chopped flat-leaved parsley

Fillet the fish, then remove the skin. Your fishmonger can do this, or you can do it if you prefer. Save the bones, skin, and heads.

Heat the oil in a medium shallow pan, add the garlic, hot pepper flakes, bell pepper, and parsley and sauté over moderate heat until the garlic begins to take on color. Add the tomatoes, salt and pepper to taste, and oregano. Cover and simmer for 10 minutes.

Meanwhile, finely chop the fish fillets and combine with the pesto, egg whites, and grated cheese, if using, in a mixing bowl. Form into balls 1½ inches in diameter. (The balls will be soft and more difficult to handle than meatballs; try wetting your hands or rubbing them with olive oil.)

After the sauce has cooked for about 10 minutes, add the fish heads, skins, and bones. (If you wish, wrap them in cheesecloth before adding to the sauce.) Cover and simmer for 20 minutes, then remove the heads, skins, and bones and discard. Add the fish balls to the sauce and cook very slowly over low heat for about 5 minutes. Carefully remove the fish balls with a slotted spoon and keep them warm.

Cook the pasta in rapidly boiling salted water for 6 minutes. Drain and add the pasta to the sauce. Add the brandy, turn up the heat, and finish cooking the pasta in the sauce, stirring often. As the pasta cooks, regulate the heat under the sauce so that most of the sauce is absorbed by the time the pasta is al dente, about 4 minutes. Serve a few fish balls with each portion of pasta and garnish with parsley.

Vermicelli with Anchovies and Walnuts

Serves 4.

2 tablespoons olive oil
3 cloves garlic, finely chopped
2 tablespoons finely chopped flat-leaved parsley
6 anchovy fillets, coarsely chopped (salted anchovies are preferable to tinned)
1½ cups chicken broth, preferably homemade (page 194)
¾ pound vermicelli or spaghettini

15 walnuts (about ½ cup shelled)
Garnish: 1½ cups fresh bread crumbs, browned*
Chopped flat-leaved parsley
2 red bell peppers, roasted, peeled, and sliced into ½-inch strips (page 48)
Extra virgin olive oil (optional)

In a medium-to-large skillet, heat the oil, then add the garlic, parsley, and anchovy fillets, and sauté over moderate heat, stirring often, until the garlic begins to take on color. Add the broth and bring to a boil. Set aside.

* To brown, mix 2 tablespoons olive oil and salt and pepper to taste with the bread crumbs. Spread on a baking tray and brown them under the broiler.

Vermicelli
with
Anchovies
and
Walnuts
(continued)

Cook the pasta in rapidly boiling salted water for 5 minutes.

Finely chop the walnut meats (I use a food processor). Drain the pasta and add it to the broth mixture in the skillet. Continue cooking over a moderate to high heat, stirring often, until the pasta is done al dente; add more broth if necessary. Mix in the walnut meats. Serve immediately on heated plates, garnished with the browned bread crumbs, a little chopped parsley, and the sliced, roasted red peppers.

Note: If the dish is too dry, add a little extra virgin olive oil to each portion.

Pasta Shells with Mushrooms, Tomatoes, and Peas

Serves 4.

3 tablespoons olive oil
3 cups sliced mushrooms
¾ onion, finely chopped
1 tablespoon finely chopped
    flat-leaved parsley
¾ cup coarsely chopped
    tomatoes
Salt and hot pepper flakes to
    taste

1½ cups peas
1½ cups chicken or beef broth,
    preferably homemade (for
    chicken broth, see page 194)
¾ pound pasta shells or other
    cut pasta
Garnish: Freshly grated
    Parmesan (optional)

Heat the oil in a medium skillet until hot, add the mushrooms and onion and sauté until the liquid from the mushrooms cooks out. Add the parsley, tomatoes, and salt and hot pepper flakes to taste; cover and simmer for 20 minutes.

Meanwhile, cook the peas in the broth until tender, about 8 minutes. Transfer the tomato-mushroom sauce to a large skillet, add the peas and broth, and simmer, covered, for about 5 minutes.

While the peas are cooking, cook the pasta in a large pot of rapidly boiling salted water for 5 minutes, drain, and add to the sauce. Cook over moderate heat, stirring often, until the pasta is done al dente. Garnish each portion with freshly grated Parmesan, if desired.

═══ BAKED PASTAS ═══

Lasagna with Eggplant, Mushrooms, and Meat Sauce My Way

Serves 12 (amply) as a first course, 8 as a main course.

The sauce:

6 tablespoons olive oil
4 cups chopped onions
2 cups chopped carrots
4 cloves garlic, peeled and
  crushed
2 quarts seeded and chopped
  tomatoes
3 tablespoons chopped fresh
  basil, or 1½ tablespoons
  dried

1 cup water
Salt and freshly ground black
  pepper to taste
1½ pounds coarsely ground
  lean pork
½ cup dry white wine
10 cups thinly sliced
  mushrooms

3 medium eggplants, unpeeled
Flour for dredging
Corn oil for frying
1 tablespoon olive oil
1 pound lasagna pasta,
  preferably imported Italian,
  either green or yellow

½ teaspoon freshly grated
  nutmeg
1 cup half-and-half cream
Freshly grated Parmesan

For the sauce: Heat 3 tablespoons of the olive oil in a medium-to-large saucepan, then sauté the onions and carrots over a medium heat until the onions begin to brown. Add the garlic and continue to sauté for a minute more. Add the tomatoes along with the basil, water, salt, and pepper; cover, lower the heat, and simmer for 15 to 20 minutes.

*Lasagna
with
Eggplant,
Mushrooms,
and Meat
Sauce
(continued)*

Pour into a food processor and puree. Return the sauce to the pot and continue to cook over medium heat.

Meanwhile, prepare the meat for the sauce. Brown the pork, seasoned with salt and pepper, in a large skillet over medium heat, stirring often. Add the wine, cover, and cook over a low heat until the wine evaporates. Add the pork to the tomato sauce. Simmer, covered, over low heat for 45 minutes, stirring often.

To prepare the mushrooms for the sauce, while the sauce is simmering, heat the remaining 3 tablespoons of oil in the skillet that was used to brown the pork. Add the mushrooms and cook, uncovered, until the liquid cooks out. Season with salt and pepper to taste, then mix into the tomato sauce. Simmer, covered, for an additional 45 minutes.

Slice the eggplants into ¼-inch-thick pieces. Layer the slices on a tray with paper towels between each layer. Allow to stand for 15 minutes.

Lightly dust the eggplant slices in flour. Heat approximately ¾ inch of corn oil in a medium skillet, and brown the eggplant slices on both sides. Drain on paper towels. Or, bake eggplant slices as in the Light Eggplant Lasagne recipe that follows.

Meanwhile, preheat the oven to 475°.

Bring a large pot of salted water to a boil. Add 1 tablespoon olive oil and drop the lasagna sections into the water one at a time so they will not stick together. Boil the pasta for 5 minutes. Run cold water into the pot to cool off the pasta, then remove the strips one at a time and spread them out in a single layer on a smooth surface. You will need approximately ¾ pound of pasta for this recipe, but some strips may break, so you might as well cook a pound and select the best pieces.

To assemble the lasagna: Spoon some sauce onto the bottom of a baking dish (about 14 by 10 by 2½ inches), add a layer of pasta, a layer of eggplant, a layer of sauce, another layer of pasta, eggplant, sauce, nutmeg, and cream and repeat the process until the dish is filled. Top the lasagna off with a layer of pasta, sauce, and grated Parmesan. Cover with foil and bake for approximately 35 minutes. Allow to rest for several minutes before serving.

Note: You will have about 1½ cups of sauce left over, enough for 1 pound of pasta.

Light Eggplant Lasagna

I think you will find that this is the lightest ricotta lasagna you have ever tasted! The eggplant slices are baked rather than fried.

Serves 14

The sauce:

¼ cup olive oil

5 cups coarsely chopped onions

1 cup sliced carrots

3 cloves garlic, coarsely chopped

6 cups chopped tomatoes

1½ pounds thinly sliced
   mushrooms

1 cup water

2 tablespoons chopped fresh
   basil, or 1 tablespoon dried

Salt and freshly ground black
   pepper to taste

3 medium eggplants, unpeeled,
   cut into ¼-inch-thick slices

¼ cup olive oil

The filling:

2 pounds fresh ricotta

2 egg whites, lightly beaten

2 tablespoons finely chopped
   flat-leaved parsley

½ teaspoon freshly grated
   nutmeg

Salt and freshly ground black
   pepper to taste

1 pound green lasagna,
   preferably imported Italian

For the sauce: Heat the oil in a medium shallow pan, add the onions and carrots and sauté them over medium heat until the onions begin to brown. Add the garlic and continue to sauté a minute, then add the tomatoes, cover, and simmer over a medium heat, stirring often, for 20 to 25 minutes. Put the sauce in a food processor and blend until smooth. Return the sauce to the pan and add the mushrooms, water, basil, salt, and pepper. Cover and simmer gently for 30 minutes, stirring often. (This can be done up to 3 days in advance if kept refrigerated. It can be frozen for 3 months.)

Meanwhile, preheat the oven to 500°.

Cut the eggplant into ¼-inch-thick slices and place as many slices as you can snugly fit on two oiled baking trays and drizzle a little olive oil from the bottle or can over them. Bake until the eggplant browns on the bottom side, then with a metal spatula flip the slices over to the other side and brown. Remove to a platter and repeat until all of the eggplant slices are browned. (This step can be done a day in advance. Cover and refrigerate.)

Prepare the filling: Combine the ricotta, egg whites, parsley, nutmeg, and salt and pepper until well blended.

For the pasta, bring a large pot of salted water to a boil. Slide the lasagna sheets into the boiling water one at a time, stir with a long-handled spoon, and cook for 5 minutes. Drain the pasta and rinse in cold water.

Preheat oven to 400° for lasagna.

To assemble the lasagna: Ladle some of the sauce over the bottom of a 14- by 17- by 3-inch baking pan. Put a layer of pasta on the sauce, then a layer of half the eggplant slices, and spread half the ricotta mixture over the eggplant slices. Put a layer of pasta over the ricotta, then a layer of sauce. Make another layer of eggplant and ricotta and continue this process, ending with a layer of pasta and sauce. You will have some pasta left over, but it is best to make more than you may need because some of the pieces will break.

Cover with foil and bake the lasagna in the preheated oven for 30–45 minutes, until liquid on top has been boiling for 5 minutes. Remove from the oven and allow it to rest for 10 to 15 minutes before serving.

VARIATION WITHOUT RICOTTA: If you want to eliminate the ricotta, you can use **6 cups blanched broccoli, cauliflower, or a combination,** drained and sautéed in **olive oil,** or an equal amount of sautéed cut-up **asparagus.**

Cannelloni

I use dried cannelloni tubes (Del Verde, imported from Italy, which you do not have to precook), and I find them excellent. You can make your own pasta dough—simply cut the sheets into squares 3 inches by 5 inches, stuff the centers, and fold over the sides.

The stuffing can be made with any combination of vegetables and meat, or you can use all vegetables. Vary this recipe as you like: spinach for Swiss chard, veal or beef for pork, and so on.

Serves 6.

The stuffing:

6 cups coarsely chopped Swiss
    chard
3 tablespoons olive oil
1 medium leek, sliced into
    ½-inch sections
1 pork chop, about ¾-inch
    thick, cut into ¾-inch
    cubes

1 chicken breast, cut into cubes
    ¾-inch square
1 small onion, chopped
⅓ cup dry white wine or dry Marsala
Salt and freshly ground black
    pepper to taste
1 teaspoon dried marjoram
1 egg, lightly beaten

1 package dried cannelloni
    (12 cannelloni), preferably
    Del Verde

The sauce:

1 cup basic tomato sauce or meat
    sauce (any marinara or meat
    sauce will do, see page 107)
¾ cup half-and-half cream

Freshly ground nutmeg
½ small potato, peeled
4 or more tablespoons freshly
    grated Parmesan

Preheat the oven to 400°.

For the stuffing: Boil the Swiss chard in salted water for 5 minutes. Drain, let cool, then squeeze out remaining moisture.

Heat the oil in a small skillet, then sauté the leek, pork, chicken, and onion over medium heat until golden brown. Add wine, salt and pepper to taste and marjoram and simmer, covered, until the wine cooks out.

Grind the meat, onion, leek, and Swiss chard together (they should be finely ground, so you can use a food processor). Add the egg and blend—taste for salt.

Stuff the dried cannelloni with this mixture—you do not have to precook Del Verde cannelloni because they are so thin. (If you use another brand or your own pasta, cook in a large pot of boiling salted water until just done al dente; then drain well.) Place the stuffed cannelloni in a lightly oiled baking dish.

Meanwhile prepare the sauce: Put the marinara or meat sauce in a saucepan with the cream, nutmeg, and the piece of peeled raw potato, cover, and simmer for about 10 minutes. (The potato keeps the sauce from curdling.) Remove the potato and pour the sauce over the cannelloni. Dust with cheese, cover lightly, and bake for about a half hour.

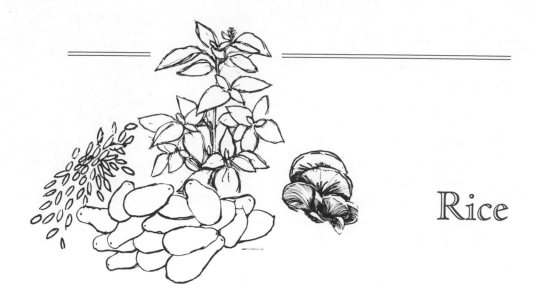

Rice

I prepare rice three ways:

1. If I am simply cooking plain rice, I use one part long-grain Carolina rice to two parts water, and steam it. Sometimes I serve it garnished with vegetables or meat and vegetables, and I use it as the foundation of a rice salad.

2. If I want to cook rice with fresh vegetables, such as peas, zucchini, tomatoes, etc., I usually use long-grain Carolina rice and cook it in broth or water along with the vegetables (see page 132). The result is a rice dish looser than risotto—more like a stew.

3. For a real risotto, I use Italian Arborio rice (available in Italian markets and gourmet stores). It is a short-grain, glutinous rice that makes a very creamy dish. The rice is invariably cooked in broth, added slowly while you stir the rice, and is often cooked in combination with vegetables and/or seafood, poultry, or meats. I use Arborio rice as a vehicle for whatever vegetables are in season. I am not of the school that you have to stand over risotto nursemaiding it as it cooks, but there are some guidelines to follow (see Basic Risotto recipe, page 134).

STEAMED RICE DISHES

Steamed Rice

Makes about 3 cups, serving 3 or 4.

1 cup good-quality rice,
  preferably Carolina

2 cups water
½ teaspoon salt

Put the rice, water, and salt in a small saucepan and bring to a boil. Lower the heat and cover by first placing a paper towel over the pan and then putting on the lid to make a tight seal. Cook for 10 minutes, then look at it and taste. If it has absorbed all the water, it should be tender. If it isn't, cover and cook a minute or two longer. Stir with a fork to fluff up.

Summer Rice Salad

Serves 4.

2 cups chicken broth, preferably homemade (page 194)
1 cup rice
6 to 8 tablespoons extra virgin
  olive oil
About 20 medium-thick
  asparagus spears, cut into
  1-inch sections (about 3 cups)
Salt to taste
1 cup peas, blanched until
  tender

6 ounces canned Italian-style
  tuna (in olive oil), preferably
  home-canned (page 268),
  drained
3 scallions, thinly sliced
3 tablespoons finely chopped
  flat-leaved parsley
Juice of 1 lemon
¾ cup thinly sliced onions*
Freshly ground black pepper to
  taste

* Vidalia onions are very sweet and good.

In a small pot, bring the broth to a boil, add the rice, cover tightly, and cook according to instructions on page 129.

In a small skillet heat 2 tablespoons of the oil and sauté the asparagus pieces over moderate heat until tender; season with salt.

In a large bowl toss the rice with the remaining ingredients, including the sautéed asparagus. Serve at room temperature and do not refrigerate.

VARIATION WITH SMOKED TROUT OR WHITEFISH: Instead of tuna, use an equivalent amount of **smoked trout or whitefish** cut into bite-sized pieces. Other lightly cooked vegetables may also be substituted for asparagus.

Rice Garnished with Sausages, Pork, and Cabbage

Serves 6 to 8.

2 tablespoons olive oil
½ pound lean ground pork
½ pound Italian-style sausage, preferably homemade (page 270)
1 medium onion, coarsely chopped
1 rib celery, coarsely chopped
1 tablespoon finely chopped flat-leaved parsley
½ cup dry white wine
2 cups chopped tomatoes

2 tablespoons chopped fresh basil, or 1 tablespoon dried
4 cups shredded savoy cabbage, blanched for 5 minutes and drained
Salt and freshly ground black pepper or hot pepper flakes to taste
8 cups chicken or beef broth, preferably homemade (for chicken broth, see page 194)
4 cups rice

Heat the oil in a medium shallow saucepan and slowly brown the pork and the sausage. When browned, drain off and discard fat. Stir in the onion, cover, and continue cooking over low heat, until the onion becomes translucent. Add the celery, parsley, and wine, cover, and simmer until the wine cooks out—about 10 minutes. Add the tomatoes and basil, cover, and simmer for another 15 minutes. Add the cabbage, season with salt and pepper or hot pepper flakes to taste, and continue to cook, covered, for 15 minutes more.

Meanwhile, bring the broth to a boil in a medium, deep pot, add the rice and cook as in the preceding recipe. Correct seasonings.

Put a mound of rice on a heated plate. Fish out the sausage and slice it. Ladle the cabbage sauce and sausages over each portion of rice.

Rice with Cranberry Beans

Serves 4.

The sauce:

2 tablespoons olive oil

2 tablespoons chopped
　prosciutto

1 small onion, coarsely chopped

2 fat cloves garlic, unpeeled

1 tablespoon finely chopped
　flat-leaved parsley

1 rib celery, coarsely chopped

1 cup chopped tomatoes

2 cups shelled fresh cranberry
　beans or other shell beans

½ cup diced carrots

2 teaspoons chopped fresh
　oregano, or 1 teaspoon dried

2 cups chicken or beef broth,
　preferably homemade (for
　chicken broth, see recipe
　page 194), or water

1 cup rice

Salt and freshly ground black
　pepper or hot pepper flakes
　to taste

Garnish: Finely chopped flat-
　leaved parsley or freshly
　grated Parmesan

For the sauce: Heat the oil in a medium soup pot and sauté the prosciutto and onion until the onion becomes translucent. Add the garlic along with the parsley and celery and continue to sauté for several minutes. Stir in the tomatoes, beans, carrots, and oregano, cover, lower the heat, and simmer for about 2½ hours.

About 30 minutes before serving time, bring the broth to a boil in a small, deep pot, stir in the rice and salt and pepper or pepper flakes, and cook according to instructions on page 129.

Add the cooked rice to the bean mixture, mix well and serve. Garnish with parsley or freshly grated cheese.

RICE STEWS

Rice with Eggplant, Peas, and Asparagus

Serves 4 to 6.

5 tablespoons olive oil
1 medium eggplant, diced
   (about 4 cups)
1 medium onion, finely
   chopped
2 cups peeled, seeded, and
   chopped tomatoes
1 cup peas
1 tablespoon chopped fresh
   basil, or 1½ teaspoons dried
Salt and freshly ground black
   pepper to taste

1 cup rice
2 cups chicken broth,
   preferably homemade (page
   194), or water
¼ pound asparagus, cut into
   1-inch pieces, yielding about
   1½ cups
Garnish: Finely chopped flat-
   leaved parsley

In a medium skillet heat 3 tablespoons of the oil until hot. Add the eggplant and sauté over moderate heat, stirring often, until it begins to brown. Remove from the skillet and set aside.

Heat the remaining 2 tablespoons oil in the same skillet and sauté the onion until it begins to brown. Add the tomatoes along with the basil and salt and pepper to taste. Cover, lower the heat, and simmer for 10 minutes.

In a saucepan combine the rice with the tomato mixture, the eggplant, peas, and half the broth and simmer, stirring often, for 8 to 10 minutes. Once the broth is absorbed, add more, as necessary. Add the asparagus and cook, stirring often until the rice is tender and the asparagus is cooked al dente. Garnish with the parsley before serving.

VARIATION:
Rice with Swiss Chard

Serves 4 to 6.

3 tablespoons olive oil

2 medium onions, coarsely chopped

½ cup coarsely chopped celery

⅓ cup coarsely chopped fresh basil

2 cups coarsely chopped tomatoes

2 medium potatoes, peeled and diced

Hot pepper flakes to taste (optional)

4 cups water

12 cups coarsely chopped Swiss chard (about 2 pounds), stalks stringed (page 78)

2 cups peas, blanched

Salt to taste

½ cup rice

Garnish: Extra virgin olive oil

In a medium saucepan, heat the olive oil and sauté the onions, celery, and basil until the onions are translucent. Add the tomatoes, potatoes, and hot pepper flakes to taste, if desired, and cook, covered, stirring occasionally, for 5 minutes. Add 4 cups water, the Swiss chard, blanched peas, and season with salt to taste. Bring to a boil and simmer, covered, for about 15 to 20 minutes. Toss in the rice and continue to cook, covered, over low heat until the rice is done. Ladle into soup bowls and serve at room temperature with a little extra virgin olive oil drizzled over the top. Do not refrigerate.

VARIATION:
Rice with Tomatoes

Serves 4 to 6.

3 tablespoons olive oil

1 medium onion, finely chopped

1½ cups rice

3 cups chicken broth, preferably homemade (page 194)

Salt and freshly ground black pepper to taste

1½ cups peeled, seeded, and chopped tomatoes

1½ tablespoons chopped fresh basil

Garnish: Freshly grated Parmesan or a few drops extra virgin olive oil

Heat the olive oil and sauté the onion until it begins to brown, then mix in the rice. Stir in the chicken broth and salt and pepper to taste, cover, and cook over a low heat for 5 minutes. Add the tomatoes and basil and continue cooking over low heat until the rice is tender, but not overcooked—approximately 6 minutes. Garnish each portion with freshly grated Parmesan or a few drops of extra virgin olive oil; I prefer the olive oil.

VARIATION:
With Other Fresh Vegetables

You may want to add one of the following vegetables during the last 6 minutes of cooking time:

1½ cups peas, blanched and
  drained
½ pound spinach, chopped

1½ cups diced zucchini
1½ cups chopped asparagus, cut
  into 1-inch pieces and sautéed

RISOTTOS

Basic Risotto

Serves 3.

2 tablespoons olive oil
1 medium onion, finely
  chopped
1 cup Arborio rice

2½ cups or more hot chicken broth,
  preferably homemade (page
  194)*
Salt and freshly ground black
  pepper to taste

In a medium saucepan, heat the olive oil, then sauté the onion until translucent. Add the rice and sauté for several minutes, stirring to coat

---

* Any kind of broth may be used—fish, beef, etc.

all the grains. Pour in ¼ cup of the hot broth and simmer over medium-low heat, stirring constantly, until the liquid is absorbed. Add ¼ cup more of the hot broth, and as the rice absorbs it, continue to add more broth, always stirring and scraping from the bottom of the pan. The rice is ready when the grains are tender but al dente, firm to the bite, and enrobed in the starch-thickened reduced broth, which has become creamy and luscious. It will take 15 to 20 minutes. Taste and season with salt and pepper.

Risotto with Green Beans

Serves 4.

> 1 cup 1-inch pieces green beans
> 4 tablespoons olive oil
> 1 small onion, finely chopped
> 1 cup peeled, seeded, and chopped fully ripe tomatoes
> 2 tablespoons finely chopped flat-leaved parsley
>
> 1 cup Arborio rice
> 2 cups hot chicken broth, preferably homemade (page 194)
> 1 tablespoon freshly grated Parmesan or 2 tablespoons grated Pecorino Romano

Blanch the beans in boiling water for 1 minute. Drain and set aside.

In a medium skillet heat 2 tablespoons of the olive oil and sauté the onion until translucent. Add the tomatoes along with the parsley, cover, and simmer for 5 minutes. Add the blanched beans, cover, and simmer for 10 minutes more.

Meanwhile, in a medium saucepan, heat the remaining 2 tablespoons olive oil, add the rice, and stir constantly for several minutes to coat the grains. Pour in ¼ cup of broth and continue to stir the rice over low to moderate heat until the liquid is absorbed. Continue cooking according to preceding basic instructions for approximately 6 minutes. Add the tomato-bean mixture and stir in more stock. Cook until the rice is tender and creamy. Mix in the grated cheese and serve at once.

VARIATIONS WITH OTHER VEGETABLES: Blanched **asparagus, cauliflower, peas, broccoli,** etc., may be used instead of the beans. Or sauté **mushrooms,** instead of tomatoes, with the onions and add when you add the tomato-bean mixture.

VARIATION:

Risotto with Chicken

Serves 3.

1 pound chicken parts (dark or white meat or a combination of the two), cut into 1-inch pieces, with bones intact

Salt and freshly ground black pepper

1 teaspoon chopped fresh or dried rosemary

1 tablespoon vegetable oil

2 cloves garlic, crushed

2 tablespoons extra virgin olive oil

1 medium onion, finely chopped

4 cups sliced wild or cultivated mushrooms

1 cup Arborio rice

½ cup dry vermouth

2 cups hot chicken broth, preferably homemade (page 194)

12 asparagus spears, cut into 1-inch pieces

3 tablespoons freshly grated Parmesan cheese

2 tablespoons finely chopped flat-leaved parsley

Season the chicken with salt and pepper, and sprinkle with rosemary. In a medium skillet, heat the 1 tablespoon vegetable oil until hot, then sauté the chicken until nicely browned and cooked through. A few minutes before the chicken is done, add the garlic. Remove the chicken from the skillet to a plate and keep it warm.

In a medium saucepan, heat the 2 tablespoons extra virgin olive oil and sauté the onion and mushrooms until the onion becomes translucent. Add the rice and continue to sauté for several minutes, stirring often. Add the vermouth and simmer, stirring constantly, until the vermouth cooks out. Continue cooking, adding hot broth according to the basic instructions on page 134 for approximately 6 minutes. Add the chicken and asparagus and continue cooking, adding more broth as necessary. Cook until the rice is tender and creamy but not overcooked. Mix in the cheese and chopped parsley before serving.

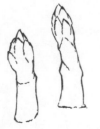    

Risotto with Shellfish and Peas

Serves 6.

*The fish stock (makes about
4 to 5 cups):*

10 cups water
1 medium onion
2 carrots, coarsely chopped
2 ribs celery, cut into 3-inch
  pieces
2 tablespoons coarsely chopped
  flat-leaved parsley

1 bay leaf
Salt and freshly ground black
  pepper to taste
1 tablespoon fennel seeds
2 to 3 pounds bones from lean
  fish, including heads, gills
  removed

The shellfish mixture:

3 tablespoons olive oil
1 pound squid, cleaned (page
  157) and cut into ½-inch-
  wide strips
2 tablespoons finely chopped
  flat-leaved parsley
2 cloves garlic, finely chopped
2 cups chopped tomatoes
1 tablespoon chopped fresh mint

Salt to taste
Hot pepper flakes to taste
  (optional)
1½ cups peas, blanched for 3
  minutes and drained
¾ pound shrimp, shelled
¾ pound sea scallops

The risotto:

3 tablespoons olive oil
1 medium onion, finely
  chopped
1 tablespoon finely chopped
  flat-leaved parsley
1¾ cups Arborio rice
½ cup dry white wine

About 4 cups fish stock
Salt and freshly ground black
  pepper to taste
Garnish:
Chopped flat-leaved parsley
Extra virgin olive oil (optional)

Make the fish stock: In a stockpot combine all of the stock ingredients, except the fish bones and heads, and bring to a boil. Boil, uncovered, for 20 minutes, then add the fish bones and heads, cover, and simmer for 25 minutes. Strain the stock into a bowl and discard all the solids.

Make the shellfish mixture: In a saucepan, heat the oil over moderate heat until hot. Then sauté the squid and parsley, stirring often, for about 5 minutes. Add the garlic and cook several minutes more. Add the tomatoes, mint, salt to taste, and hot pepper flakes, if using; cover, and simmer for about 5 minutes. Add the peas, cover and cook 15 minutes. Finally, add the shrimp and scallops and cook until the shrimp are tender, about 3 to 4 minutes more. Set the pan aside, partially covered.

Make the risotto: In a pan heat the oil until hot, then sauté the onion over moderate heat until it becomes translucent. Stir in the parsley and rice and continue to cook for several minutes, stirring often. Add the wine and cook until it cooks out. Add about 1 cup of the fish stock and salt and pepper to taste and cook, stirring continuously with a wooden spoon, until the stock is incorporated. Continue cooking and adding stock according to basic instructions on page 134 until the rice is tender but al dente.

With a soup ladle, scoop out a portion of the risotto onto a warm plate. Make a depression in it and ladle a generous amount of the shellfish mixture over the top. Serve at once.

Garnish with chopped Italian parsley. A little extra virgin olive oil is a nice touch.

Risotto Mold with Asparagus

A risotto can always be molded and it will hold its shape when turned out. You can use different seasonal vegetables to fill the center.

Serves 4.

4 tablespoons olive oil
2 medium onions, finely chopped
1½ cups chopped asparagus, cut into 1-inch pieces
1½ cups coarsely chopped mushrooms
1 tablespoon finely chopped flat-leaved parsley

3 cups chicken broth, preferably homemade (page 194)
Salt and freshly ground black pepper to taste
2 cups Arborio rice
2 tablespoons freshly grated Parmesan

Heat 2 tablespoons of the olive oil in a medium skillet until hot, then sauté half of the onions, the asparagus pieces, and the mushrooms, uncovered, over moderate heat for about 5 minutes. When the onions begin to brown, add the parsley, ⅓ cup of the broth, and salt and pepper. Cover and simmer until most of the broth cooks out, about 10 minutes. Set aside.

In a medium saucepan heat the remaining 2 tablespoons oil until hot and sauté the remaining chopped onions over moderate heat, uncovered, stirring constantly, for about 2 or 3 minutes. Add some of the remaining broth and cook the rice according to the directions for making risotto on page 134. The rice should be cooked but firm. Taste for salt and pepper and stir in the cheese.

Pack the rice firmly into a lightly oiled 6- to 8-inch-diameter ring mold. Cover the top of the mold with a plate and invert. Carefully remove the mold; the rice should be perfectly formed into a ring. Fill the center of the ring with the vegetable mixture, reheated if necessary. Serve each portion of rice with some of the asparagus mixture spooned over it.

VARIATION: The shellfish combination in Risotto with Shellfish and Peas (page 137) can be used in the center of the mold in place of the vegetables used above.

Polenta

I love polenta, which is really the same thing as cornmeal mush. It's always amazed me that southerners in the United States have never done more with their cornmeal mush, other than frying it; they aren't creative about adding vegetables and aromatics to give it flavor and texture or combining it with fish, fowl, or meats and letting the juices mingle. To me, polenta is one of the great carriers of flavors, always enhanced by good things from the garden.

You can use either fine- or coarse-ground cornmeal. The fine cooks much more quickly so it is easier to prepare; by the time you add the last handful, the water is almost absorbed and it is cooked. Coarse-ground will take at least 20 minutes to cook and must be stirred almost constantly.

If you let the cornmeal flow from your hand in a slow, steady stream into the boiling water as you are stirring, it will not lump. Imported Italian cornmeal, or polenta, as it is usually labeled, is always reliable, as are Canadian cornmeals. But I have tested several popular American brands and found that their texture was more flourlike and therefore difficult to release from the hand in a steady flow. As a result, the polenta became lumpy and too dense. The only exception was Aunt Jemima's pure cornmeal, and I found that that worked almost as well as a fine-ground imported product.

There are three ways of serving polenta:

First, loose polenta—that is, the cooked cornmeal is poured onto individual plates or a large board, then garnished with plain sauce or with strewed meats and vegetables.

Second, set polenta—that is, the cooked cornmeal is poured (sometimes mixed with vegetables) onto a baking tray or pie plate and allowed to set. Then a little olive oil is sprinkled over it and it is broiled until the top is crusted. The polenta can also be poured into a bowl, allowed to set about 10 minutes, and then unmolded to serve.

Third, grilled polenta—that is, the cooked cornmeal is poured onto a tray and allowed to set about 15 minutes. Then it is cut into squares, usually with a wire or a string, and the pieces are grilled on all sides; they can also be grilled under the broiler.

Basic Polenta

My rule of thumb in making polenta is to use 1 cup water per serving. Each cup of boiling water absorbs approximately ⅓ cup cornmeal and that makes an ample serving. You know when to stop pouring more cornmeal into the water when it reaches the right consistency.

Serves 3.

    3 cups water
    2 teaspoons kosher salt, or 1
        teaspoon table salt
    1 cup, more or less, cornmeal,
        fine or coarse, preferably
        imported (see preceding
        remarks)

Bring the water and salt to a gentle boil in a 2-quart (or larger) heavy saucepan. Add the cornmeal to the boiling water gradually by letting it trickle from your hand in a slow, steady stream, stirring constantly with a wooden spoon in your other hand. Continue until you have used as much of the cornmeal as necessary to make a polenta that is the consistency of thick porridge. If you are using fine-ground cornmeal, it will be almost done by the time you have added the final grains. Continue to cook about 1 minute. If you are using coarse-ground cornmeal, continue cooking, stirring all the time, making sure to scrape from the bottom of the pan, for about 20 minutes.

Polenta with Mixed Vegetables

This recipe and those that follow are excellent with broiled foods. An artist friend of mine said his father often made polenta and always made a cross on the surface before broiling.

Serves 6.

1 cup chopped string beans, cut into 1-inch sections
4 cups loosely packed spinach
1 medium onion, coarsely chopped

1 tablespoon olive oil plus extra for sprinkling
Salt to taste

The polenta:

1 cup cornmeal, fine or coarse
4 cups water
1 teaspoon table salt

Freshly ground black pepper to taste

Cook the string beans in salted boiling water in an uncovered pot until they are tender but firm, about 4 minutes. Cook the spinach in boiling water for 2 minutes, drain, cool, and squeeze out all excess moisture.

Sauté the onion in the olive oil until it begins to brown, then mix with the beans and spinach and season with salt to taste.

Preheat the broiler to hot.

For the polenta: Cook the cornmeal, water, and salt according to the instructions for polenta on page 141.

As soon as the polenta is cooked, add the vegetables and mix them in. Immediately pour the polenta and vegetable mixture into a 10-inch pie plate. Smooth the surface with a spatula and sprinkle with olive oil and pepper. Place under the broiler until its surface is lightly charred.

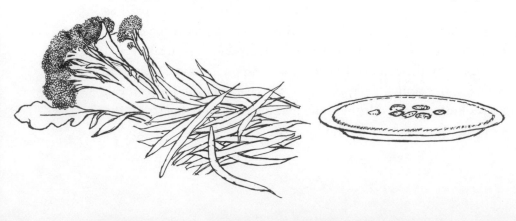

VARIATION:
Polenta with Rape

You may use spinach, dandelion greens, or sautéed asparagus with peppers instead of rape for this recipe.

Serves 6.

12 cups chopped rape
2 cloves garlic, finely chopped
Hot pepper flakes to taste

2 tablespoons olive oil plus
  extra for sprinkling

The polenta:

1 cup cornmeal, fine or coarse
4 cups water
Pepper

2 tablespoons kosher salt, or 1
  teaspoon table salt

Cook the rape in salted boiling water about 3 minutes, drain, and mix with the garlic, hot pepper flakes to taste, and olive oil. Cook over medium heat for 5 minutes, adding a little water if needed. Set aside.

For the polenta: Cook according to the instructions on page 141.

As soon as the polenta is cooked, add the vegetables and mix them in. Immediately pour the mixture into a 10-inch pie plate, sprinkle with olive oil and pepper, and broil until lightly charred.

VARIATION:
Polenta with Rape and Sausages

Serves 6.

¾ pound Italian-style sausage

For the polenta:

1 cup cornmeal, fine or coarse
4½ cups water

1 tablespoon kosher salt

2 cups rape, cooked
Olive oil for sprinkling

Pepper

Prick the sausage and brown in a skillet, uncovered, until cooked through, about 20 minutes. Cut into ¼-inch-thick slices and set aside.

Prepare the polenta as instructed above. As soon as the polenta is cooked, add the sausage and rape, cooked as in the preceding variation. Mix well, and immediately pour the polenta mixture into a 10-inch pie plate, sprinkle with olive oil and pepper, and broil as above.

VARIATION:

Polenta with Mashed Potatoes

Serves 6.

1 pound whole potatoes, preferably Idaho, unpeeled	2 tablespoons olive oil plus extra for sprinkling
3 cups thinly sliced onions	

For the polenta:

1 cup cornmeal, fine or coarse	2 tablespoons kosher salt, or 1 teaspoon table salt
4 cups water	
Pepper	

Cook the potatoes in boiling salted water until cooked but firm; drain, peel, and force through a potato ricer. Set aside.

Sauté the onions in the olive oil until they begin to brown. Mix with the potatoes.

For the polenta: Prepare as instructed on page 141.

As soon as the polenta is cooked, add the potato and onion mixture. Mix well and immediately pour the polenta mixture into a 10-inch pie plate, sprinkle with olive oil and pepper, and broil until lightly charred.

Sausage with Sauerkraut and Polenta

This recipe is from a mountainous region of Northern Italy. Use a light, superior sauerkraut; I use my homemade sauerkraut (page 64). I think you will be delighted with this satisfying winter dish.

Serves 4.

Vegetable oil	½ cup dry white wine
1 pound Italian-style sausage	2 cups sauerkraut, drained

The polenta:

6¾ cups water

1½ tablespoons kosher salt, or
   2½ teaspoons table salt

1½ cups cornmeal, fine or
   coarse

Rub the bottom of a medium skillet with vegetable oil. Prick the sausage, place it in the skillet, and brown on both sides over low heat, about 20 minutes. Drain all of the fat from the skillet, then add the wine and sauerkraut to the sausage. Turn up the heat and cook until the wine cooks out. Set aside and keep warm.

For the polenta: Cook according to the instructions on page 141. Pour onto a heated serving plate so that it is approximately ¾ inch thick.

Cut the sausage into 1-inch sections and place on the polenta. Pour the sauerkraut and juices over all and serve immediately.

Polenta with Ground Meat

It needs 2 hours' cooking time and, of course, you can prepare the dish ahead.

Makes enough sauce for polenta for 4 and an additional pound of pasta.

The sauce:

2 tablespoons olive oil

1 medium onion, finely chopped

1 pound lean ground beef (top
   of the round)

Salt and freshly ground black
   pepper to taste

1 ounce dried Italian mushrooms, covered with warm
   water and soaked at least 10
   minutes, or 10 ounces mushrooms, thinly sliced

½ cup dry white wine

4 cups seeded and chopped
   tomatoes

2 tablespoons chopped fresh
   basil, or 1 tablespoon dried

The polenta:

2¼ cups whole or skim milk

2¼ cups water

1 tablespoon kosher salt, approximately, or 1 teaspoon table salt

1 cup fine cornmeal

3 to 4 tablespoons freshly
   grated Parmesan

For the sauce: Heat the oil in a medium saucepan and sauté the onion until it begins to brown, then add the beef. Season with salt and pepper to taste and cook, uncovered, over high heat, until the meat changes color. Add the mushrooms (if using dried mushrooms, strain and reserve the soaking liquid), and cook over medium heat until all of the liquid cooks out. Add the wine and cook, uncovered, until the wine cooks out, then add the tomatoes along with the basil and the soaking liquid from the mushrooms, if you used dried, and adjust the seasonings. Cover and simmer for 2 hours.

Prepare the polenta: Use the milk and water as your liquid and follow the cooking instructions on page 141.

To assemble: Pour the cooked polenta into a 7- by 9-inch dish and spoon a generous amount of sauce over the surface, then sprinkle with some grated Parmesan. Pour the remaining polenta over the sauce, spoon more sauce over the polenta, and sprinkle with more grated cheese. Serve hot or at room temperature.

Pea and Polenta Mold

This recipe from Northern Italy makes a very attractive presentation and a light, elegant first course.

Serves 4 to 6 as a first course or as an accompaniment.

The polenta:

2½ cups cornmeal, fine or coarse	2½ tablespoons kosher salt, or 4 teaspoons table salt
7¼ cups water	
2 cups peas, boiled in salted water for 5 minutes and drained	4 cups meat sauce (page 107) ¼ cup freshly grated Pecorino Romano

For the polenta: Cook the polenta according to the instructions on page 141.

Pour the peas into a bowl about 9 to 10 inches in diameter and about 4 to 5 inches deep. Try to spread the peas out so they are in a single layer, then pour ¾ of the polenta over the peas and cover the polenta with a ¾-inch layer of sauce. Sprinkle the sauce with grated cheese, then spread the remaining polenta over the top. Let the mold stand for about 10 minutes, place a plate over the bowl, and carefully but quickly turn the bowl over to unmold it. Serve by cutting wedges as you would a cake.

VARIATION:

Polenta with a Layer of Spinach and Topped with Tomato-Mushroom Sauce

In this recipe, rather than using the sauce as a layer, you pour it over the mold.

Serves 4 to 6.

⅓ pound spinach
Salt and coarsely ground black
   pepper to taste
1 clove garlic, finely chopped

2 tablespoons freshly grated
   Parmesan
Dash of freshly grated nutmeg

The sauce:

2 tablespoons olive oil
1 medium onion, finely
   chopped
4 cups sliced wild mushrooms,
   such as boletus or honey
   mushrooms, or 4 cups sliced
   cultivated mushrooms plus
   1 ounce dried Italian
   mushrooms, soaked in warm
   water for 15 minutes,
   soaking water strained and
   reserved

1 cup chopped tomatoes
1 tablespoon finely chopped
   flat-leaved parsley
Salt and freshly ground black
   pepper to taste

The polenta:

2 cups fine cornmeal
9 cups water

2½ tablespoons kosher salt, or
   4 teaspoons table salt

Polenta
with
Spinach and
Tomato-
Mushroom
Sauce
(continued)

Boil the spinach in salted water, uncovered, for 5 minutes. Drain, cool, and squeeze out all of the moisture. Chop coarsely, add salt and black pepper to taste along with the garlic, grated cheese, and nutmeg. Set aside.

For the sauce: Meanwhile, heat the olive oil and sauté the onion and mushrooms (if using dried mushrooms, strain and reserve the soaking liquid), cover, and cook over medium heat for about 5 minutes, until the vegetables have wilted. Add the tomatoes, the soaking liquid from the mushrooms, if you used dried, and the parsley. Taste for salt and pepper. Simmer, covered, stirring often for about 15 minutes. Set aside.

For the polenta: Prepare the polenta using the instructions in the basic recipe on page 141. Make a mold of polenta as in the recipe above with a layer of spinach in the middle. When the polenta is unmolded, pour the tomato-mushroom sauce over it and serve in wedges.

Fish
and
Shellfish

Fish

About Trash Fish

Up until the late 1960s, the fishing fleets going out of Provincetown
fished primarily for mackerel, yellowtail flounder, and some haddock.
Practically everything else caught in the nets was discarded as trash fish
—whiting, blowfish (sea squab), skate, monkfish, squid, butterfish, and
so on. But I would go down to the pier when the boats came in and
pick up a bounty of those fish before the dump trucks delivered them
to cat food canneries and to mink farms. They made the best stews and
fritto misto imaginable.

It was during the 1960s and 1970s that the Russian and Eastern
bloc nations fished (vacuum style) close to the shore, and it
wasn't long before these trash fish became scarce.

Whiting, for instance, has always been a favorite fish in
Mediterranean countries. It is one of the most expensive
fish sold in Italy, where it is considered a delicacy.
But it is still reasonably priced in the United States
compared with other fish. It is found only in
the North Atlantic and is especially good
in the spring, because the ocean is cold
and, therefore, the flesh of the fish
remains firm and succulent.

Steamed Whiting with Primavera Sauce

Serves 2 or 3.

Uncooked Primavera Sauce:

4 cups chopped
  (unrefrigerated) tomatoes
¼ cup extra virgin olive oil
1 tablespoon chopped flat-
  leaved parsley

2 tablespoons chopped basil
2 to 4 garlic cloves, chopped
Salt and freshly ground pepper
  to taste

1½ to 2 pounds whole whiting,
  gutted, scaled, with head on

Salt and freshly ground black
  pepper to taste

In the bowl of a food processor, purée the ingredients for the Primavera Sauce.

Steam the whiting in a steamer for about 10 minutes. When it is
cooked, remove and discard the head, then carefully lift the skin off the
fish and remove the flesh from the bones. Divide the fish into portions,
sprinkle with salt and pepper, and top with the sauce.

VARIATION WITH FRESH CORIANDER OR PARSLEY SAUCE:
Serve steamed whiting with the Fresh Coriander or Parsley Sauce on
page 229.

Baked Whiting and Asparagus

Serves 2.

2 medium whitings (about
  1 pound each), scaled,
  washed, and cleaned with
  heads left on, or other
  medium fish, such as red
  snapper or black bass
8 to 10 medium-thick
  asparagus spears
2 fat cloves garlic, finely chopped

2 tablespoons finely chopped
  fresh mint
1 tablespoon finely chopped
  flat-leaved parsley
Salt and hot pepper flakes to
  taste
½ cup dry white wine
Garnish: Extra virgin olive oil

Preheat the oven to 450°.

Arrange the whiting and asparagus spears in one layer in a baking pan. Sprinkle the garlic, mint, parsley, and salt and hot pepper flakes to taste over the top and pour the wine into the pan. Cover tightly and bake for about 10 to 15 minutes, until the fish comes easily off the bone when tested. Do not overcook.

With a spatula, carefully transfer each fish to a warm plate and remove and discard the heads. Split both fish down the sides and with the tip of the knife lift out each backbone. Distribute the asparagus spears evenly between the plates, pour the pan juices over the fish, and garnish with a drizzling of olive oil. Serve at once.

Fried Skate Wing and Zucchini Blossoms

The body of a skate is pencil thin and the good meat is found in the wings between the membrane or soft bones. Most people comb the flesh off the bones with a fork, but I eat the bones along with the meat.

Serves 4.

Batter (page 76—double the amount), refrigerated
12 large zucchini blossoms, inspected for insects
Flour for dredging
Corn or other vegetable oil for frying

1 skate wing (about 1½ pounds), skinned, boned, and cut into 2-inch-wide strips
Salt to taste
Garnish: Lemon wedges

Stir the batter well to mix and drop in an ice cube or two. Dust the zucchini blossoms with flour, dip them, one at a time, into the batter, and heat the oil and fry them according to the directions on page 77. Let drain on paper towels and keep warm.

Skim any brown particles from the oil with a slotted spoon. Dust the skate pieces with flour, dip them, one at a time, into the batter, and fry until golden brown. Let drain briefly on paper towels, combine on a platter with the blossoms and sprinkle with salt. Serve at once with the lemon wedges.

Baked Skate Wing San Benedetto Style

This recipe is nice with a wedge of polenta (see grilled polenta, page 141) or Bruschetta (page 294).

Serves 4.

2 tablespoons olive oil
1 medium onion, coarsely
   chopped
2 cloves garlic, finely chopped
1 tablespoon finely chopped
   flat-leaved parsley
4 or 5 fresh plum tomatoes,
   skinned, seeded, and chopped
Salt and freshly ground black
   pepper or hot pepper flakes
   to taste

2 tablespoons capers, drained
2 tablespoons white wine
   vinegar
3 medium potatoes, boiled with
   their skins on
2 pounds skate wing, skinned
   on both sides and cut into
   3 pieces

Preheat the oven to 450°.

Heat the oil in a medium skillet until hot, then sauté the onion over moderate heat until it begins to brown. Add the garlic, sauté about 30 seconds, and then add the parsley along with the tomatoes, salt, and pepper or hot pepper flakes. Cover and lower the heat to a simmer, cook for 5 minutes, then add the capers and vinegar and simmer for 10 minutes more.

Peel the potatoes and place them with the skate sections in a shallow baking dish large enough for the skate and potatoes to fit snugly. Pour the sauce over all, cover the dish, and bake for 20 minutes. Serve immediately.

VARIATION:

Baked Skate Wing with Peas and Potatoes

Serves 3.

2 medium potatoes, unpeeled
1 cup peas
1 cup chopped tomatoes

1 cup thinly sliced scallions
3 tablespoons finely chopped
   flat-leaved parsley

2 pounds skate wing, skinned on both sides and cut into 3 pieces

3 tablespoons olive oil

2 teaspoons chopped fresh oregano, or 1 teaspoon dried

Hot pepper flakes (optional)

Salt and freshly ground black pepper to taste

Preheat the oven to 450°.

Boil the potatoes for 10 minutes, then drain, peel, and cut into thirds. Blanch the peas in boiling water for 3 minutes, then drain. Put the chopped tomatoes, scallions, and parsley in the bottom of a baking dish, then lay the skate, peas, and potatoes on top. Drizzle the olive oil over, and sprinkle on the oregano, optional hot pepper flakes, and salt and pepper to taste. Bake for 20 minutes.

Skate Wing with Peas and Cauliflower

Serves 3.

3 tablespoons olive oil

1 onion, finely chopped

2 tablespoons finely chopped flat-leaved parsley

2 fat cloves garlic, finely chopped

2 cups peeled, seeded, and chopped tomatoes

Hot pepper flakes to taste (optional)

2 tablespoons coarsely chopped fresh mint

2 potatoes, peeled and cut into thirds

1 cup peas, blanched for 1 minute and drained

1½ pounds skate wing, skinned on both sides

5 cups cauliflower flowerets, blanched for 1 minute and drained

Salt to taste

In a shallow saucepan heat the oil until hot, then sauté the onion and parsley until the onion is translucent. Add the garlic and cook for 1 minute. Add the tomatoes, hot pepper flakes, if using, and mint, and simmer for 10 minutes. Add the potatoes along with the peas, cover, and cook 10 minutes more.

Rinse and cut the skate wing into thirds. Add the skate and cauliflower to the pan, salt to taste, cover, and cook over low heat for about 10 minutes.

Sea Squab with Fresh Peas

Sea squab, also called blowfish, is sold skinned and boned during the spring in many fish markets. If it is not available, catfish can be substituted.

Serves 3.

3 tablespoons olive oil
2 cloves garlic, finely chopped
1½ tablespoons finely chopped
 flat-leaved parsley
6 medium sea squabs, rinsed in
 cold water

1½ cups peas, blanched for
 5 minutes and drained
½ cup thinly sliced scallions
⅓ cup dry white wine
Salt and freshly ground black
 pepper to taste

In a skillet just large enough to hold the sea squabs in one layer, heat the oil until hot and sauté the garlic and parsley over moderate heat until the garlic just begins to color. Add the sea squabs and cook for about 1 minute on each side, then add the rest of the ingredients, cover, and cook over moderate heat about 4 minutes. Serve at once.

Monkfish with Tomatoes and Potatoes

The head of the monkfish is enormous, and what you eat is the tail. Serve this dish with a green vegetable that is in season.

Serves 2.

2 tablespoons olive oil
1 medium onion, thinly sliced
Hot pepper flakes to taste
 (optional)
2 cups chopped tomatoes
1 teaspoon finely chopped flat-
 leaved parsley

2 teaspoons chopped fresh
 oregano, or 1 teaspoon dried
2 medium potatoes, unpeeled
1½ pounds monkfish, skinned
Salt to taste

Heat the oil in a medium skillet until hot, and sauté the onion and hot pepper flakes, if using, until the onion begins to brown. Add the tomatoes, parsley, and oregano, cover, and simmer for 20 minutes.

Meanwhile, boil the potatoes for 20 minutes. Drain, cool, peel, and cut crosswise into thirds.

Preheat the oven to 500°.

Place the fish in a baking dish so that it fits with a little room to spare. Pour the tomato sauce over the fish. Place the potatoes around the fish and sprinkle with salt. Cover the dish tightly and bake for 20 minutes or until the fish separates easily from the bone. Serve immediately.

Monkfish with Rape

Serves 2.

2½ pounds monkfish, skinned
8 cups rape, peeled and
   blanched (page 61)*
3 tablespoons olive oil
3 cloves garlic, finely chopped

18 dried black olives
Salt to taste
Hot pepper flakes to taste
   (optional)

Preheat the oven to 500°.

Place the monkfish in a baking dish and surround with the rape. Sprinkle with olive oil, garlic, olives, salt, and hot pepper flakes, if using. Cover tightly and bake for 20 minutes or until the fish separates easily from the bone. Serve immediately.

* Broccoli can be used if rape is not available.

Squid

There are two kinds of squid available in the Northeast—summer squid and bone squid. Summer squid is reddish in color and has a thin skin and a strong taste. Bone squid is usually larger, although it also appears in the markets small; it has thicker skin, is white, and has a more delicate taste than summer squid. I much prefer the bone squid.

To prepare squid if it has not been done at your market, separate the head with the tentacles from the body tube, remove the insides (including the celluloidlike bone) from the tube, and wash well. Peel off and discard any purple outer skin from the tube, cut the tentacles off just before the eye, squeeze out and discard the beak where the tentacles begin. Wash several times (always in cold water) to be sure all of the sand is removed.

Polenta-Stuffed Squid with Cauliflower and Tomatoes

Serves 8.

The polenta stuffing:

1 tablespoon olive oil

1 medium onion, finely chopped

1½ cups water

¾ cup fine cornmeal

1 tablespoon finely chopped flat-leaved parsley

2 tablespoons freshly grated Parmesan

Salt and freshly ground black pepper or hot pepper flakes to taste

4 large squid, about 10 inches long

5 tablespoons olive oil

2 large tomatoes, peeled, seeded, and coarsely chopped

6 cups cauliflower flowerets

2 cloves garlic, coarsely chopped

4 teaspoons chopped fresh oregano, or 2 teaspoons dried

2 tablespoons finely chopped flat-leaved parsley

Salt and hot pepper flakes to taste

Prepare the squid for stuffing as described on page 157.

To make the stuffing: Heat the oil in a medium skillet and sauté the onion until it becomes translucent. Use the water and cornmeal to make polenta according to the directions on page 141. To the hot polenta mixture, add the sautéed onion, parsley, cheese, and salt and pepper or hot pepper flakes to taste. Mix well.

Preheat the oven to 400°.

Stuff the squid with the filling and sew up the ends of the squid. Sew on the tentacles. Put the squid on a baking tray and drizzle it with 5 tablespoons olive oil. Top with tomatoes, cauliflower flowerets, garlic, oregano, parsley, and salt and hot pepper flakes. Cover and bake for 30 minutes. Remove the cover and bake 15 minutes more. Serve immediately.

VARIATION WITH BREAD-CRUMB AND CHEESE STUFFING: In a food processor, blend **1½ cups fresh bread crumbs, 2 teaspoons chopped flat-leaved parsley, 2 cloves garlic, finely chopped, ¼ cup grated Parmesan, 2 lightly beaten egg whites, 2 medium tomatoes, coarsely chopped,** and **salt and freshly ground black pepper or hot pepper flakes** to taste. Clean and stuff **4 large squid** according to the instructions above. Put the squid in a baking dish, surround with **4 cups thinly sliced peeled potatoes,** then sprinkle with **olive oil, 2 teaspoons chopped fresh or dried rosemary,** and a little **salt.** Cover and bake at 400° for 30 minutes or until the potatoes are tender. Serve with lemon wedges.

Catfish with Shrimp and Green Tomatoes

Catfish is now being farmed all over America and is relatively inexpensive. When fresh and cooked with some imagination, catfish is delicious.

Serves 2.

3 tablespoons olive oil
1 red bell pepper, thinly sliced
1 small onion, thinly sliced
2 cloves garlic, finely chopped
Hot pepper flakes to taste
  (optional)
¼ cup white wine vinegar
2 cups seeded and chopped
  half-green tomatoes

1 tablespoon coarsely chopped
  fresh basil
Salt to taste
2 medium catfish, heads
  removed, cleaned, and
  skinned
8 shrimp, shelled

In a skillet heat the olive oil and sauté the red pepper and onion until the onion becomes translucent, then add the garlic and cook several minutes; stir in the hot pepper flakes, if using, and vinegar, cover, and cook for 3 minutes. Add the tomatoes, basil, and salt to taste, cover, and cook for 10 minutes. Nestle the catfish into the sauce, cover, and simmer until the fish are tender, about 10 minutes. Add the shrimp and cook 2 to 3 minutes more or just until the shrimp are pink. Taste and adjust for salt, then serve immediately.

Fish Stew with Almond Pesto

This recipe is of Southern Italian origin. Any combination of fish may be used; monkfish, cod, and striped bass are ideal. The almond pesto can be made with a mortar and pestle—finely chop the almonds, and then work in the garlic, parsley, and oil to form a paste. Mix the paste with 1 cup of the broth from the stew and blend.

Serves 4 to 6.

The stew:

2 tablespoons olive oil

1 large onion, finely chopped

2 tablespoons finely chopped flat-leaved parsley

1 pound squid, cleaned (page 157) and cut into 1-inch strips

¼ cup dry white wine

2 tablespoons chopped fresh basil, or 1 tablespoon dried

2 cups skinned, seeded, and chopped fresh tomatoes or canned tomatoes

Salt and a generous amount of freshly ground black pepper to taste

2 pounds skate wing, skinned on both sides, cut into 4 sections

½ pound sea scallops

12 mussels, debearded and scrubbed

½ pound shrimp (I use Maine shrimp with the heads still on)

The almond pesto:

½ cup almonds, blanched and skinned

2 fat cloves garlic, finely chopped

2 tablespoons extra virgin olive oil

Heat the olive oil in a medium skillet and sauté the onion and 1 tablespoon of the parsley until the onion begins to brown. Add the squid and wine, cover, and lower the heat and cook until the wine cooks out. Add the basil and tomatoes, cover, and simmer for 10 minutes. Season with salt and pepper to your taste and transfer the squid and sauce to a large, shallow pan and add the skate wing sections. Cover and simmer the fish and sauce for 5 minutes. Turn the wing sections over occasionally and add some extra salt and pepper if you wish. Add the scallops, mussels, and shrimp to the stew. Cover and cook over a medium heat until the mussels open.

Put the almonds, remaining parsley, garlic, and extra virgin olive oil into a food processor; add 1 cup of the sauce from the fish stew, and blend this mixture to a creamy consistency. Add salt and pepper to taste. Serve the stew in warm soup plates, garnished with almond pesto.

Other Fish

Baked Shad

In the Northeast fresh shad are available in the spring. I suggest buying them already filleted. Because of the unusual bone structure of the shad, after boning, each fillet is left with a flap on either side where the bones were. The flaps can be opened to hold stuffing and folded back over the stuffing.

I like to serve this shad recipe with asparagus, which you can bake along with the fish. Arrange about 1 pound trimmed asparagus in the dish at the same time and drizzle a little olive oil over.

Serves 3.

1 shad fillet or side
3 cloves garlic, finely chopped
3 tablespoons chopped fresh
 mint
½ cup thinly sliced scallions
Hot pepper flakes to taste
 (optional)

3 tablespoons wine vinegar
1 tablespoon capers
Salt to taste
Garnish: Lemon wedges

Preheat the oven to 450°.

On the counter spread open the fillet flaps and sprinkle inside with the garlic, mint, scallions, and hot pepper flakes, if using. Close up so that the filling is covered. Place the fillet gently in a shallow oiled baking dish and sprinkle the fish with the vinegar, capers, and salt. Bake, uncovered, until the fish separates easily when tested with a fork, about 15 minutes. Serve immediately, with the lemon wedges.

Shad Roe

The roe, or the eggs, of shad come in two large attached lobes, and one of the halves serves one person adequately. I like this dish with a mélange of green beans, tomatoes, and potatoes (page 56), or baked asparagus.

Serves 1 or 2.

2 tablespoons olive oil
Salt and freshly ground black
  pepper to taste
1 pair shad roe
Flour for dredging
½ cup sliced scallions

1 clove garlic, finely chopped
½ cup dry white wine
1 tablespoon finely chopped
  flat-leaved parsley
Garnish: Lemon wedges

Heat the oil in a small skillet. Salt and pepper the roe, then dust with flour. Sauté the roe, turning it over when it begins to take on color, being careful not to puncture the membrane that encloses the roe. Sauté the other side in the same way, then add the remaining ingredients, cover, and lower the heat. Simmer for 10 minutes. Garnish with lemon wedges.

Fried Sardines

Fresh sardines from Maine are available in the Northeast, but there is not much market for them. I find them sweet and delicious. You eat them with your fingers, nibbling the flesh off the bones like corn from the cob. We should rely more on the sensitivity of our mouths.

Serves 3.

The batter:
  ½ cup flour
  Pinch of baking powder

1 egg white, lightly beaten
½ cup dry white wine

¾ pound fresh sardines
Corn oil for frying

Garnish: Salt to taste
Lemon wedges

Prepare the batter: mix the flour, baking powder, egg white, and wine in a bowl and refrigerate for at least one hour.

Split the sardines leaving the head on, gut, and rinse them.

Pour approximately ¾ inch of corn oil into a medium skillet. As the oil heats, remove the batter from the refrigerator and drop a couple of ice cubes into it. Dip the fish into the batter; fry, uncrowded in the skillet, until light brown, about 1 minute, depending on the size of the fish.

Blot the cooked fish on a paper towel and serve immediately with salt and lemon wedges.

Grilled Sardines with Orange Slices

You can use any small fish, such as smelts, but fresh sardines are best. The fish can be broiled indoors, but I prefer them cooked over hot coals.

Serves 2.

> 1 pound fresh sardines, cleaned (see above) with the heads left on
> 3 cloves garlic, finely chopped
> Juice of ½ lemon
> Salt to taste
> Hot pepper flakes to taste (optional)
>
> 1 tablespoon olive oil
> 1 orange, cut into ¼-inch-thick slices (with rind on)
> *Garnish:* 1 tablespoon flat-leaved parsley or fresh chopped coriander (cilantro)

Put the sardines in a bowl and add the garlic, lemon juice, salt, and hot pepper flakes, if using. Marinate, in the refrigerator, for at least 2 hours. Remove the sardines, reserving the marinade, and coat the sardines with the oil. Grill over hot coals or broil for about 1 minute on each side, depending on the size of the sardines. Be sure not to overcook them. Baste the fish with the marinade.

Serve the sardines with the orange slices and garnish them with chopped parsley or leaf coriander.

VARIATION WITH WHITE WINE VINEGAR AND HOT PEPPER SAUCE: Make a marinade of **2 fat cloves garlic, finely chopped,** ½ **cup good white wine vinegar, Hot Pepper Sauce** (page 52) or **hot pepper flakes** to taste, and **salt** to taste. Marinate **1 pound sardines** and grill or broil according to the instructions above.

Cod with Potatoes and Cabbage

I like to serve this dish with a few drops of extra virgin olive oil drizzled over each serving.

Serves 4.

3 tablespoons olive oil
2 medium onions, thinly sliced
3 cloves garlic, finely chopped
Hot pepper flakes to taste
  (optional)
2 cups coarsely chopped
  tomatoes

1 medium cabbage, preferably
  savoy, cored and quartered
4 medium potatoes, peeled and
  cut in half
4 pieces fresh cod or other
  white-fleshed fish, such as
  halibut, about 1 inch thick

Heat the oil in a medium saucepan and sauté the onions until translucent, then add the garlic and hot pepper flakes, if using. Continue to sauté until the garlic begins to color, then add the tomatoes and cook, covered, for 5 minutes.

Cook the cabbage and potatoes in boiling salted water for 5 minutes. Drain well and add both to the tomato mixture. Cook, covered, over low heat until the potatoes are cooked but firm.

Preheat the oven to 400°.

Transfer the ingredients from the saucepan to a shallow ovenproof dish and arrange the fish slices in a single layer on the top. Do not overlap the slices. Bake, covered, until the fish separates from the bone when tested with a fork, about 10 to 15 minutes. Serve at once.

Baked Scrod with Tomatoes and Mint

Serves 2.

3 tablespoons olive oil
1 small onion, finely chopped
2 cloves garlic, finely chopped
1 tablespoon finely chopped
  flat-leaved parsley
Hot pepper flakes to taste
  (optional)

1 cup coarsely chopped
  tomatoes
Dry white wine if needed
1 tablespoon chopped fresh
  mint, or 1 teaspoon dried
¾ pound fresh scrod or
  flounder

Heat the oil in a small skillet and sauté onion until it begins to wilt. Add garlic, parsley, and hot pepper flakes, if using. Stir and cook several minutes, then add the tomatoes, cover, and cook over low heat for about 10 minutes. Add a little dry white wine if the mixture is too dry.

Preheat the oven to 450°.

Put the fish into a shallow baking dish, pour the tomato mixture over, and bake, covered, until tender, about 20 minutes. Serve with boiled potatoes.

Scrod with Wild Mushrooms, Tomatoes, and Potatoes

Serves 2.

3 tablespoons olive oil
4 cups sliced wild or
   cultivated mushrooms
   (I use honey mushrooms)
1 medium onion, finely
   chopped
1 cup chopped tomatoes
Salt to taste
Hot pepper flakes to taste
   (optional)

2 potatoes, boiled, peeled, and
   cut into ½-inch slices
¾ pound fresh scrod, cod, or
   striped bass fillets, cut into
   1½-inch-long pieces
Garnish: 1 tablespoon finely
   chopped flat-leaved parsley
Extra virgin olive oil

In a medium skillet, heat the oil and sauté the mushrooms over high heat for 15 minutes, stirring often. Add the onion and cook, uncovered, until it begins to brown. Add the tomatoes and salt and optional hot pepper flakes to taste, cover, and cook over moderate heat for about 7 minutes. Add the potatoes and fish and cook, covered, over moderate heat until the fish is done. Be careful not to overcook. Garnish each portion with some parsley and a drizzle of extra virgin olive oil.

VARIATION: Blanch any or all of the following to make 4 cups total and add them when you add the tomatoes: **cauliflower, broccoli,** and **peas.**

Scrod with Cauliflower and Peas

Serves 2.

1 pound scrod fillets

3 cups cauliflower flowerets, boiled for 2 minutes and drained

1 cup peas, boiled in salted water for 10 minutes and drained

2 tablespoons finely chopped shallots

2 cloves garlic, finely chopped

¼ cup sliced scallions

1 tablespoon finely chopped flat-leaved parsley

3 tablespoons capers, drained

3 tablespoons olive oil

Salt and freshly ground black pepper to taste

2 cups rice, freshly cooked (page 129)

Preheat the oven to 500°.

Place the scrod fillets in a shallow baking dish. Arrange the cauliflower and peas around the fish. Distribute the remaining ingredients, except the rice, over the fish and vegetables. Cover the dish with foil and bake for about 10 to 15 minutes or until the flesh of the fish flakes easily with a fork.

To serve, place a portion of rice on each plate and ladle the liquid, cauliflower, and peas over the rice, then add a serving of fish on the side.

Baccalà

Baccalà, dried salted codfish, is a favorite in the Mediterranean countries. It is very common for families to eat it once a week in parts of Italy, since it is plentiful and does not spoil.

I use dried salted cod in certain recipes even if fresh cod is available, because of its distinctive flavor and because dried cod does not fall apart the way fresh cod would when cooked a fairly long time. The dried cod can be stewed without destroying its identity, and as a result it makes a rich, flavorful stew.

To prepare baccalà for cooking: First you need to soak it in a pot of cold water for 2 to 3 days, depending on the thickness of the fish, changing the water as often as possible. Then wash, drain, and blot dry.

It's easy to oversalt when cooking baccalà, so be very careful.

Baccalà with Tomatoes, Wild Mushrooms, and Potatoes

The original recipe for this dish does not include potatoes, but I think they improve it.

Serves 6.

2 tablespoons safflower or other vegetable oil

2 medium onions, thinly sliced

Hot pepper flakes to taste (optional)

2 cups seeded and chopped tomatoes

4 cups sliced mushrooms (I use any wild mushroom)

½ cup dry white wine

1 tablespoon finely chopped flat-leaved parsley

2 teaspoons chopped fresh oregano, or 1 teaspoon dried

1½ pounds baccalà, prepared as described on opposite page

2 tablespoons pine nuts

Salt to taste

4 medium potatoes, peeled and cut in half

Garnish: Extra virgin olive oil

Preheat the oven to 450°.

In a medium saucepan or skillet, heat the oil and sauté the onions and hot pepper flakes, if using, until the onions begin to brown. Add the tomatoes, mushrooms, wine, parsley, and oregano, cover, and cook the sauce over moderate heat for 5 minutes.

Place the fish in a baking dish that holds the pieces snugly, then add the pine nuts, vegetable sauce, and some salt—but be careful not to oversalt this dish. Cover the pan tightly and bake for approximately 45 minutes. Add the potatoes, cover, and bake an additional 30 minutes. Remove the cover and bake for 10 minutes more. Garnish each portion with a drop or two of extra virgin olive oil before serving.

Baccalà Portuguese Style

Serves 4.

1 pound baccalà, prepared as
  described on page 166, cut
  into 2-inch-wide pieces
5 tablespoons olive oil
1 medium onion, finely
  chopped
2 red bell peppers, cored and
  cut into ½-inch-wide strips

Hot pepper flakes to taste
  (optional)
2 cups chopped tomatoes
2 tablespoons chopped fresh
  basil, or 1 tablespoon dried
Salt to taste
2 cups 1-inch-thick sliced,
  peeled potatoes

Preheat oven to 400°.

Place the prepared baccalà pieces on a baking tray, sprinkle with approximately 2 tablespoons oil, and broil close to the heat until the fish begins to brown.

Meanwhile, heat 3 tablespoons of oil in a medium skillet and sauté the onion and peppers until the onion begins to brown. Add the hot pepper flakes, if using, tomatoes, and basil, cover, and simmer for 10 minutes. Add salt to taste—but be careful not to oversalt.

Place the baccalà in a baking dish so that the pieces fit snugly in the bottom. Add the potatoes and pour the tomato mixture over them. Cover and bake for 45 minutes.

Baccalà Salad

This recipe was given to me by a lovely Portuguese lady.

Serves 3.

1 pound baccalà, prepared as
  described on page 166
6 tablespoons olive oil
1 onion, finely chopped and
  soaked in cold water for 10
  minutes
24 dried black olives, pitted
  and sliced

1 teaspoon dried oregano
1 tablespoon finely chopped
  flat-leaved parsley
Freshly ground black pepper
  or hot pepper flakes to taste

Preheat the broiler.

Cut the baccalà into 2-inch-wide sections and sprinkle them with 3 tablespoons of the olive oil. Broil the baccalà strips close to the heat until they begin to brown.

Break up the baccalà strips with your hands and rinse them in cold water. Drain the chopped onion and mix the remaining 3 tablespoons olive oil and all of the other ingredients together with the fish in a serving bowl.

Serve this salad at room temperature.

VARIATION: Boil the soaked **baccalà** until just tender instead of broiling, then break up and mix with the remaining ingredients, or boil **baccalà** with **4 cups Swiss chard** cut into 1-inch sections, and **2 potatoes** cut into 1-inch wide sections. Garnish with **1 large onion thinly sliced** and cooked with **6 tablespoons of olive oil** and **parsley.**

Baccalà with Fennel and White Beans

This is a wintertime dish, since that is when fennel is available. And I always have on hand white beans, such as Tuscan (Great Northern will do as well), that I have dried to serve with boiled potatoes or rice.

Serves 6 to 8.

3 tablespoons olive oil
1 medium onion, sliced
2 fat cloves garlic, crushed
Hot pepper flakes to taste
   (optional)
2 cups chopped tomatoes
2 teaspoons chopped fresh
   mint, or 1 teaspoon
   dried

2 medium bulbs fennel, cut in
   half, cored, and cut into
   ½-inch-thick slices
2 pounds baccalà, prepared as
   described on page 166, cut
   into 2-inch-wide pieces
1 cup cooked white beans
   (page 73)
Salt to taste

Preheat the oven to 425°.

Heat the oil in a medium skillet and sauté the onion over medium heat until it begins to brown, then add the garlic and hot pepper flakes, if using, and cook several more minutes. Add the tomatoes, cover, and simmer over low heat for 5 minutes, then add the mint along with the fennel and cover and simmer for 10 minutes more.

In a baking dish, arrange the prepared fish in a single layer, pour the tomato and fennel mixture over the fish, add the cooked beans and salt to taste, cover, and bake for 45 minutes.

VARIATION WITH FRESH COD, MONKFISH, OR BASS: Make the tomato and fennel sauce as above and cook for about 35 minutes, then place 3 pounds **fresh cod, monkfish, or bass** in a baking dish, pour the sauce over it, and bake at 425° for about 10 to 15 minutes or just until the flesh of the fish flakes with a fork.

Fresh Tuna or Mako Shark with Peas

Serves 3.

The sauce:

2 tablespoons olive oil
1 medium onion, finely chopped
2 cups chopped tomatoes
2 teaspoons chopped fresh
  oregano, or 1 teaspoon dried

Hot pepper flakes to taste
  (optional)
1 cup peas, blanched for
  1 minute and drained

2 tablespoons olive oil
Salt and freshly ground black
  pepper to taste
1¼ pounds (approximately)
  fresh tuna or mako shark
  steak, sliced 1 inch thick

Flour for dredging
¼ cup white wine vinegar
Garnish: 1 tablespoon finely
  chopped flat-leaved parsley

Make the sauce: Heat 2 tablespoons olive oil in a shallow medium pot and sauté the onion until it begins to brown; add the tomatoes, oregano, and hot pepper flakes, if using. Cover and simmer for 10 minutes, then add the peas and simmer for 5 minutes more.

Meanwhile, heat 2 tablespoons olive oil in a medium skillet. Lightly salt and pepper the fish, then dust lightly in flour. Brown the fish on both sides over medium to high heat, then add vinegar, lower the heat, and cook, covered, until the vinegar cooks out. Remove half the pea-and-tomato sauce from the pot and add fish; then pour the sauce back on top. Cover and cook over medium heat an additional 20 minutes. Garnish with chopped parsley.

Tuna Rolls

Serves 4.

4 slices fresh tuna, about
½ inch thick

Salt and freshly ground black
pepper to taste

The stuffing:

2 tablespoons finely chopped
flat-leaved parsley

3 cloves garlic, finely chopped

Grated zest of 1 lemon

Salt and freshly ground black
pepper to taste

3 tablespoons olive oil

Juice of 1 lemon

Garnish: Lemon wedges

Place each slice of tuna between sheets of wax paper. Press a rolling
pin gently over the tuna, being careful not to press so hard that the
fibers of the fish separate. Press the slice until it is about ³⁄₁₆ inch thick.
Salt and pepper both sides of each slice.

For the stuffing: Mix together the stuffing ingredients. Spread about
¼ of the stuffing across the center of each slice, then carefully roll up
each slice and fasten it with toothpicks.

Heat the olive oil in a medium skillet until hot, then add the tuna
rolls. Cook over high heat, carefully turning them, for several minutes.
Add the lemon juice and cook, uncovered, for about 30 seconds. Serve
immediately with lemon wedges for garnish.

Swordfish with Capers and Olives

Serves 3.

2 medium potatoes, unpeeled

2 tablespoons olive oil

1 medium onion, finely chopped

1 rib celery, finely chopped

2 cups seeded and chopped
tomatoes

2 teaspoons chopped fresh
oregano, or 1 teaspoon dried

Salt and freshly ground black
pepper to taste

6 green olives, pitted and
sliced*

2 tablespoons capers, drained

1 pound fresh swordfish, skin
removed and cut into
2-inch-wide pieces

* I use my own canned olives. For the recipe see page 316.

Boil the potatoes, and when they are cooked but firm, peel them and cut into ½-inch-thick slices; set aside.

Heat the oil in a medium skillet, add the onion and celery and sauté until the onion begins to brown. Then add the tomatoes, oregano, and salt and pepper, cover and simmer for 10 minutes. Add the olives and capers and simmer, covered, for 5 minutes more. Add the swordfish along with the potatoes, cover, and continue to cook over low heat, gently stirring occasionally, for 8 minutes.

Cubed Swordfish with Clams and Fresh Peas

Other shellfish, such as mussels and shrimp, can be substituted for the clams in this recipe. Add them at the same time as you would the clams.

Serves 3.

3 tablespoons olive oil	1 cup thinly sliced scallions
2 cloves garlic, finely chopped	½ cup dry white wine
1 swordfish steak (about 1 pound), about 1 inch thick, cut into 1-inch cubes	2 tablespoons finely chopped flat-leaved parsley
1 cup peas, blanched and drained	2 tablespoons coarsely chopped fresh mint
Hot pepper flakes to taste (optional)	9 littleneck clams, scrubbed
	Salt to taste

In a medium skillet heat the olive oil until hot, add the garlic and the swordfish cubes, and cook over moderate heat, uncovered, stirring often, until the fish just begins to color. Add the peas, hot pepper flakes (if using), scallions, white wine, parsley, mint, and clams. Cover the skillet and cook, stirring occasionally, until the clams open. Add salt to taste. With a slotted spoon remove the swordfish cubes and clams to a serving bowl and keep them warm. Reduce the sauce, if desired, to a thicker consistency. Pour the sauce over the fish combination and serve at once.

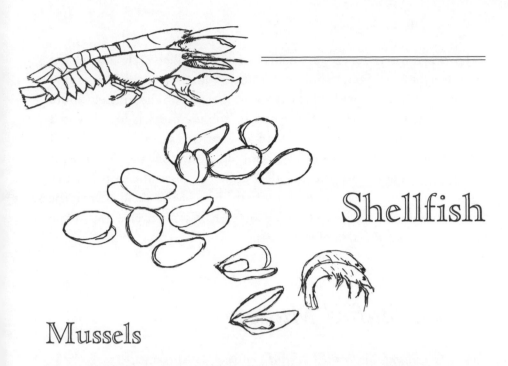

Shellfish

Mussels

During the Depression, my father, my godfather Tomasso, and their friends would drive to New Haven, Connecticut, to gather mussels. They gathered mussels most of the year, and they gathered them by the bushel, bringing them home tied securely on the running board of the Model T Ford one of them owned. My father used to take me with them, and I remember all of the wonderful discoveries I made while gathering the mussels. The fascinating tidal pools teeming with life, the snails, the starfish, an occasional horseshoe crab—it was worlds apart from the drab factory town we lived in. The women would wait for our return. Then they would wash the mussels—laughing and gossiping all the while—and prepare the sauces and stuffing for them. The men would deftly open the mussels with their pocketknives (and they all had pocketknives) as they drank my father's wine, smoked Italian cigars, and chatted about their gardens or their own wine.

I suppose I remember those occasions because they were joyous, and I tend to think of the Depression with some nostalgia. The gathering and preparing of the food was a group effort, and everyone was loving and open. People had their priorities in order then—survival and dignity were the norm. Perhaps that is why I have a special reverence for food; it is not a matter of gluttony (I have never been overweight). But because so many happy experiences of my childhood were directly related to food, for me, sitting at the table is always a very special communal occasion.

To test mussels for good quality, be certain that each mussel has some weight to it. Simply hold one in the palm of your hand; the best mussels will be those with the heaviest weight. Scrub the mussels under cold running water with a stiff brush, or rub the mussels together in a pan of cold water to remove the sand and barnacles.

Carefully open the mussels by prying open the concave side of each one with a small, sharp, thin-bladed knife. Remove the beard (hairy appendages) and loosen the flesh on both sides of the shells. Leave the mussel on one shell, discarding the other half. When cleaning make sure to scrub out the side of the shells.

Broiled Stuffed Mussels

This same stuffing can be used to stuff clams *or* mushrooms.

Serves 4 as an antipasto.

16 mussels
½ cup fresh bread crumbs
2 teaspoons finely chopped
   fresh oregano, or 1 teaspoon
   dried
1 tablespoon finely chopped
   flat-leaved parsley
2 tablespoons freshly grated
   Parmesan or Pecorino
   Romano

3 tablespoons olive oil
Salt and freshly ground black
   pepper or hot pepper flakes
   to taste
6 tablespoons dry white wine

Preheat the broiler.

Place prepared mussels (above) on a baking tray. Mix all of the remaining ingredients, except 2 tablespoons of the wine, together in a bowl. Sprinkle a generous amount of the stuffing over the mussels and pour the remaining wine into the bottom of the baking tray.

Broil the mussels close to the heat until the crumbs begin to brown. Serve immediately.

VARIATION:
Mussels and Wine

Serves 4 to 6.

1 cup thinly sliced scallions
¼ cup olive oil
½ cup finely chopped flat-
leaved parsley
3 tablespoons chopped fresh
basil, or 1 tablespoon dried
4 fat cloves garlic, finely chopped
½ cup coarsely chopped green
bell peppers

2 tablespoons chopped fresh
oregano, or 1 tablespoon
dried
1 cup dry white wine
Salt and hot pepper flakes to
taste
5 pounds mussels

Put all the ingredients, except the mussels, in a large pot, bring to a boil, add whole, scrubbed mussels, and cover tightly. Cook over high heat until the mussels open, about 8 minutes.

Strain the broth, removing all sand, into cups and serve it with the mussels. As you eat, dip the mussels into the broth. Serve with crusty Italian bread.

VARIATION WITH THIN PASTA: Prepare the mussels and broth as above. Remove the mussels, strain the broth, removing all the sand, and set it aside. Cook **thin pasta,** such as **spaghettini,** for about 4 minutes in salted boiling water and drain; bring the mussel broth to a boil and finish cooking the pasta in it until done al dente, and drain. (Should there not be enough broth in which to cook the pasta, simply add water.) Remove most of the mussels from their shells (reserving about 3 or 4 per person for garnish) and serve them with or over the pasta.

Asparagus and Shellfish Soup

The first time I tried this lovely creation was in a wonderful Italian restaurant in New York City called Toscana. This is a fairly accurate interpretation of the recipe. It is easy and elegant, and a good example of an Italian "creamed soup" without cream or butter. You can use shrimp or other shellfish in the recipe if you like.

Serves 4.

3 tablespoons olive oil
1 small onion, finely chopped
3 shallots, finely chopped
1 tablespoon chopped flat-
  leaved parsley
1½ pounds asparagus, cut into
  2-inch sections
About 2 cups fish stock (page
  118) or chicken broth (page
  194)

1 teaspoon chopped fresh mint
Salt and freshly ground black
  pepper to taste
8 littleneck clams, scrubbed
8 mussels, scrubbed and
  debearded
8 medium sea scallops

Heat the olive oil in a medium soup pot, add onion, shallots, and parsley and sauté, uncovered, until onion becomes translucent, then add the asparagus and continue to sauté until the asparagus is tender. Add 1½ cups stock or broth, mint, and salt and pepper. Simmer over low heat for 5 minutes. Pour into a food processor and puree. The soup should be the consistency of light pea soup; use the rest of the stock or broth as needed to thin the soup. When you are ready to serve, bring the soup to simmer and add the clams and mussels. As each clam or mussel opens, remove it and keep it warm. When all of the clams and mussels are done, add the scallops and cook just until tender—about 3 minutes. Portion the soup and scallops into soup bowls and add 2 clams and 2 mussels (in their shells) to each serving. It makes a better presentation if the shells are not completely submerged in the soup. Serve immediately.

Clams

When I was a child we used to dig clams when we went mussel hunting on the Connecticut shore. But what I remember most is digging clams in Provincetown during the late 1940s and the 1950s.

Residents in Provincetown were issued licenses to dig clams, and the clams were wonderful. I would take a gallon of my father's wine to the clam flats in late summer and dig clams with my friends. We would eat the clams as we dug them up and wash them down with cold white wine.

The clams were naturally cold, sweet, and nutty in flavor. We would then take our allotted bucket of clams home and eat them in different ways during the week.

One warning about clams in general: Do not buy clams that are not tightly closed.

Littleneck clams	small	best raw
Cherrystone clams	medium	best cooked
Sea clams	large	best for sauces and stews
Steamer clams (soft-shelled)		always eaten cooked, best steamed with a sauce or drawn butter

Razor clams are a treat that you find a few times a year. They look like an old-fashioned razor in its sheath. I buy local ones whenever I see them in Chinatown or on Ninth Avenue in New York.

Razor Clams and Soft-Shelled Crabs

Razor clams are usually available in early summer where I live, although I don't know of any reason that they should not be sold more often. Soft-shelled crabs are in the markets at the same time; I think they make a lovely seasonal marriage.

Serves 3.

3 tablespoons olive oil
3 cloves garlic, finely chopped
Hot pepper flakes to taste (optional)
1 cup thinly sliced scallions
6 live soft-shelled crabs, cleaned (see page 184, or have your fishmonger clean them)
4 tablespoons coarsely chopped fresh mint

⅓ cup dry white wine
Salt to taste
1½ pounds live razor clams (available in ethnic—Italian and Chinese—neighborhood markets), well washed in cold water
Garnish: 2 to 3 tablespoons chopped flat-leaved parsley

In a skillet large enough to hold all the ingredients, heat the olive oil until hot and add the garlic, hot pepper flakes, if using, and scallions; sauté over moderate heat, uncovered, stirring often, for about 30 seconds. Add the crabs and cook, uncovered, for about 1 minute on each side. Add the mint, wine, salt, and razor clams. Cover the skillet tightly and cook over high heat until the clams open. Serve at once.

Garnish with parsley.

Oysters

Some years ago when we had a house in Provincetown, we would sometimes gather oysters known as Wellfleets. They are small, sweet, and so popular that the townspeople jealously guard their oyster beds, since they are not available commercially. I remember a sense of well-being in having a bushel of freshly gathered Wellfleet oysters on the back terrace under the grape arbor, cooling off beneath a cover of wet burlap.

It was fun having quantities of fresh oysters to experiment with, but no matter how you prepare oysters, they are best raw. The following recipe is for the more inhibited who prefer their oysters cooked. The sauce also happens to be wonderful on clams or mussels on the half shell.

Baked Oysters in Green Sauce

Serves 2 to 4 as a first course.

3 tablespoons olive oil
2 tablespoons finely chopped
   onions
1 cup packed spinach
1 teaspoon finely chopped
   flat-leaved parsley

1 tablespoon pine nuts
1 tablespoon bread crumbs
Salt and freshly ground black
   pepper to taste
1 teaspoon dry sherry
8 medium oysters

In a small skillet heat the oil until hot and sauté the onions until they begin to brown, then add the spinach, parsley, pine nuts, bread crumbs, salt and pepper to taste, and sherry, cover, and simmer over low heat for 5 minutes. Transfer the mixture to a food processor and blend until smooth (or pound it to a paste in a mortar with a pestle).

Preheat the oven to 450°.

With a small, very sharp knife, and taking care, open the oysters. Slide the knife under the oysters to loosen them slightly. Leave each oyster on one shell, discarding the other half. Spread about 1 teaspoon of the green sauce evenly over each oyster so that it is covered completely. Bake about 6 minutes and serve at once.

Sea Scallops with Asparagus

Serves 4.

6 tablespoons olive oil
1 large onion, finely chopped
1 pound medium-thick
   asparagus spears, cut into
   1½-inch pieces
Salt and freshly ground black
   pepper to taste
1½ pounds sea scallops
Juice of 1 lemon
2 fat cloves garlic, finely
   chopped

1 bunch scallions, cut into
   1-inch pieces
2 tablespoons coarsely chopped
   fresh mint
1½ tablespoons finely chopped
   flat-leaved parsley or
   coriander (cilantro)
Hot pepper flakes to taste
   (optional)

In a medium skillet heat 3 tablespoons of the olive oil until hot. Add the chopped onion and the asparagus and salt and pepper to taste and sauté, uncovered, over moderate heat until the asparagus is tender but not overcooked. With a slotted spoon remove the vegetables from the skillet to a plate.

Add the remaining oil to the skillet and heat until hot, then sauté the scallops, uncovered, over high heat, turning often with a metal spatula, for about 2 minutes. Add the lemon juice, garlic, and scallions and cook about 1 minute. Add the mint, parsley or coriander, and hot pepper flakes, if using, and continue to cook, uncovered and stirring constantly, for about 1½ minutes. Return the asparagus and onion to the skillet and reheat for about 1 minute. Serve at once. Excellent with rice or pasta.

Lobster with Monkfish

One way to make expensive lobster go further is to combine it with monkfish, which has a similar texture and will absorb the flavor of the lobster.

Serves 4 to 6.

3 live lobsters (about 1 pound each)

3 tablespoons olive oil

3 cloves garlic, finely chopped

3 tablespoons finely chopped shallots

2 tablespoons finely chopped flat-leaved parsley

Hot pepper flakes to taste

1½ cups dry white wine

1 cup finely chopped fennel bulb

Salt to taste

2 teaspoons chopped fresh oregano, or 1 teaspoon dried

1 cup thinly sliced scallions

1½ pounds monkfish, boned and cut into 6 pieces

Extra virgin olive oil for bread slices

6 slices crusty white bread, such as Italian or French

Kill each lobster by inserting a sharp knife between the eyes. Rinse well, cut off the tail section and claws, and then chop each lobster into 4 pieces.

Heat the oil in a large skillet and add the garlic, shallots, parsley, hot pepper flakes, and lobster sections. Cook uncovered over moderate heat, mixing often, until the shallots and garlic begin to brown. Add 1 cup of the wine, the fennel, salt, and oregano. Cover, lower the heat, and cook for 5 minutes, then add the scallions and cook another 5 minutes. Add the monkfish along with the remaining wine, cover, and cook until the monkfish is done, about 8 minutes. Remove the lobster sections and monkfish with a slotted spoon.

Put the sauce into a food processor and blend. Set the sauce aside and keep it warm.

Sprinkle some oil on the bread slices and toast them. Place each slice of toast on a heated plate. Put 1 piece of monkfish on the toast and ladle some of the sauce on top. Place some lobster sections alongside the toast and serve immediately.

Crayfish Soup

Crayfish are another gift of nature. They are prevalent today in our ponds and lakes and are easy to trap.

This soup and the recipe that follows make for messy eating—each diner breaks the shell of the crayfish and sucks out the meat—but it's fun and satisfying. I make this with capellini—meaning thin hair that is rolled into a nest. It's wonderful in soups and can be found in Italian groceries.

Serves 4.

2 tablespoons olive oil
1 medium onion, finely
   chopped
1 rib celery, finely chopped
1½ tablespoons finely chopped
   flat-leaved parsley
3 cloves garlic, finely chopped
1½ cups chopped tomatoes

½ cup dry white wine
8 cups water
16 to 18 live crayfish, rinsed
   well in cold water
Salt and freshly ground black
   pepper to taste
6 capellini (thin pasta) nests

In a medium soup pot, heat the oil until hot, add the onion, and sauté over moderate heat until it becomes translucent. Add the celery and parsley and cook until the onion browns, then stir in the garlic and cook for 1 minute. Add the tomatoes and cook for 5 minutes, stirring often, then add the wine, cover, and cook for 5 minutes. Puree through a food mill and return pureed mixture to the pot along with the water, crayfish, and salt and pepper, cover, and boil gently for 5 minutes.

Remove the crayfish from the soup with a slotted spoon, and when they are cool enough to handle, separate the heads from the tails (bodies) and return the heads to the soup. (Refrigerate the tails until needed.) Boil the soup and the heads gently for 45 minutes, and then remove the heads from the soup with a slotted spoon and let cool. Squeeze the juice from the heads back into the pot by pressing on the shells. Discard the heads.

Return the reserved tails to the soup and cook for about 2 minutes. Add the capellini and cook until al dente. Put some pasta and crayfish tails into each soup bowl and ladle more soup over them.

Crayfish with Wine

Serves 2.

2 tablespoons olive oil
3 cloves garlic, finely chopped
4 scallions, thinly sliced
Hot pepper flakes to taste
2 tablespoons coarsely chopped
    fresh mint

2 tablespoons finely chopped
    flat-leaved parsley
½ cup dry white wine
Salt to taste
2 pounds live crayfish, rinsed
    well in cold water

In a shallow saucepan, heat the olive oil until hot, add the garlic and
sauté over moderate heat for 30 seconds, being careful not to burn it,
then add the scallions, hot pepper flakes, mint, and parsley and continue
to sauté, uncovered, for several minutes to combine flavors. Add the
wine, salt, and crayfish, cover, and cook, stirring occasionally, for about
5 minutes, or until the crayfish are deep red. Serve hot or at room
temperature with crusty Italian or French bread or Bruschetta (page
294) to mop up the sauce.

Mixed Fry with Soft-Shelled Crabs

*For this recipe I use a combination of half corn oil and half other vegetable
oil in which to deep-fry the ingredients.*

*You will see that I add an ice cube or two to an already chilled batter.
What this does is further chill the batter, so that when it makes contact with
the very hot oil the reaction, or seal, is instantaneous. It makes for a very
light, crispy batter.*

*Serve this mixed fry with a green or cooked-vegetable salad, dressed with
oil and vinegar. Tomato Horseradish Sauce (page 53) is excellent served
with fried fish.*

Serves 3.

The batter:
1 cup flour
¾ cup dry white wine
¼ teaspoon baking powder

1 egg white, lightly beaten
Salt and hot pepper flakes to
    taste (optional)

Corn oil and/or other vegetable oil for deep-frying

9-ounce package frozen artichoke hearts, or 8 small fresh artichokes,* blanched, cooled, and quartered

Flour for dredging

6 medium mushrooms, stems removed

3 live soft-shelled crabs, cleaned (see page 184, or have your fishmonger clean them)

Garnish: Lemon wedges

Make the batter: In a bowl mix all of the batter ingredients, then refrigerate for at least 1 hour.

Pour 1¼ inches of oil into a large skillet and heat until very hot. Remove the batter from the refrigerator and add an ice cube or two to it.

Dust each artichoke quarter with flour, dip into the batter, and carefully place it in the hot oil. Fry until light golden brown on all sides. When done, remove them from the skillet with tongs and let them drain in one layer on paper towels. Fry the mushrooms in the same way.

With a slotted spoon, remove the particles from the oil. Dust each crab with flour, dip into the batter, then fry in the hot oil until golden brown on both sides. (The crabs will sputter, so be careful of the hot oil.) Remove the crabs with tongs and blot on paper towels. Serve at once with the vegetables and lemon wedges.

* Should small fresh artichokes be available, use them instead of frozen. Remove the tough outer leaves, quarter the artichokes, then blanch them in boiling water, and let cool before battering and deep-frying them as directed.

Soft-Shelled Crabs with Scallions, Mint, and Tomatoes

I remember in the month of May my father and his friends used to fish on Long Island Sound for soft-shelled crabs. To me, there is no finer delicacy. When buying soft-shelled crabs, be sure they are alive.

Serves 2.

4 live soft-shelled crabs
3 tablespoons olive oil
3 cloves garlic, finely chopped
1 cup coarsely chopped
    tomatoes
1 cup thinly sliced scallions

3 tablespoons coarsely chopped
    fresh mint
Hot pepper flakes to taste
    (optional)
½ cup dry white wine
Salt to taste

To clean soft-shelled crabs: Lift up the side flaps on each crab and remove and discard the gills. Snip off the eyes with scissors and remove and discard the bottom flap. Wash, drain, and pat the crab dry. (You can instead ask your fishmonger to clean the crabs for you.)

In a medium skillet heat the oil until hot. Add the garlic and cook it, uncovered, until it begins to take on color. Add the tomatoes, scallions, mint, and hot pepper flakes, if using, cover, and cook over moderate heat, stirring occasionally, for about 5 minutes. Add the wine, cover, and simmer for 8 to 10 minutes. Add the crabs and salt to taste, cover, and simmer for about 8 minutes in all (4 minutes on each side). Serve the crabs at once on heated plates.

Chicken
and
Other Birds

Chicken

My mother and father never bought a dead chicken. They either raised their own or bought them live in a local poultry store. After the chicken was killed, my mother would pluck it, and when she opened it up, she would know whether it was healthy or not. If a fryer was too fat, she would say it was not healthy; young chickens should be lean. Needless to say, the chicken we ate when I was a child was far superior to the fat, tasteless, bloated chickens that we see in the supermarket today. They are difficult to cook because of all that fat and excessive moisture. When I was a young man, a broiler weighed from 1½ to 2 pounds. The broilers were lean and tasty. Today 3½-pound chickens are sold as broilers.

When I lived in Italy as a student, I enjoyed wonderful chicken at my relatives' homes. I remember what a pretty sight it was to see my uncle turning the rich earth over with a plow pulled by two enormous white oxen. There would be about 50 chickens following close behind the plow, picking up all of the goodies in the turned earth.

Because of the poor quality of commercial birds, for many years now we have been raising a variety of chickens at our place in Katonah. We found that the best setting chickens are bantams. A bantam hen can hatch a dinosaur egg.

One year a friend gave me 12 fertile mallard eggs. When I put them in the nest of our bantam hen (she was getting ready to set), she fussed and moved the eggs about until she was able to completely cover them with her body and wings. Duck eggs are much larger than bantam eggs, so she looked very funny perched on top of the eggs. It was a confusing situation for her after she hatched the eggs. The ducklings followed her about like obedient children and slept under her wings at night. They would quack and waddle after her, but the minute they saw water, they headed toward it and to her dismay would happily swim about. She would stand on the bank squawking, trying to get them to come ashore.

Bantams as well as other chickens make wonderful pets. For years we raised chickens in a coop with a fenced-in yard. Later, my wife built a chicken coop near her studio to keep pet chickens. She let them out of the coop every day, and they wandered about all day, returning to their coop before dusk. We discovered each chicken had a personality. They were more intelligent and affectionate than we realized, and they produced more eggs than the chickens that we fenced in. They also lived longer; although roosters generally live about 4 to 5 years in a hen house, we had one that lived for 9 years before he was killed by a coon and another that lived 10 years before dying a natural death.

The old hens and roosters make wonderful soup, and though the meat is a little tough, it is much tastier than supermarket chicken.

We usually order our chicks from Sears Roebuck. It has a variety of chickens, ducks, geese, guinea fowl, and so on that are sent to you by mail. They must be kept warm for a few weeks; a heat lamp will do—they'll huddle around it when they are cold. They will grow rapidly and will be ready to eat as broilers when they are about 6 to 8 weeks old.

How to Butcher and Dress Chickens

To kill a chicken: There are three ways to kill a chicken—wring its neck, cut its throat, or chop off its head.

If you wring the chicken's neck, you must hold the wings and tie its feet, then turn the neck, and pull to break it. Hang the chicken by its tied feet (it will flap its wings before it dies). The blood will run to its head. Some people tie the neck so that the blood does not escape while the chicken is cleaned.

If you prefer, tie its feet, and, holding its wings between your legs, use a sharp knife to slit its throat or cut off the head. (If you want to use the head later don't cut it off now.) After you have killed the chicken, I suggest you put it into a basket so that it does not thrash about as chickens do for several minutes before they die.

To pluck a chicken: You should pluck the chicken as soon as it dies; the longer you wait, the harder it is. It is a messy job that is best done outdoors.

There are two ways to pluck a chicken—dry-pluck (simply pull out the feathers immediately after killing the chicken) or wet-pluck (dip the freshly killed chicken in boiling water). I have heard Italian women say the chicken tastes better if it is dry-plucked, but that is more difficult. The easiest way to pluck a chicken is by submerging it in boiling water, then plucking off all the feathers after it cools off. Leave the chicken in only until the water soaks through the feathers to the skin. If you leave it in the water too long, especially if it is young, the skin will come off with the feathers.

I like to save the feet and head as they are excellent in soups and sauces. Remove all of the feathers from the head, cut off the beak, and pull out the tongue. To prepare the feet, cut them off, then cut off the nails and dip into boiling water to skin.

To clean a chicken: Make a slit at the base of the neck, then cut out the feed bag in the chest and pull out the windpipe. Clean out the carcass by cutting a slit about 2 inches long under the chicken's anus. Put your hand in and pull out everything in the cavity. Disconnect the gizzard from the intestinal tract, cut the gizzard in half lengthwise, and pull out the coarse skin holding the digested feed from the gizzard and discard. Wash the cleaned gizzard and set aside. Remove the heart and liver and carefully cut away the green sac (the gallbladder) from the liver and discard. Wash both organs and set them aside. Discard everything else in the cavity. Turn the carcass over and make a wedge-shaped incision at the base of the tail and remove and discard the gland. Wash the carcass well in cold water. Now it is ready for cooking. Allow the chicken to cool completely before cooking or refrigerating it. The heart, liver, gizzard, feet, neck, and head should be used in soups and sauces.

It is messy cleaning a chicken. I do not enjoy doing it but in my opinion the results are worth the effort. There is a logic to cleaning a chicken, and it will come to you once you try it. But if you can't bear the whole messy business of killing, plucking, and cleaning, that's no reason not to raise chickens. In the country there is always someone who will do the job for you.

Roast Chicken Stuffed with Polenta

I like to serve this roast chicken with roasted peppers (page 48).

Serves 4.

The stuffing:

2 cups spinach
2 tablespoons olive oil
1 small onion, finely chopped
1 rib celery, finely chopped
1 chicken gizzard, coarsely chopped
1 chicken heart, coarsely chopped
1 chicken liver, coarsely chopped

2 teaspoons chopped fresh tarragon, or 1 teaspoon dried
Salt and freshly ground black pepper to taste
Polenta made with 1 cup water, salt to taste, and ½ cup cornmeal

1 chicken (3½ to 4½ pounds), washed and excess fat removed
2 fat cloves garlic, cut into slivers
1 tablespoon chopped fresh or dried rosemary

Salt and freshly ground black pepper to taste
1 cup dry white wine
1 cup water
4 medium potatoes
3 tablespoons white wine vinegar

Preheat the oven to 450°.

To make the stuffing: Wash the spinach, drop into boiling water for 1 minute, drain, cool, squeeze out all moisture, and chop. Set aside.

Heat the oil in a medium skillet, add the onion along with the celery and gizzard, and sauté until the onion becomes translucent. Add the heart and liver and continue to cook until the liver changes color, about 1 minute. Add the tarragon and salt and pepper to taste and mix.

Make the polenta according to the instructions on page 141. Pour into a medium mixing bowl and stir in the sautéed onions and chicken organs along with the chopped spinach.

Using a large spoon, pack the polenta stuffing into the chicken, slip garlic slivers under the breast skin, truss, and rub with rosemary, salt, and pepper.

Put the chicken on a rack in a medium roasting pan. Pour the wine and water into the pan and roast, uncovered, for 20 minutes, basting occasionally. Turn the chicken over and cook an additional 20 minutes.

Meanwhile, peel the potatoes, cut lengthwise, place in a bowl, and cover with water.

Turn the chicken back to its original position. Drain the potatoes and place them around the chicken. Pour in the vinegar, cover, and lower the heat to 375°. Roast for about 40 minutes more, basting often, then remove the chicken and keep it warm. If the potatoes are not cooked, turn up the oven to 500° and cook them uncovered until they are easily pierced by a fork. Defat the pan juices and serve with the chicken.

VARIATION:

Swiss Chard and Ricotta Stuffing for Roast Chicken

1 pound Swiss chard, strings
   removed
1 tablespoon olive oil
½ medium onion, finely
   chopped
1 chicken gizzard, diced
1 chicken liver, diced
1 chicken heart, diced

1 egg white, lightly beaten
¼ teaspoon freshly grated
   nutmeg
1 tablespoon finely chopped
   flat-leaved parsley
1 cup fresh ricotta
Salt and freshly ground black
   pepper to taste

1 chicken (3½ to 4½ pounds),
   washed and excess fat
   removed
2 fat cloves garlic, cut into slivers
Salt and freshly ground black
   pepper

1 tablespoon chopped fresh or
   dried rosemary
1 cup dry white wine
1 cup water

Cook the Swiss chard in boiling water for 10 minutes, then drain and chop (you should have about 1 cup). Heat the olive oil and sauté the onion and diced gizzard until the onion becomes translucent. Add the diced liver and heart and sauté for 1 minute more. Remove from the heat and mix in the egg white, nutmeg, parsley, ricotta, and salt and pepper to taste. Prepare the chicken as described in the preceding recipe by stuffing, placing garlic slivers under the breast skin, trussing, and rubbing with salt and pepper and rosemary. Roast as above, adding the white wine and water to the pan and basting often.

Chicken with Asparagus

When asparagus is in season, I use it as often and in as many ways as possible. Chicken and asparagus make a perfect marriage.

Serves 6.

1 chicken (3 to 3½ pounds), cut into 8 pieces
4 tablespoons olive oil
Salt and freshly ground black pepper to taste
2 tablespoons chopped fresh or dried rosemary
1 medium onion, coarsely chopped
2 ounces dried Italian mushrooms, covered with warm water and soaked for 15 minutes, drained

3 whole cloves garlic, unpeeled
½ cup dry Marsala
1½ pounds asparagus, cut into 2-inch pieces
1 tablespoon finely chopped fresh flat-leaved parsley

Wash the chicken and pat dry. Heat 2 tablespoons of the olive oil in a large skillet and add the chicken, skin side down. Season with salt, pepper, and rosemary and cook, uncovered, over moderate heat, turning the chicken often. When the chicken begins to brown, drain off all fat and add the onion, drained mushrooms, and garlic. Continue to cook until the onion becomes translucent. Add the Marsala, cover, and simmer for about 10 minutes.

Meanwhile, heat the remaining oil in a skillet, add the asparagus and chopped parsley, and season with salt and pepper to taste. Sauté over medium heat for about 8 minutes, tossing occasionally, or until the asparagus is crisp-tender. Mix in with the chicken and cook an additional 4 minutes. The cook may either enjoy the pleasure of eating the garlic squeezed onto a bit of bread or squeeze it back into the sauce.

VARIATION WITH VEGETABLE COMBINATIONS: Instead of asparagus, use 1½ **pounds cooked vegetable combinations** such as **tomatoes and peas,** or **tomatoes, peppers, and onions,** or **cauliflower and onions.** The vegetables should always be cooked separately and combined with the chicken after it has browned and the wine has been added.

Chicken Smothered in Vegetables

I make this recipe with an older chicken. However, you can use a fryer if you wish. The cooking time will vary with the age of the chicken.

Serves 6.

1 chicken (3 to 3½ pounds), cut into 8 pieces
2 tablespoons olive oil
Salt and freshly ground black pepper to taste
2 tablespoons chopped fresh or dried rosemary
1 medium onion, coarsely chopped
2 ounces dried Italian mushrooms, covered with warm water and soaked for 15 minutes, drained

½ cup dry white wine
3 whole cloves garlic, unpeeled
1 pound tomatoes, chopped
2 ribs celery, chopped
½ pound fresh vegetables of your choice, such as asparagus, peas, peppers, and/or cauliflower, cut into bite-sized pieces
2 or 3 small potatoes, peeled and sliced
Garnish: 1 tablespoon finely chopped flat-leaved parsley

Wash the chicken and pat dry. Heat the olive oil in a large skillet, and add the chicken, skin side down. Season with salt, pepper, and rosemary and cook, uncovered, over moderate heat, turning the chicken often.

When the chicken begins to brown, drain off all fat and add the onion and drained mushrooms. Continue to cook until the onion becomes translucent, then add the wine and garlic and cook, covered, for 10 minutes. Stir in the tomatoes, celery, and vegetables of your choice. Cover, and simmer until the chicken is tender, between 45 minutes and 1½ hours, depending on the age of the chicken. Add the sliced potatoes during the last 10 minutes of cooking. Serve hot, garnished with chopped parsley.

Boiled Chicken

This recipe is of Chinese origin. If you are fond of boiled chicken, then I think you will be very pleased with this recipe. I like to serve it with a green sauce (page 231). I also like to use it in Chicken and Potato Salad (page 202).

Serves 4.

2 large carrots, scraped
1 medium leek, slit and washed
1 medium onion
1 rib celery

Salt to taste
1 chicken (about 3½ pounds),
    washed and trussed
Cold water

Put the carrots, onion, celery, salt, and chicken in a large pot and pour in just enough water to cover the chicken. Now remove the chicken and set it aside for the moment. Bring the water to a boil, return the chicken to the pot, and boil for 1 minute. Cover the pot, turn off the heat, and let the chicken rest in the water for 1 hour. Do not remove the cover during this time. After an hour remove the chicken from its broth and bone and skin it. Serve the chicken warm or at room temperature.

For chicken broth: Put the skin, bones, and carcass back into the broth and simmer them, partially covered, for 2 to 3 hours more. Strain and defat the broth and discard the solids. This broth will make excellent soup.

Chicken Wings with Broccoli

I like this dish served with rice (page 129) or polenta (page 141).

Serves 5.

2 tablespoons vegetable oil
Salt and freshly ground black
    pepper to taste
15 chicken wings (about
    3 pounds), washed, patted
    dry, and with tips turned
    back

1 tablespoon chopped fresh or
    dried rosemary
½ cup dry white wine
2 tablespoons olive oil
1 large onion, thinly sliced
3 cups sliced mushrooms
2 cups seeded and chopped tomatoes

1 bunch broccoli, with stems peeled and cut into quarters, flowerets cut into manageable pieces (about 5 cups)

Preheat the oven to 400°.

Heat the vegetable oil in a large skillet. Salt and pepper the chicken wings, and when the oil is hot, add the chicken and rosemary. Sauté, uncovered, over moderate heat, turning the wings often, until they begin to brown. Discard all of the oil and fat from the skillet and add the wine. Cover and cook over moderate heat until the wine cooks out.

Meanwhile, heat the olive oil in a medium skillet and sauté the onion until it becomes translucent, then add the mushrooms and cook, uncovered, over a moderate heat until the onion begins to brown. Add the tomatoes, cover the skillet, and simmer for 10 minutes.

Meanwhile, blanch the broccoli in boiling salted water for 2 minutes, drain, and set aside.

Place the chicken wings in a shallow baking pan so they fit snugly but do not overlap. Pour the tomato sauce over the wings and place the broccoli around them. Adjust the salt and pepper to taste, cover with foil, and bake for 10 to 15 minutes. Serve hot.

Chicken Wings with Chickpeas

This dish goes very nicely with rice.

Serves 4.

2 tablespoons olive oil
1 medium onion, finely chopped
½ medium green bell pepper, coarsely chopped
2 tablespoons chopped fresh basil, or 1 tablespoon dried
4 cups peeled, seeded, and chopped tomatoes
4 cups water
1 teaspoon chopped fresh or dried rosemary
2 bay leaves

1 cup dried chickpeas, soaked for 24 hours in 3 cups water (change water after 12 hours)
1 piece Parmesan or Pecorino Romano rind (optional)
1 medium carrot, finely chopped
Salt and freshly ground black pepper to taste
2 pounds chicken wings (about 10), washed and with tips folded back

Heat the oil in a medium-heavy saucepan, then add the onion, pepper, and basil and sauté until the onion browns. Add the tomatoes, cover, and simmer for 5 minutes. Add the water along with the rosemary, bay leaves, drained chickpeas, cheese rind (if using), carrot, and salt and pepper, cover, and simmer for 2 hours, until the chickpeas are tender. Add the chicken wings and simmer for about 40 minutes, until the wings are tender.

Chicken Breast on a Skewer

Serves 2.

The marinade:

2 cloves garlic, finely chopped

1 teaspoon chopped fresh or
   dried rosemary

Freshly ground black pepper to
   taste

Juice of ½ lemon

2 tablespoons olive oil

1 whole chicken breast, split,
   skinned, boned and each
   half cut into 3 sections

Salt to taste

4 scallions, thinly sliced

2 tablespoons olive oil

2 tablespoons coarsely chopped
   fresh mint

Garnish:

Extra virgin olive oil

1½ tablespoons coarsely
   chopped fresh mint

2 lemon wedges

For the marinade: Combine the marinade ingredients in a medium bowl and add the chicken pieces. Marinate for several hours in the refrigerator.

Preheat the oven broiler or light the coals in a grill.

Spear each chicken section on a skewer. Season with salt to taste.

To broil in the oven: Use the broiler pan with about ¼ inch of water in the bottom. Be sure the skewers are above the water level. Broil the breasts for about 2 minutes on each side or until the chicken is no longer pink in the middle.

If using a barbecue grill, simply grill over hot coals for about 2 minutes on each side or until the chicken is no longer pink in the middle.

Remove the chicken from the skewers and put it into a mixing bowl. Toss with the scallions, oil, and mint. Serve hot or at room temperature, garnished with a little extra virgin olive oil, chopped mint, and lemon wedges.

Chicken Breasts with Shrimp and Edible Pea Pods

Serves 4.

5 tablespoons olive oil
½ pound mushrooms, thinly sliced
1 pound asparagus, cut into 2-inch lengths
½ pound edible pea pods, ends and strings removed
Salt to taste (if using lemon juice instead of soy sauce, below)
2 whole chicken breasts, skinned, boned, and cut into ½-inch strips

½ pound shrimp, shelled
2 tablespoons soy sauce or juice from 1 lemon
Hot pepper flakes to taste (optional)
¼ cup thinly sliced scallions
2 tablespoons finely chopped flat-leaved parsley
1 tablespoon chopped fresh mint

In a heavy skillet or wok, heat 3 tablespoons of the oil until hot, add the mushrooms, and stir-fry over high heat for several minutes. Add the asparagus and stir-fry over moderate heat for 5 minutes. Toss in the pea pods, season with salt (only if you will be using lemon juice instead of soy sauce), and continue stir-frying for about 5 minutes more. With a slotted spoon, remove the vegetables from the skillet and reserve.

Turn up the heat and add the remaining 2 tablespoons oil. When the oil is hot, add the chicken and shrimp and cook over very high heat, stirring and tossing constantly, for about 3 minutes or until the chicken is opaque and the shrimp are pink. Do not overcook. Add the mushrooms and asparagus along with the soy sauce or lemon juice, hot pepper flakes (if using), scallions, parsley, and mint. Stir-fry for an additional minute to heat through. Serve immediately.

Chicken Breasts with Zucchini and Tomatoes

This version of the preceding stir-fry recipe uses only summer vegetables instead of shrimp, and the chicken strips are marinated first in soy sauce, garlic, and hot pepper.

Serves 4.

   1 whole chicken breast (about 1
      pound), boned, skinned, and
      cut into ½-inch strips

The marinade:

   3 tablespoons soy sauce
   2 cloves garlic, finely chopped

   1 teaspoon hot pepper flakes

   3 tablespoons vegetable oil
   1 medium onion, thinly sliced
   1 cup seeded, skinned, and
      chopped tomatoes
   2 cups sliced zucchini, cut in
      ¼-inch slices

   2 tablespoons finely chopped
      flat-leaved parsley
   Salt to taste

For the marinade: Put the strips of chicken in a small bowl with the soy sauce, garlic, and hot pepper flakes. Refrigerate and let marinate for at least 1 hour.

Heat 2 tablespoons of the oil in a medium-to-large skillet or wok, then add the onion and stir-fry for several minutes. Add the tomatoes, zucchini, parsley, and a little salt. Cook, stirring occasionally, over medium heat for about 6 minutes. Remove the vegetables with a slotted spoon and set aside.

Heat the remaining oil in the same skillet, remove the chicken from the marinade, and cook the chicken, stirring, over high heat for 2 to 3 minutes until opaque; do not overcook. Now return the vegetables to the pan and heat through, stirring to mix. Serve warm or at room temperature.

Grilled Chicken Breasts with Country-Style Tomato Sauce

Serves 4.

3 whole chicken breasts,
    skinned and boned

The marinade:

Juice from 3 lemons
3 cloves garlic, peeled and
    sliced
2 tablespoons chopped fresh
    rosemary, or 1 tablespoon
    dried

3 tablespoons olive oil
Salt and freshly ground black
    pepper to taste

The sauce:

2 medium tomatoes, cut in half
3 tablespoons coarsely chopped
    fresh basil
2 tablespoons coarsely chopped
    flat-leaved parsley

1 teaspoon chopped garlic
2 tablespoons olive oil
Grated zest of 1 lemon
Pinch of salt and freshly
    ground pepper

For the marinade: Put the chicken breasts in a bowl with the lemon juice, garlic, rosemary, olive oil, and salt and pepper to taste. Let marinate for several hours.

Grill the chicken breasts over hot coals for about 3 minutes on each side—do not overcook. Thin breasts will cook faster. Remove from the grill and keep warm.

For the sauce: Briefly grill the tomato halves over the hot coals. Squeeze out the seeds and coarsely chop the tomatoes, then puree them in a food processor with the rest of the sauce ingredients. (Do not make ahead and refrigerate.) Pour the sauce on the grilled breasts.

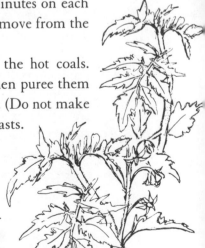

Spinach-Stuffed Honeyed Chicken Legs

While raising bees might not be everyone's idea of good fun, my wife, Ellie, has enjoyed doing it for years and thus assures us of a good and constant supply of home-produced honey.

Serves 4.

The stuffing:

4 cups spinach

2 cups sliced mushrooms

1 small onion, finely chopped

1 tablespoon finely chopped shallots

6 tablespoons fresh bread crumbs

1 egg white, lightly beaten

2 tablespoons freshly grated Parmesan

Salt and freshly ground black pepper to taste

4 chicken drumsticks (with or without the thigh)

Salt and freshly ground black pepper to taste

½ cup imported Marsala

4 tablespoons honey

Make the stuffing: Blanch the spinach in boiling salted water to cover for 30 seconds and drain well. Let cool and squeeze the remaining water out with your hands. Chop fine. Combine the spinach with the remaining stuffing ingedients.

Preheat the oven to 450°.

Bone the chicken drumsticks. Starting at the thick end of the leg, with a sharp paring knife cut around the bone and push the flesh down until you get about 1 inch from the foot joint. At that point, chop off the bone and pull the meat back up.

Fill each leg cavity with the stuffing and gently press the openings closed. Arrange the stuffed legs on a lightly oiled baking tray and bake them, uncovered, for about 40 minutes. Drain the fat from the tray and season the chicken legs with salt and pepper to taste. Pour the Marsala over the legs and cover the tray tightly. Bake, basting occasionally, for 15 minutes. Pour 1 tablespoon of honey over each chicken leg and bake 15 minutes more. Increase the oven temperature to 500° and brown the legs for about 5 minutes. Serve at once.

Oriental-Style Chicken with Eggplant and Peppers

I never peel eggplant. I find that the peel cooks to a very beautiful color, and it is particularly important in this dish because the peel holds the flesh of the eggplant together. Use long, thin eggplant so that you get some of the peel on each strip.

Serves 4.

2 tablespoons vegetable oil
2 tablespoons olive oil
2 cups strips of eggplant 2 to
  3 inches long
2 cups ¾-inch slices of frying
  peppers
1 medium onion, thinly sliced

4 tablespoons light soy sauce
1 whole chicken breast (about
  3½ pounds), skinned, boned,
  and cut into ½-inch strips
1 clove garlic, finely chopped
Freshly ground black pepper to
  taste

In a medium skillet heat 1 tablespoon each of the vegetable and olive oil until hot, then add the eggplant, frying peppers, and onion. Sauté, uncovered, over high heat, stirring often, for about 5 minutes. Add 2 tablespoons of the soy sauce and toss several times. Remove the vegetables to a plate.

Heat the remaining 2 tablespoons oil in the skillet, add the chicken and garlic, and cook over high heat, stirring often, for about 2 minutes. Season with the black pepper, drizzle the remaining 2 tablespoons soy sauce over the top, and toss. Add the eggplant and pepper mixture. Cook, tossing often, to combine and to heat through. Serve at once.

Chicken with Green Olives

This recipe is a specialty of the area in Italy that my mother and father came from. It is a region famous for its giant green olives, called olive verde Ascolane. *My aunt's mother made chicken with olives every Sunday. I have not been able to reproduce her marvelous recipe exactly, but this is a close second. She always cut the chicken into 2-inch sections, but you can cook it cut up in the usual way.*

Serves 4 to 6.

3 tablespoons olive oil
1 frying chicken (2½ to
    3 pounds), cut into serving
    pieces or into 2-inch pieces
Giblets (gizzard, heart, and
    liver), cut into ½-inch pieces
4 fat cloves garlic, unpeeled
¼ cup chopped prosciutto
¾ tablespoons chopped fresh
    or dried rosemary

Salt and freshly ground black
    pepper to taste
Hot pepper flakes to taste*
10 large home-cured green
    olives (page 316),† pitted
    and cut into quarters
    lengthwise
1 medium onion, coarsely
    chopped
1 cup dry white wine

Heat the oil in a skillet large enough to hold the chicken, then add the chicken, giblets, garlic, prosciutto, rosemary, and salt, pepper, and hot pepper flakes to taste. Cook for about a half hour, uncovered, over low to moderate heat, turning the chicken often. Pour off the fat, leaving a glaze of oil in the pan. Add the olives and onion and continue cooking for about 10 minutes. Add the wine, turn up the heat, and when the wine boils, reduce the heat to medium, stir often, and cook until the wine cooks out—about 20 minutes. The cook may eat the garlic squeezed onto a bit of bread or may squeeze it back into the sauce.

* My aunt's mother did not use hot pepper, but I like a taste of it.
† You may buy 20 large cured green olives and soak in cold water for 15 minutes before using. The home-cured olives aren't as bitter.

Chicken and Potato Salad

Serves 4.

The dressing:

5 tablespoons extra virgin olive
    oil

1½ cups shredded boiled
    chicken (page 194)
2 medium carrots, halved, boiled,
    and cut into ½-inch pieces
2 potatoes, boiled, peeled, and
    sliced ¼-inch thick

4 tablespoons wine vinegar
1 tablespoon prepared mustard

3 scallions, thinly sliced
1½ tablespoons coarsely
    chopped fresh mint
Salt and freshly ground black
    pepper to taste

Make the dressing: In a small bowl whisk the olive oil, vinegar, and mustard.

In a serving bowl mix together the remaining ingredients, then toss gently with the dressing. Serve at room temperature.

Ground Chicken Patties

As mentioned earlier, I kill chickens year-round, so it is not unusual for me to have extra chicken on hand. Ellie collects honey in the spring and fall, so it was one spring day that I decided to combine the two, which resulted in the following recipe. If you have no Honey Sauce or another sauce that you care to use, Dijon mustard makes a fine substitute.

Serves 3.

Enough leftover cooked chicken to make 2 cups ground, or 2 whole chicken breasts, broiled, skinned, and boned

2 egg whites, lightly beaten

1½ tablespoons finely chopped flat-leaved parsley

2 cloves garlic, finely chopped

Salt and freshly ground black pepper to taste

Vegetable oil as needed

Honey Sauce:

½ cup or more orange juice

¼ cup honey

1 teaspoon Dijon mustard

Preheat the broiler.

Cut the leftover chicken or chicken breasts into ½-inch cubes, then grind them in a meat grinder. (This should yield about 2 cups ground chicken.)

In a bowl combine the ground chicken with the remaining ingredients. Form the mixture into balls about the size of golf balls. Flatten the balls gently into patties and place the patties in an oiled baking pan. Drizzle a little of the oil over each patty and broil under high heat for about 2 or 3 minutes on each side. Meanwhile mix together the ingredients for the Honey Sauce. Add more orange juice if you want a thinner sauce.

Chicken Gizzards with Beans

Serves 4 to 6.

3 tablespoons olive oil

1 medium onion, coarsely chopped

1½ cups chopped red bell peppers

1½ pounds chicken gizzards, washed and boiled in water for 5 minutes, then drained

1 tablespoon chopped fresh or dried rosemary

Salt and freshly ground black pepper to taste

1 ounce dried Italian mushrooms, covered with tepid water and soaked 15 minutes, then drained

1 cup chopped tomatoes

2 tablespoons chopped fresh basil, or 1 tablespoon dried

1 cup chicken broth, preferably homemade (page 194)

2 cups cooked kidney beans (page 73), or one 20-ounce can

Heat the oil in a medium shallow saucepan. Add the onion and red peppers and sauté over a medium heat, uncovered, stirring often, until the onion begins to brown. Add the gizzards, rosemary, and salt and pepper and cook for several minutes more. Add the mushrooms, tomatoes, basil, and broth and simmer for 1 hour, stirring often. Add the beans, cover, and simmer for 45 minutes more, stirring occasionally.

VARIATION WITH POTATOES AND BRUSSELS SPROUTS: In a medium skillet, heat **3 tablespoons olive oil** and sauté the **gizzards** (boiled 5 minutes as above) along with **1½ cups coarsely chopped onions** and **hot pepper flakes to taste** until the onions begin to brown. Add **3 cloves garlic, finely chopped, 1½ teaspoons chopped fresh or dried rosemary,** and **½ cup white wine vinegar, or ¾ cup dry white wine.** Cover and simmer until the vinegar or wine cooks out. Add **3 cups chopped tomatoes** and **1 tablespoon chopped fresh basil, or 1½ teaspoons dried,** and bring to a gentle boil. Add **½ pound brussels sprouts, blanched,** and **3 medium potatoes, peeled and cut into ½-inch slices.** Cover and simmer for approximately 45 minutes. Add some **water or broth** if the mixture gets too dry while cooking.

Devilish Young Chickens or Cornish Hens

This recipe is made in Italy with spring chickens weighing no more than 1½ pounds dressed, but because young spring chickens are difficult to find, I discovered that Cornish hens are a fine substitute.

Serves 2.

2 spring chickens or 2 fresh
  Cornish hens, split, with
  excess fat removed
½ cup wine vinegar for
  marinade, plus additional
  ½ cup for cooking liquid

3 tablespoons vegetable oil
Salt to taste
2 tablespoons chopped fresh or
  dried rosemary
Hot pepper flakes or coarsely
  ground black pepper to taste

Marinate the hens in ½ cup wine vinegar for several hours, turning occasionally, then remove the birds, reserving the marinade, lay them on a large plate, and cover them with wax paper. Flatten them by weighting them down with two bricks wrapped in wax paper or plastic wrap or by laying a large flat plate or clean board over the chickens and filling a pot with water and setting it on top. (I put them in an old woodblock press.) Keep the chickens weighted for 20 minutes or so.

Heat the oil in a large skillet. Sprinkle salt and rosemary over the hens and rub hot pepper flakes or pepper on them. Place the hens in the hot oil skin side down and put a brick on each hen (or set a large pot filled with water on top of them). If you do not have a skillet large enough to hold both hens, use two skillets. Cook the hens over moderate heat, turning over every 5 minutes until both sides are golden brown. Keep the weights on the hens while they are cooking. When the hens are brown, add the reserved marinade plus additional ½ cup of vinegar and cook, uncovered, until the vinegar cooks out, about 30 to 40 minutes. Serve hot.

Cornish Hens Baked in Bread

Plan to make this wonderful dish when you are preparing bread dough for some other purpose and start it the night before. You will use only half the amount of dough that Ellie's Italian-Style Bread (page 289) yields.

Serves 4.

1 recipe bread dough (page 289)
2 tablespoons olive oil
2 plump lean Cornish hens
2 tablespoons fresh or dried rosemary

1 or 2 cloves garlic, cut in slivers
Salt and freshly ground black pepper to taste

The sauce:

1 small onion, or ½ medium onion, finely chopped
2 tablespoons olive oil
Giblets from the hens
1 tablespoon finely chopped flat-leaved parsley

½ cup sweet sherry
Salt and freshly ground black pepper to taste

Make the bread dough the night before and refrigerate, covered. Turn the dough out and knead it, adding more flour as necessary. Return to the bowl, cover, and let rise while you are preparing the birds.

Preheat oven to 450°.

Heat 1 tablespoon of the olive oil in the bottom of a roasting pan large enough so that the hens fit snugly. Rub the birds with crumbled rosemary, garlic, salt, and pepper. Put them in the pan, breast side down, and drizzle a little olive oil over them. Roast in the preheated oven 15 minutes, then turn the birds breast side up and roast 15 minutes more. Allow the birds to cool, drain them well, and pour off the juices from the pan. Skim off the fat and reserve the pan juices.

Reduce oven temperature to 400°.

Turn the risen dough out onto a floured work surface. Using about ¼ of the dough, roll it out to ½ inch thickness. Place one of the hens in the center of the dough and fold the sides of the dough up over the bird, overlapping the ends and pinching them together for a tight seam; cut away any excess dough. Place the dough-wrapped hen on an oiled baking sheet. Repeat with the other hen. Bake for 20 to 30 minutes or until the bread is browned, throwing an occasional ice cube on the oven floor to create steam.

For the sauce: Meanwhile, make the sauce. Sauté the onion in the olive oil, then add the giblets, parsley, reserved juices from the roasting pan, ¼ cup of the sherry, and salt and pepper to taste. Simmer, covered, over low heat for 20 minutes. Remove the giblets and cut them into small cubes. Defat the sauce by pouring it into a transparent defatting pitcher, and when the fat rises to the top, pour it off. Put the defatted sauce into a small saucepan, add the cubed giblets and the remaining sherry, and bring to a boil. Reserve.

When the birds are done, arrange them on a large platter and present to your guests. Then with a sharp knife slit the bread through the middle lengthwise, spread it open, and remove it from the birds. Put it back in the oven or under a broiler to dry out the damp interior. Cut the birds in half and serve with the sauce and chunks of the bread.

Ducks

We have a pond in front of our house and we usually have ducks. In addition to our small flock of domestic white ducks, wild mallards and Canadian geese usually stop by in the spring and nest on the island in the pond. We do not kill the mallards and Canadian geese—after all, they are our guests. But we do eat our own domestic ducks. Actually we don't have much choice. The ducks are "sitting ducks" in the winter (pardon the pun) when the pond freezes, and they are helpless, quickly becoming the victims of coons, dogs, foxes, and so on. So we usually herd them into the chicken coop and kill them as we need them.

Unlike chickens, ducks are miserable when they are cooped up. They are messy, and, without water to swim in, they are not very healthy. We do not let them linger long. The following spring we buy a new flock. We let them eat what they please; they have plenty of water to swim in and feed in, and we supplement their diet with corn. Needless to say, the meat is superior to the ducks sold in supermarkets.

Use the same technique to kill, pluck, and eviscerate a duck as you use for a chicken (page 188). Ducks are more difficult to pluck because their outer feathers are waterproof and their plumage is much thicker, but with patience it is not so difficult and it is certainly worth the effort.

Grilled Duck Breasts

I like to serve this recipe with small steamed artichokes.

Serves 2.

The marinade:

3 cloves garlic, thinly sliced
1 tablespoon chopped fresh or
    dried rosemary
Juice of 1 lemon

2 tablespoons brandy (optional)
1 tablespoon good mustard
Salt and freshly ground black
    pepper to taste

2 good-sized duck breasts*
Olive oil

Garnish: Lemon wedges

Make the marinade: Mix the marinade ingredients together in a glass baking dish. Place the duck breasts, meat side down, in the marinade and allow to sit for at least 2 hours; 4 hours is better. Sprinkle the skin side of the breasts with olive oil.

Grill the breasts over hot coals, first the flesh side down and then the skin side. Do not overcook the duck. The flesh should be cooked only until it is pink, about 5 minutes on each side for a large breast.

Cut the breasts into thin slices and serve with lemon wedges.

* Mallards, as well as domestic ducks, may be used. Save the legs, wings, and carcass for soup.

Duckling with Lentils

Serves 4 to 6.

1 duckling (4 pounds)	½ cup finely chopped celery
Salt and freshly ground black pepper to taste	½ cup finely chopped carrots
2 tablespoons olive oil	2 tablespoons finely chopped flat-leaved parsley
1 medium onion, finely chopped	2 bay leaves
3 cloves garlic, finely chopped	¾ cup dry white wine
	1 teaspoon dried marjoram

The lentils:

1 medium onion, finely chopped	½ cup coarsely chopped celery
2 tablespoons olive oil	2 tablespoons chopped fresh basil, or 1 teaspoon dried
Liver from the duckling, coarsely chopped	1 cup lentils
1 medium carrot, coarsely chopped	Salt and freshly ground black pepper to taste

Wash the duckling in cold water and dry it. Sprinkle it with salt and pepper. Heat the olive oil in a heavy pot, then sauté the duckling over moderate heat, turning to brown all sides. Add the onion, and when it becomes translucent, add the garlic and cook 1 minute, stirring. Add the celery, carrots, parsley, and bay leaves, cover, and sauté until the vegetables are tender. Add the wine and, when it boils, the marjoram. Simmer over low heat until the wine evaporates. Now add enough hot water to cover the duckling, bring to a boil, then lower the heat and simmer gently, partially covered, for 1 hour or until the duckling is tender. Pour off 4 cups of the cooking liquid, skim off all fat, and reserve for the lentils.

Prepare the lentils: Sauté the onion in the olive oil, and when it is translucent, add the chopped liver and sauté for 1 minute. Add the reserved duck cooking liquid, carrot, celery, and basil, and when it comes to a boil, stir in the lentils. Cover and simmer over moderate to low heat, adding more liquid if necessary. Add salt and pepper to taste.

When the lentils are tender, in about 20 minutes, remove the duckling from the remaining broth and cut it up into serving pieces. Place on a heated platter with the lentils. Serve hot.

Duck Breast Meat Loaf

I used our own duck (a large old gander) for this recipe. I ground the breasts because they were tough and made soup with the carcass. You could use any elderly fowl or rabbit in place of the duck.

Serves 6.

¼ pound spinach
1 large onion, chopped
2 tablespoons vegetable oil
1½ pounds duck breasts, skinned, boned, and coarsely ground
¾ pound lean pork tenderloin or chicken breasts, ground
3 egg whites, lightly beaten
2 tablespoons chopped fresh basil, or 1 tablespoon dried

Grated zest of 1 lemon
3 tablespoons finely chopped walnuts
1 cup bread crumbs
1 tablespoon tomato paste, preferably homemade (page 31)
Salt and freshly ground black pepper to taste
¼ cup sherry

Preheat the oven to 450°.

Blanch the spinach in boiling salted water to cover for 30 seconds and drain well. Let cool and squeeze the remaining water out with your hands; chop.

Sauté the onion in the oil until lightly browned. Mix the sautéed onion and the spinach with the rest of the ingredients except the sherry. Oil a loaf pan (3½ by 9 by 2½ inches). Pack the meat mixture into the pan and form into a loaf. Cover with foil and bake about 45 minutes. Remove the foil and pour the sherry over the meat loaf. Bake uncovered for an additional 20 minutes.

Goose

We have raised geese on a number of occasions. They are interesting, bad-tempered creatures, who make wonderful watchdogs. They are afraid of neither man nor beast and ours have even attacked the tires of cars coming up our driveway. Unfortunately they are terribly messy and leave their droppings all over the place. But they are rather noble and they make wonderful food. The following recipe was given to me by Pierre Franey, and it is my favorite way of preparing goose.

Meats, including pork, goose, and duck, have been preserved in fat in Europe for centuries. Although today freezing may be a much simpler way of preserving, this method gives such a lovely flavor and texture to the meat that it is worth the effort, and you will have a treasure on hand for unexpected company. Incidentally, the fat is just a preservative and is wiped off when you use the meat in a dish. In fact, the fatty birds raised today take particularly well to this method because they render all their fat in the process.

Preserved Goose

When I used my own domestic goose, there was plenty of fat on it, enough to cure the goose properly. Then I tried this recipe with a wild goose, but because it was not nearly as fat, it did not render enough fat, so I had to use rendered pork fat to compensate for the amount of fat necessary to cover the goose parts. Use the preserved goose for stews, cassoulets, etc.

Serves 8.

1 goose 8 to 10 pounds dressed (see instructions for chickens, page 189)	2 bay leaves
	2 tablespoons dried rosemary
	½ teaspoon saltpeter
About 2 pounds fat total—the goose fat plus additional pork fat or lard, if necessary	(optional)*
	Salt and freshly ground black pepper to taste

Remove and discard the wingtips. Cut the breast away from the bone and cut off the thigh and legs. Use the carcass for soup or discard it. Remove all of the fat and reserve.

Place the goose sections and the remaining ingredients into a mixing bowl, rub the goose sections with the fat and spices, cover the bowl, and refrigerate it or put it in a cool place (at least 40°F) overnight.

The next day cut the pork and goose fat into small pieces and render the fat by cooking slowly until the fat is melted and cracklings have separated from it. Strain (you should have enough fat to cover up the meat).

---

* Saltpeter is used to keep the goose flesh pink, but it is not necessary for making this recipe a success.

In a deep skillet, place the goose sections skin side down and cook slowly for about 10 minutes, then pour in the rendered fat, completely immersing the goose sections. Cook the goose slowly, uncovered, for about 1½ hours; the fat will just bubble gently. Put the goose pieces in a crock and pour over them the fat the goose cooked in as well as the rendered fat. Store the goose completely covered by the fat, in a cool place—under 50°F; it will keep about 6 months.

Squab

We ate squab (young pigeons) when I was a child. Pigeons were easy and cheap to raise and were divine food. My father was especially fond of squab and wild mushrooms cooked in a sauce served over polenta. Believe it or not, that was Depression food.

When I was a student in Italy in the early fifties, I ate a lot of squab. It was well prepared and inexpensive. Then, when we moved to Katonah in 1961, we discovered pigeons making their home in our barn. Under my father's directions I would climb up the rafters to peek into the nests perched high up near the roof. My father below would tell me what to look for. The squab were ready when fully feathered and about to fly. At that point they were plump and almost as large as an adult bird. I would drop the squab down to my father. He would kill, dress, and cook them, and they were a delight.

The easiest way to kill a squab is to hold the bird with one hand and with the fingers of the other hand cover the air holes in the bird's beak. Death comes quickly and painlessly. You can also kill and dress squab as you do chicken (page 189), but take care if you are wet-plucking them that the water is not too hot. I've always found it better to dry-pluck squab.

Unlike chicken, pigeons are constantly laying and hatching eggs. They lay two eggs and then immediately sit on them. After their young fly off, they lay two more, and so on. We eat squab to keep the flock manageable.

Squab require very little care. They fly from the barn and around our house back to the barn in a beautiful white wave that takes our breath away. If we go away, they will just take care of themselves until our return. Of all the creatures we raise, squab are by far the most productive and the least trouble.

Squab with Peas

Serves 2 to 4.

3 tablespoons olive oil

2 cups small white onions, peeled (page 59)

2 squab, with gizzards reserved, split, washed, drained, patted dry

Salt and freshly ground black pepper to taste

2 tablespoons finely chopped shallots

2 tablespoons finely chopped flat-leaved parsley

¼ cup coarsely chopped prosciutto

1 ounce dried Italian mushrooms, soaked in warm water for 15 minutes

1¾ cups peas, cooked in boiling salted water for 5 minutes, drained

1 fat clove garlic, finely chopped

1 tablespoon crushed dried rosemary

½ cup dry imported Marsala

Heat the olive oil in a wide heavy skillet until hot. Add the onions and gizzards of the squabs, and sauté, uncovered, over moderate heat, for about 8 minutes. Remove the gizzards, chop them, and return them to the skillet. Salt and pepper the squabs, place them in the skillet, skin side down, and cook over moderate heat until the skin begins to brown. Turn the squab over, and when the second side begins to brown, add the shallots and parsley. Cook for several minutes to combine. Add the remaining ingredients, cover, and cook over moderate heat for 30 minutes, until the wine cooks out. Serve with Bruschetta (page 294).

Doves and Polenta

Serves 2 to 4 as a first course.

2 tablespoons olive oil

1 tablespoon butter

Salt and freshly ground black pepper to taste

4 doves, cleaned, plucked, and split (see method for chicken, page 189)

Flour for dredging

½ cup finely chopped onions

¼ cup imported Marsala

1 ounce dried Italian mushrooms, soaked in 1 cup hot chicken broth for 15 minutes

2 tablespoons tomato paste, preferably homemade (page 31)

1 recipe polenta using 1–1½ cups cornmeal (page 141)

Heat the olive oil and butter in a medium skillet or saucepan. Salt and pepper the birds and then lightly dust with flour and sauté over moderate heat, turning often until lightly browned. Add the onions and cook uncovered over moderate heat until the onions begin to brown, then add the Marsala, lower heat, and simmer, covered, until the wine is almost cooked out.

Meanwhile, strain the mushroom liquid into a small saucepan and cook the mushrooms in broth for 15 minutes; stir in the tomato paste and then pour the mushroom-tomato mixture over the doves. Cover and simmer over low heat for about 1¼ hours, turning the birds over often.

Cook polenta. Apportion onto hot serving plates, top with sauce and mushrooms, and place doves on each side. Serve immediately.

Pheasant My Way

Serves 4 to 6.

1 ounce dried Italian
   mushrooms
1 fat pheasant, about 3½ pounds,
   plucked and cleaned (page 189)
¼ cup olive oil
3 whole cloves garlic, unpeeled
2 bay leaves
Salt and freshly ground black
   pepper to taste
1 medium onion, finely chopped

¾ cup chopped prosciutto
2 cups thinly sliced mushrooms
   (if possible, use 4 cups wild mushrooms and no dried ones)
1 cup dry Marsala
1 teaspoon chopped fresh or
   dried rosemary
2 teaspoons chopped fresh
   mint, or 1 teaspoon dried
¾ cup chopped tomatoes

Soak the Italian mushrooms in tepid water for 15 minutes, then strain, reserving the liquid, and slice them.

Soak the pheasant in cold salted water for 2 hours. Rinse and pat dry. Cut into serving pieces as you would a chicken.

Heat the oil in a large skillet, add the pheasant pieces, and cook, uncovered, over medium heat, turning often. Add the garlic, bay leaves, and salt and pepper to taste. When the pheasant begins to brown, add the onion, prosciutto, and all of the mushrooms—the fresh and the reconstituted dried ones. Stir often with a wooden spoon. When the onion wilts, add the Marsala, rosemary, and mint. Cover, lower heat, and simmer for 10 minutes. Add the tomatoes and mushroom soaking water, cover, and continue to cook over medium to low heat for about 30 minutes or until the pheasant is tender. Discard the garlic.

Meat
and
Game

Meat

During the Depression no one was able to afford big pieces of meat. Maybe people like my family would have a roast of lamb for Easter and a fat turkey for Thanksgiving. But most of the time we had vegetables cooked with a little meat, mostly veal—the vegetables serving to stretch the meat. But it turned out that those dishes were much more interesting than the average American fare because they varied with each season. We looked forward with pleasure to the accents of spring asparagus and peas, then the summer tomatoes, peppers, and eggplant, and the fall root vegetables and cabbages and potatoes. I learned early that the secret to enjoying food is to anticipate something you like. Now when I want a piece of meat, I think of it seasonally. Our diet also turned out to be a very healthy one. So the recipes in this meat chapter are really just another excuse to eat vegetables in interesting ways.

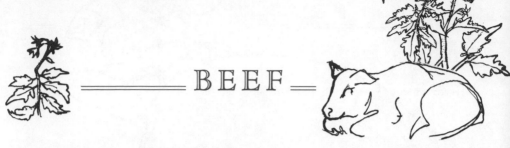

BEEF

Mixed Boiled Dinner I

I like to serve a boiled dinner with a hot pepper sauce (page 52) and green sauce (page 231). You can freeze the leftover broth for future use. I deliberately let some of my chickens get old so I can enjoy them in a boiled dinner (go to a farmer—he'll be glad to let you have an old hen). A boiled dinner can be made from many different types of meat: veal head, tongue, rabbit, etc.

Serves 6 to 8.

3½ pounds beef shank or short
   ribs
12 cups cold water
4 bay leaves
2 large onions, whole
2 ribs celery, cut into 3-inch
   sections
1 soup chicken (about
   4–4½ pounds), trussed
4 carrots, scraped

4 medium potatoes, peeled and
   cut in half
1 pound cotechino in 1 piece
   (page 278), optional
4 parsnips, scraped
10 ounces brussels sprouts
4 fat leeks, trimmed
   (page 59)
Salt and freshly ground black
   pepper to taste

Put the beef and the water in a large soup pot along with the bay leaves, onions, and celery and gently boil, covered, for 1 hour. Skim off the scum as it rises. Add the chicken and cook for 30 minutes. Add the carrots and potatoes and cook for 30 minutes more; add the cotechino along with the parsnips, brussels sprouts, leeks, and salt and pepper to taste. Cook just until the parsnips are tender, about 20 to 30 minutes; at this point the potatoes should also be cooked.

Carefully remove the meat from the broth and cut the cotechino into ¾-inch slices. Remove the vegetables with a slotted spoon and keep them warm. Strain the soup and skim off all of the fat.

You can serve the broth alone or with thin bird's nest pasta (Nidi) cooked in it as a first course, if you wish. Serve the meat and the vegetables as a second course with a sauce (page 228, or see index).

VARIATION:
Mixed Boiled Dinner II

When you don't have an old soup chicken and cannot get your hands on good cotechino, this boiled dinner is a fine alternative.

Serves 6 to 8.

1½ pounds beef shank, bone in
12 cups water
1 large onion, chopped
2 ribs celery, cut in 2-inch
    pieces
2 medium carrots,
    scraped
2 bay leaves
1 cup chopped tomatoes

1 piece Parmesan or Pecorino
    Romano rind, scraped, about
    3 inches by 2 inches or larger
Salt to taste
2 pounds mixed chicken parts
2 medium parsnips, scraped
3 or 4 medium potatoes, peeled
15 brussels sprouts
Fresh lemon juice

Combine the first 8 ingredients in a soup pot, add salt to taste, and boil gently for 1 hour. Add the chicken parts and cook 45 minutes more, then add the parsnips, potatoes, and brussels sprouts and cook until the vegetables are done. Skim off the fat, correct seasonings, adding a little lemon juice, and serve as above. Cook about ¼ cup rice or 2 to 3 ounces thin pasta in the broth to serve it as a first course.

Sauce for Boiled Meat

Makes 1½ cups, enough for 4 servings.

2 carrots, boiled
1 medium onion, boiled
2 teaspoons prepared mustard
2 tablespoons white wine vinegar
1 tablespoon finely chopped
    flat-leaved parsley

½ cup scallions, thinly sliced
2 tablespoons capers, drained
2 tablespoons extra virgin olive
    oil
Salt and freshly ground black
    pepper to taste

Blend the carrots, onion, mustard, and vinegar in a food processor or with a mortar and pestle. Add the parsley, scallions, capers, oil, and salt and pepper. Mix all of the ingredients and serve the sauce at room temperature with boiled meat. More oil may be added if you desire.

Boiled Beef with Cauliflower

If you have boiled beef left over from your Mixed Boiled Dinner I (page 218), try this recipe with cauliflower.

Serves 2.

2 tablespoons olive oil
1 medium onion, coarsely
    chopped
½ medium green bell pepper,
    coarsely chopped
2 cups chopped tomatoes
2 tablespoons finely chopped
    flat-leaved parsley

4 cups cauliflower flowerets,
    blanched
1 to 1½ cups boiled beef, cut
    into large pieces
Salt to taste
Hot pepper flakes to taste
    (optional)

Heat the oil in a medium skillet and sauté the onion and pepper until the onion beings to brown. Add the tomatoes and parsley, cover, and simmer for 10 minutes. Add the cauliflower, boiled beef, salt, and hot pepper flakes, if using. Cover and boil gently for 10 minutes.

Meatballs with Eggplant

Serves 4.

The meatballs:

½ pound lean ground beef
1 egg white, lightly beaten
⅓ cup fresh bread crumbs
2 to 3 teaspoons chopped fresh
    oregano, or 1 teaspoon dried
2 tablespoons finely chopped
    flat-leaved parsley

Salt and freshly ground black
    pepper to taste
Dash of freshly grated nutmeg
1 medium onion, finely
    chopped

The sauce:

2 tablespoons olive oil
1 small onion, thinly sliced

2 cups chopped tomatoes
Hot pepper flakes to taste (optional)

2 small to medium eggplants,
    sliced into ¼-inch-thick rounds

For the meatballs: In a medium bowl mix the ground beef, egg white, bread crumbs, oregano, parsley, salt, pepper, nutmeg, and the chopped medium onion; form into 18 balls about 1 inch in diameter.

Place the meatballs on a lightly oiled baking tray and broil them close to the heat, turning occasionally until they are brown all over.

Preheat the oven to 500°.

For the sauce: Heat the olive oil in a medium skillet and sauté the sliced small onion over a moderate heat until translucent. Add the tomatoes and hot pepper flakes (if using), cover, and simmer for 5 minutes. Add the meatballs, cover, and simmer for 15 minutes more.

Meanwhile, lightly oil a baking tray, spread the eggplant slices on it, and place in the oven. When the slices are lightly browned on both sides, add them to the meatballs and cook for 15 minutes more. Taste and adjust for salt.

Tripe with Raisins, Pine Nuts, and Potatoes

This is one of the innards that people concerned with cholesterol can eat. When the tripe is boiled briefly, it is easier to remove the outside fat and to cut it up. I find the flavor of tripe very delicate. It is not only healthy but it is also extremely versatile and inexpensive.

Serves 5 or 6.

¼ cup olive oil
1½–2 medium-sized onions, finely chopped
3 cloves garlic, finely chopped
3 cups chopped tomatoes
1½ cups beef or chicken broth, preferably homemade (for chicken broth, see 194)
3 pounds tripe, prepared as in recipe introduction, cut into 3- by ¼-inch strips

Salt to taste
3 tablespoons chopped fresh basil, or ½ tablespoon dried
1½ teaspoons chopped fresh or dried rosemary
Hot pepper flakes (optional)
3 tablespoons white raisins, soaked in tepid water for 15 minutes, then drained
3 tablespoons pine nuts
12 small potatoes, peeled

Heat the olive oil in a shallow saucepan and sauté the onions until translucent, then add the garlic and continue to sauté several minutes.

*Tripe with
Raisins,
Pine Nuts,
and
Potatoes
(continued)*

Stir in the tomatoes and the broth. Add the tripe and season with salt to taste, basil, rosemary, and hot pepper flakes, if using. Cover, bring to a boil, and simmer for 1½ hours. Add the raisins, pine nuts, and potatoes, cover, and cook 20 to 30 minutes more until potatoes are done. Serve hot.

VARIATION:

Tripe with White Beans, Savoy Cabbage, and Tomatoes

Serves 5 or 6 with hearty portions.

2 tablespoons olive oil
1 tablespoon salt pork, chopped
1 large onion, finely chopped
1½ tablespoons finely chopped
    flat-leaved parsley
1 medium carrot, finely
    chopped
1 rib celery, finely chopped
2 medium cloves garlic, finely
    chopped
2 cups fresh or canned chopped
    tomatoes
1 cup chicken broth, preferably
    homemade
1½ teaspoons chopped fresh or
    dried rosemary
2 tablespoons chopped fresh
    basil, or 1 tablespoon dried
Salt and freshly ground black
    pepper to taste

1½ pounds tripe, cut into ½-
    inch-wide sections (see
    recipe introduction,
    page 221)
2-inch piece Parmesan rind,
    scraped (optional)
1 cup dried cannellini or Great
    Northern beans, soaked in
    3 cups cold water overnight,
    drained
5 or 6 medium potatoes, peeled
    and cut in half crosswise
½ large or 2 small head savoy
    cabbage (about 1 pound), cut
    into 5 or 6 sections, with
    core removed
Garnish: Freshly grated
    Parmesan or hot pepper
    flakes

Heat the olive oil and salt pork in a large skillet and sauté the onion and parsley for 5 minutes. Add the carrot and celery and continue to sauté for 7 minutes more. Add the garlic and cook another minute, then add the tomatoes and cook for 5 minutes more. Pour in the chicken broth and season with the rosemary, basil, and salt and pepper.

Cover and simmer for approximately 20 minutes. Add the tripe, optional cheese rind, and beans, cover, and continue to boil gently for another 1½ hours, occasionally stirring from the bottom of the skillet.

Meanwhile, boil the potatoes and cabbage in salted water, together, until the potatoes are tender but firm. Place two potato halves and one section of cabbage on the bottom of each soup bowl and ladle the tripe and beans over it. Serve with grated cheese or hot pepper flakes.

VARIATION:

Tripe with Lima Beans and Rape or Broccoli

Serves 5 or 6.

2 tablespoons olive oil

1 large onion, finely chopped

4 cups chopped tomatoes

4 tablespoons chopped fresh basil, or 2 tablespoons dried

1 tablespoon chopped fresh or dried rosemary

2 teaspoons chopped fresh marjoram, or 1 teaspoon dried

1½- by 2-inch piece Parmesan rind, scraped

Salt and freshly ground black pepper or hot pepper flakes to taste (I prefer hot pepper)

2 cups water

3 pounds tripe, cut into ½- by 2-inch strips (see recipe introduction, page 221)

1 cup large dried lima beans, soaked overnight in 3 cups water, drained

4 cups rape or broccoli flowerets, blanched

Heat the olive oil in a sauce pot and sauté the onion until it begins to brown, then add the tomatoes, basil, rosemary, marjoram, cheese rind, and salt and pepper or hot pepper flakes to taste. Simmer, covered, for 5 minutes. Pour in the water and add the tripe, cover, and simmer for a half hour. Add the lima beans to the tomato-tripe mixture, cover, and continue to simmer as above, or boil gently, for 1½ hours. Then add the rape or broccoli and cook for another 15 minutes. Serve hot.

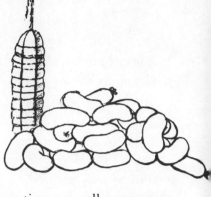

PORK

When I was younger and seemed to have more time as well as more family at home, I used to buy a whole pig—about 150 pounds dressed. I would hang it on our back porch with sticks to keep the cavity open so that the cold winter air could circulate freely. I would hang the pig for about 5 days, then I butchered it for sausages, prosciutto, salt pork, liver sausages, head cheese, and so on. The meat was so much better than the pork we buy in supermarkets. Most of the recipes that follow are designed to make the pork we get today taste a little better.

To Make Salt Pork

Simply pour a generous amount of coarse salt over the fatty side of the pork sections. Leave in a cool, airy place or in the refrigerator, occasionally rubbing the skin side with more salt. The pork will be cured in 3 weeks. Store in the refrigerator, where it will keep for a long time.

Stuffed Pork Chops with Green Tomato Sauce

We like this dish with a boiled potato and a green vegetable like broccoli or rape.

Serves 4.

4 pork chops, about ¾ inch thick

The stuffing:

¼ pound spinach
¼ cup bread crumbs
1 egg white, lightly beaten
2 tablespoons freshly grated Parmesan
1 teaspoon chopped fresh oregano, or ½ teaspoon dried

Salt and freshly ground black pepper to taste
2 tablespoons safflower or corn oil

Salt and freshly ground black pepper to taste
1 tablespoon olive oil
1 small onion, finely chopped

¼ cup white wine vinegar

The sauce:

2 tablespoons olive oil
1 small onion, finely chopped
3 cups sliced green tomatoes
Salt and freshly ground black pepper to taste

1 tablespoon finely chopped flat-leaved parsley

Trim off all of the excess fat from the pork chops. With a sharp knife, cut horizontally through each chop to the bone, butterfly fashion. Pound each side of the chop with a meat pounder to flatten it out a bit, and set the chops aside.

Make the stuffing: In a medium saucepan, bring 1 cup of water to a boil, add the spinach and boil 1 minute. Drain the spinach, squeeze out all excess moisture, chop it, and place it in a mixing bowl. Stir in the bread crumbs, egg white, cheese, oregano, and salt and pepper.

*Stuffed
Pork Chops
with Green
Tomato
Sauce
(continued)*

Heat 1 tablespoon of olive oil in a small skillet and sauté the onion until it begins to brown. Mix the onion with the spinach–bread crumb mixture.

Stuff the cut pocket of the pork chops and secure each individual chop with a toothpick or two. Salt and pepper the chops.

Heat the safflower or corn oil in a medium skillet and brown the pork chops on each side, over low heat and uncovered, for about 10 minutes. Add the vinegar, cover, and simmer, turning the chops occasionally, until the vinegar cooks out.

Meanwhile, make the sauce: Heat 2 tablespoons olive oil in a small skillet and sauté the onion until it begins to brown, then add the tomatoes and salt and pepper to taste. Cover and cook over low to moderate heat for 15 minutes. Remove from the heat, add the parsley and mix well. Serve alongside the pork chops.

Pork Rolls

Serves 2 to 4.

> 1 pound pork loin, cut into 4-
> ounce slices, or 1 pound thin
> pork chops

The stuffing:

2 tablespoons raisins

6 tablespoons bread crumbs

1 egg white, lightly beaten

1 tablespoon finely chopped
flat-leaved parsley

2 tablespoons milk

2 tablespoons freshly grated
Parmesan

Salt and freshly ground black
pepper to taste

Salt and freshly ground black
pepper to taste

2 tablespoons corn oil

1 medium onion, finely
chopped

1 rib celery, finely chopped

2 cups chopped tomatoes

2 teaspoons chopped fresh
basil, or 1 teaspoon dried

¾ cup chicken or beef broth,
preferably homemade (for
chicken broth, see page 194),
or water

Using a meat pounder, pound to flatten the slices of pork loin to ⅛-inch thick. Or bone a thin pork chop, remove the outer fat, butterfly the meat, and pound to flatten.

Make the stuffing: Combine the raisins, bread crumbs, egg white, parsley, milk, cheese, and salt and pepper.

Sprinkle each flattened pork cutlet with salt and pepper and place an equal amount of the stuffing in the center of each. Roll the meat up and tie it closed.

Heat the oil in a medium saucepan and brown the pork rolls over moderate to high heat. Add the onion and continue cooking until it begins to brown. Stir in the celery, tomatoes, basil, and broth or water, cover, and simmer 1 hour.

Grilled Pork Loin Slices

I like this dish served with either boiled potatoes or grilled polenta slices (page 141) and a mixed green salad.

Serves 4.

The marinade:

3 tablespoons light soy sauce
Juice of 1 lime
1 tablespoon chopped fresh or
  dried rosemary
2 cloves garlic, finely chopped

Salt and freshly ground black
  pepper or hot pepper flakes
  to taste (I prefer hot pepper
  flakes here)

1½ pounds pork loin, cut into
  ½-inch slices

For the marinade: Combine all of the marinade ingredients in a shallow baking dish large enough to hold the pork slices in one layer. Thoroughly coat the pork with the marinade and marinate for at least 2 hours.

Meanwhile start a fire (page 243). Grill the meat over hot coals or wood embers for about 3 minutes on each side, basting with the marinade.

VARIATION WITH BROILED PORK LOIN SLICES: Prepare in the same way and cook 3 minutes each side under a hot broiler.

Pesto

A pesto is simply an uncooked or lightly cooked sauce that has been blended to a paste, traditionally made with a mortar and pestle. Nowadays, using a food processor, you can make pestos very easily, and with fresh herbs at hand, you can produce a lovely, intense-tasting sauce in a matter of minutes to dress a pasta or enhance a dish of meat, poultry, or fish.

What has become known in America as the classic pesto is made with basil, pine nuts, garlic, and olive oil. I prefer to use the small-leaved basil if available (page 26), which is sweeter and more tender than the large-leaved variety, and I often substitute walnuts or even pecans for pine nuts, which are expensive and sometimes hard to get. It is essential to use extra virgin olive oil and to be sure that your garlic is fresh (aging garlic gives a bitter, strident accent).

But, as you can see, there are many other kinds of pesto. Here is an assortment, and others are to be found in different chapters; check the index.

Traditional Pesto

Makes about 2 cups.

5 cups tightly packed fresh
  basil leaves, preferably
  small-leaved
2 tablespoons coarsely
  chopped flat-leaved parsley
2 tablespoons chopped garlic

½ cup pine nuts or walnuts
  or pecans
1 teaspoon salt
½ cup freshly grated Pecorino
  or Parmesan
¼ cup extra virgin olive oil

Put all the ingredients in a food processor and blend until just pureed; be careful not to overprocess. Or put the basil, parsley, garlic, nuts, and salt in a mortar and grind to a paste with a pestle. Slowly add the olive oil, stirring with the pestle, until blended. To store, put the pesto in a jar, pour about ½ inch olive oil on top, cover tightly, and refrigerate (it will keep for up to 6 months). Some people like to freeze pesto, but I don't recommend it. If you are using pesto as a sauce for pasta, thin it to the consistency of thin cream with a little of the pasta cooking water.

VARIATION:
Mint Pesto

1 pint.

12 cups fresh basil leaves
3 cups fresh mint, preferably spearmint
⅓ cup pine nuts

6 cloves garlic, chopped
¼ cup extra virgin olive oil
Salt and freshly ground black pepper to taste

Blend all the ingredients as above. This is very good on pasta, vegetables, fish, and lamb.

VARIATION:
Fresh Coriander or Parsley Sauce

Makes enough for 4 servings.

¼ cup chopped fresh coriander or flat-leaved parsley
2 cloves garlic, chopped

Juice of 2 lemons
¼ cup extra virgin olive oil
Salt and freshly ground pepper to taste

Blend all the ingredients in a mini-chopper. Serve on fish.

VARIATION:
Pistachio Pesto

Makes enough for 4 servings.

1 cup plain pistachios, shelled
2 tablespoons chopped fresh
    mint
1 tablespoon extra virgin olive
    oil

3 anchovy fillets, chopped
Juice of 1 lemon
Freshly ground black pepper
    to taste

Blend as above. This is excellent on broiled or boiled fish. This is also good with lamb.

VARIATION:
Pine Nut Sauce

Makes enough for 3 or 4 servings.

2 tablespoons pine nuts
2 tablespoons extra virgin
    olive oil

3 anchovy fillets
Juice of 1 lemon

Put all of the ingredients in a food processor or mini-chopper and blend. Serve on fish.

VARIATION:
Tomato, Tuna, and Nut Sauce

Makes enough for 4 servings.

Half a 7-ounce can tuna,
    packed in olive oil, drained
¼ cup walnuts or pine nuts
1 tablespoon chopped flat-
    leaved parsley
3 tablespoons extra virgin
    olive oil

1½ cups fresh seeded and
    coarsely chopped ripe
    tomatoes
1 tablespoon chopped fresh
    mint

Blend all the ingredients in a food processor. Good with boiled or broiled meats and fish and especially with ricotta-stuffed veal breast (page 238).

VARIATION:

Green Sauce

Makes enough for 10 to 12 servings.

4 cups thinly sliced scallions
1 cup coarsely chopped fresh
  mint
3 cloves garlic, chopped
3 tablespoons extra virgin
  olive oil

¼ cup pine nuts
Salt and freshly ground black
  pepper to taste

Blend all the ingredients in a food processor. Delicious on boiled meats or simple poached fish.

VARIATION:

Summer Sauce

Makes enough for 10 to 12 servings.

2 cups tightly packed chopped
  rucola (arugula)
⅓ cup chopped fresh mint
1 fat clove garlic, coarsely
  chopped
1 cup coarsely chopped
  cucumber

2 tablespoons white wine
  vinegar
1 tablespoon prepared
  mustard
Salt and freshly ground black
  pepper to taste

Blend all the ingredients in a food processor. Serve with broiled fish or meats, particularly lamb.

VARIATION:
Tuna Sauce

Serves 4.

Half a 7-ounce can tuna,
   packed in olive oil, drained
1 teaspoon good mustard
Juice from ½ lemon
Freshly ground black pepper
   to taste

1 tablespoon extra virgin olive
   oil
Approximately ⅓ cup
   chicken or beef broth,
   preferably homemade, at
   room temperature

Put all of the ingredients into a food processor and blend until the sauce is smooth. Add more tuna if the sauce is too thin. Serve on cold meats or fish.

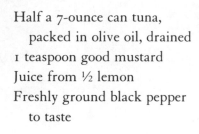

===== VEAL =====

Veal with Peas and Potatoes

Serves 3.

1 pound stewing veal, cut into
   large pieces
2 cloves garlic, coarsely chopped
Juice from ½ lemon
Salt and freshly ground black
   pepper to taste
Flour for dredging
3 tablespoons olive or other
   vegetable oil
1 medium onion, coarsely
   chopped

2 cups sliced mushrooms
½ cup dry white wine
1 teaspoon chopped fresh or
   dried rosemary
1 cup chicken or beef broth,
   preferably homemade (for
   chicken broth, see page 194)
3 medium potatoes, peeled and
   cut into ¼-inch-thick slices
2 cups peas, blanched and
   drained

Rub the veal with the garlic and lemon juice and allow to marinate, refrigerated, for several hours.

Remove the veal from the marinade and reserve the juices. Salt and pepper the veal, dust with flour, and brown it lightly in the oil in a medium skillet. Add the onion and mushrooms and continue cooking the veal over a moderate heat, uncovered, stirring often, until the onion becomes translucent. Add the marinade and cook the veal and sauce for several minutes. Then add the wine and rosemary and simmer, covered, until the wine cooks out. Pour in the broth, cover, and cook over a moderate heat for about 20 minutes more. Add the potato slices and the peas, cover, and simmer for about 30 minutes more, until the potatoes are tender.

VARIATION:
Veal with Artichoke Hearts

Serves 3.

1 pound lean veal, cut into
   1-inch cubes
Salt and freshly ground black
   pepper to taste
Flour for dredging
3 tablespoons olive oil
1 medium onion, finely
   chopped
½ cup chopped prosciutto
2 whole cloves garlic, unpeeled

⅓ cup dry Marsala
1 teaspoon fresh chopped or
   dried rosemary
2 teaspoons chopped fresh
   marjoram, or 1 teaspoon
   dried
2 cups chopped tomatoes
2 cups sliced fresh artichoke
   hearts, or 9 ounces frozen,
   thawed

Season the meat, dust lightly with flour, and brown as above. Lower heat, add the onion, prosciutto, and garlic, and cook, stirring, until the onion begins to brown. Stir in the wine, rosemary, and marjoram, cover, and cook, continuing to stir often, until the wine cooks out, about 6 minutes. Add the tomatoes, cover, and simmer for 1 hour, stirring occasionally. Add the artichoke hearts, cover, and simmer for 15 minutes. The cook may either enjoy the pleasure of eating the garlic squeezed on a bit of bread or squeeze it back into the sauce.

VARIATION:

Veal with Peas and Dried Mushrooms

Serves 3.

1 pound stewing veal, cut into
    1½-inch pieces
Salt and freshly ground black
    pepper to taste
Flour for dredging
3 tablespoons olive oil
1 small onion, finely chopped
3 tablespoons finely chopped
    carrots
⅔ ounce dried Italian mush-
    rooms, soaked in warm water
    for 15 minutes, then drained,
    or 6 to 7 ounces cultivated
    or wild mushrooms, sliced

⅓ cup vermouth
1½ teaspoons chopped fresh
    thyme, or ¾ teaspoon dried
1⅓ cups peeled, seeded, and
    pureed tomatoes
1⅓ cups peas, blanched and
    drained

Season the veal with salt and pepper to taste and lightly dust with flour. Brown quickly in the olive oil, toss in the onion, carrots, and mushrooms and sauté, uncovered, over medium to high heat until the onion becomes translucent. Add vermouth and thyme, cover, lower the heat, and simmer for 5 minutes. Stir in the tomatoes and cook, covered, for 5 minutes more. Then add the peas, cover, and continue cooking until the peas are tender, about 10 minutes more.

VARIATION:

Veal with Roasted Red Peppers

Serves 3.

1 pound lean veal, cut into
    1½-inch pieces
Salt and freshly ground black
    pepper to taste
Flour for dredging
3 tablespoons olive oil
1 medium onion, finely chopped

2 cloves garlic, finely chopped
½ cup dry white wine
1 heaping tablespoon chopped
    fresh sage, or 1 heaping
    teaspoon dried
1 cup chopped tomatoes

2 red bell peppers, roasted,
  peeled, cored, and cut into
  ½-inch strips (page 48)

Garnish: Chopped flat-leaved
  parsley

Season the meat, dust lightly with flour, and brown as above. Lower heat to medium, add the onion, and cook uncovered until the onion begins to brown. Add the garlic, cook 1 minute, then add the wine and sage, cover, and simmer over low heat until the wine is almost cooked out. Mix in the tomatoes and cook, covered, for about 1 hour and 20 minutes, stirring often. Add the red pepper strips and serve garnished with parsley on each portion.

Veal with Coarse Fresh Tomato Sauce

Serves 2.

The sauce:

3 tablespoons olive oil
2 cloves garlic, finely chopped
2 cups peeled, seeded, and chopped
  fully ripened tomatoes

2 tablespoons chopped fresh
  basil

2 tablespoons olive oil
1 pound veal from the shoulder
  or leg, cut into 1½-inch chunks
2 cloves garlic, flattened but
  left intact

Salt and freshly ground black
  pepper to taste
½ cup dry white wine
1 tablespoon chopped fresh
  oregano, or 1 teaspoon dried

Make the sauce: In a medium skillet heat 3 tablespoons olive oil until hot, then sauté the garlic until it just begins to color. Add the tomatoes and basil, cover, and simmer for 5 minutes. Remove from the heat and set aside.

In another skillet heat 2 tablespoons olive oil until hot, add the veal and sauté over high heat, uncovered, turning it often, until it begins to color. Add the garlic and salt and pepper to taste. As the veal begins to brown, add the wine and oregano and continue to cook until the wine has cooked off. Pour in the fresh tomato sauce, cover and cook over moderate heat for about 5 minutes. Remove the cover and cook the sauce down to the desired consistency.

Braised Veal Shanks

I like to serve risotto (page 134) with this particular veal dish. When you are shopping for the veal, be certain you buy good cuts of shank. Supermarkets are notorious for concealing large bones and undesirable cuts when they package veal shanks.

Serves 4.

4 center-cut veal shanks, about 1½ inches in diameter

Salt and freshly ground black pepper to taste

Flour for dredging

3 tablespoons olive or other vegetable oil

1 medium onion, finely chopped

2 cups sliced mushrooms (I use wild mushrooms, but cultivated mushrooms will do)

1 carrot, finely chopped

1 cup dry white wine mixed with 1 tablespoon high-quality tomato paste, preferably homemade (page 31)

2 teaspoons fresh marjoram, or 1 teaspoon dried

1 cup peas, blanched and drained

Chicken or beef broth if needed

Garnish: Gremolada (recipe follows) or finely chopped flat-leaved parsley

Season the veal shanks with salt and pepper and then dust them lightly with flour. Heat the oil in a heavy saucepan large enough to accommodate the veal. When the oil is hot, brown the veal on both sides, then add the onion and continue to cook, uncovered, until the onion becomes translucent. Add the mushrooms and carrot and continue cooking until the onion begins to brown. Add the wine and tomato paste mixture along with the marjoram. Cover, lower the heat, and simmer until most of the wine has cooked out, about 15 minutes. Add the peas, cover, and cook for an additional hour. Add a little chicken or beef broth to the sauce if it becomes too dry.

Garnish each portion with Gremolada or flat-leaved parsley.

  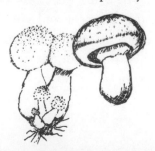

Gremolada

Makes about ¾ cup.

½ cup finely chopped lemon
  zest
2 teaspoons finely chopped
  garlic
3 tablespoons finely chopped
  flat-leaved parsley

2 tablespoons olive oil
Salt and freshly ground black
  pepper to taste

Mix all of the ingredients and add to sauces or stews during the last 5 to 10 minutes of their cooking time.

Veal Breast with Potatoes and Cabbage

Serves 4.

1 veal breast (4 to 4½ pounds)
Salt and freshly ground black
  pepper to taste
1 tablespoon chopped fresh or
  dried rosemary
1 medium onion, coarsely
  chopped
2 cloves garlic, finely chopped

½ cup dry white wine
4 cups seeded and chopped
  tomatoes
4 medium potatoes, peeled and
  cut in half crosswise
½ medium cabbage, preferably
  savoy, cut into 4 sections,
  blanched and drained

Preheat oven to 450°.

Sprinkle the veal breast with salt and pepper on both sides, then rub both sides with rosemary. Place veal in a roasting pan and bake uncovered for 45 minutes, turning occasionally until meat begins to brown. Skim off all fat. Add the onion, and when it begins to brown, add the garlic and wine. Cover and bake until the wine cooks out. Add the tomatoes, lower heat to 350°, cover, and bake for a half hour. Add the potatoes along with the cabbage, and continue to bake, covered, for 45 minutes more, basting the meat and vegetables occasionally with the sauce. Allow to rest at least 15 minutes before serving. Serve hot or at room temperature with crusty Italian or French bread.

VARIATION WITH RED WINE AND RAISINS: Prepare a veal breast with salt, pepper, and rosemary as above, place in a roasting pan along with **1 cup dry red wine,** and bake, uncovered, in a 450° oven for about a half hour, basting occasionally, until meat is browned. Remove fat, then add **2 cups chopped tomatoes** along with **2 cups chicken or beef broth,** preferably homemade, **2 tablespoons fresh basil, or 1 tablespoon dried,** and **3 whole cloves garlic, unpeeled.** Lower the heat to 350°, cover, and continue to bake about a half hour longer. Add **2 tablespoons golden raisins** and **4 medium potatoes, peeled and cut in half,** then bake another 45 minutes. (Eat the garlic on a slice of bread or squeeze it into the sauce.)

Ricotta-Stuffed Veal Breast with Red Tomato and Nut Sauce

This veal breast is boned so that it can be rolled up (be sure to have at hand a piece of cheesecloth about 18 inches long). I invariably prepare the roll a day in advance for serving; it needs that resting period. For a variation, try it with Tomato, Tuna, and Nut Sauce (page 230). I serve it at room temperature, usually in the summer.

Serves 6.

1 veal breast (about 6 pounds), boned and trimmed of all outside fat (rib bones saved for soup or stock)

Salt and freshly ground black pepper to taste
6 thin slices boiled ham

The stuffing:

2 cups whole-milk ricotta
¼ cup freshly grated Parmesan
1 tablespoon finely chopped flat-leaved parsley
1 large egg, lightly beaten

½ teaspoon freshly grated nutmeg
Salt and freshly ground black pepper to taste

Olive oil

Fresh rosemary to taste

1 cup dry white wine

¾ cup imported Marsala

Red Tomato and Nut Sauce
(page 30) as an
accompaniment

Preheat the oven to 400°.

Spread the veal breast, boned side up, out on the counter and salt and pepper it. Lay the ham slices over the surface.

Make the stuffing: In a bowl combine all of the stuffing ingredients with salt and pepper to taste.

Spread the stuffing evenly over the ham, leaving a 1-inch border, then carefully start rolling up the veal breast jelly-roll style, starting with a short end. Rub with olive oil and sprinkle with the rosemary and additional salt and pepper to taste.

Place the rolled breast in the middle of the cheesecloth, wrap securely, twist the ends, and tie them securely. Cut off any excess cheesecloth and tie with kitchen string in several places along the roll as you would a roast.

Put the veal breast in a roasting pan. Pour the white wine into the pan and roast, uncovered, basting often, for about 1 hour. (Add extra wine if the meat begins to stick.) When the meat is brown, add the Marsala and cook 20 to 30 minutes longer. Transfer the meat to a board and let it stand at least 3 hours and preferably 24 hours before serving. Serve at room temperature. Refrigerate if not served after 3 hours.

To serve, remove the cheesecloth and cut the roll into slices about ¼ inch thick. Serve with the Red Tomato and Nut Sauce.

Veal Breast with Spinach Stuffing

Look for a piece of veal breast close to the shoulder, because that's the meatier part. This is an often-neglected, inexpensive cut that is sweet and succulent when cooked until the meat falls off the bone. You can cook any number of vegetables with it the last hour or so of cooking to make a nice one-pot dish.

Serves 4.

    1 piece veal breast (4 pounds)

The stuffing:

¼ pound spinach	¾ pound lean ground veal
1 medium onion, finely chopped	1 tablespoon finely chopped flat-leaved parsley
2 cloves garlic, finely chopped	Salt and freshly ground black pepper to taste
2 egg whites, lightly beaten	
Pinch of freshly grated nutmeg	

½ cup chicken broth or water	2 cups chopped tomatoes
½ cup dry white wine	1 cup water
1 teaspoon chopped fresh or dried rosemary	2 teaspoons chopped fresh basil, or 1 teaspoon dried
Salt and freshly ground black pepper to taste	1 cup peas, blanched and drained
2 large carrots, cut in half lengthwise	2 large potatoes, peeled and cut in half crosswise

Preheat the oven to 400°.

Make a pocket in the veal breast by carefully cutting underneath the meat, close to the bone, within one inch of the sides.

Make the stuffing: Bring 3 cups of water to a boil in a 4- or 5-quart pot, drop the spinach in, stir well, and blanch for 1 minute. Drain, cool, squeeze out all excess moisture, and chop. Place the spinach in a mixing bowl along with the other stuffing ingredients and mix well.

Spoon the stuffing into the veal breast pocket and place the veal in a roasting pan, pour in the chicken broth or water and wine, along with the rosemary and salt and pepper, and bake until the surface of the veal breast browns and all of the moisture has evaporated (about 35 to 40 minutes). Add the carrots, tomatoes, water and basil, cover, lower the heat to 350° and cook for 1¼ hours. Add the peas and potatoes, adjust salt, and add more water, if needed. Cover and cook for an additional half hour, until the potatoes are cooked. Skim off all fat before serving.

VARIATION WITH MUSHROOM STUFFING: To make the stuffing, heat **1 tablespoon olive oil** and sauté **1½ cups coarsely chopped mushrooms** until they begin to brown. Add **1 tablespoon finely chopped shallots** and **3 tablespoons finely chopped onion** and cook until the onion becomes translucent. Transfer to a bowl and add ¾ **pound lean ground veal, 2 egg whites lightly beaten, 3 tablespoons bread crumbs, 1 tablespoon finely chopped flat-leaved parsley, 2 teaspoons chopped fresh sage, or 1 teaspoon dried,** and **salt and freshly ground black pepper** to taste. Mix well. Stuff and bake the veal breast as described above, adding **2 cups celery cut into 1-inch pieces** at the same time as the broth or water. Omit the peas if you wish.

Veal Heart Stew

Serve this good winter dish with plain rice or boiled potatoes.

Serves 4.

2 tablespoons olive oil	1 teaspoon dried rosemary
1 tablespoon safflower oil, or	1 teaspoon dried thyme
3 tablespoons peanut oil	2 cups thinly sliced onions
1 veal heart (about	2 cups thickly sliced
1½ pounds), with all fat	mushrooms
removed, cut in half, then in	1 cup dry white wine
pieces ½ inch thick	1 cup chopped tomatoes
Salt and freshly ground black	*Garnish:* 3 tablespoons finely
pepper to taste	chopped flat-leaved parsley

Heat the oils in a medium skillet. Add the veal and salt and pepper and cook over a high heat, stirring constantly until the meat begins to brown. Add the rosemary, thyme, onions, and mushrooms and cook until the liquid cooks out and the onions begin to brown. Add the wine, cover, and lower the heat. Simmer until the wine cooks out. Add the tomatoes, cover, and simmer over low to medium heat for approximately 30 minutes.

Garnish the stew with parsley.

Veal Kidney with Wine

Serves 2.

1 veal kidney
1 tablespoon salt
2 tablespoons olive oil
1 medium onion, finely
  chopped
1 fat clove garlic, finely
  chopped
1 tablespoon finely chopped
  flat-leaved parsley

Salt and freshly ground black
  pepper to taste
1 teaspoon crushed dried
  rosemary
2 cups sliced mushrooms, about
  ⅛ inch thick
½ cup dry white wine

Remove the fat from the veal kidney with a sharp pointed knife. (The glands in the fat produce the odor that is associated with kidneys.) Place the kidney in a bowl with the inside of the kidney facing up and pour 1 tablespoon salt over it, cover with cold water, and let rest for at least 2 hours. Wash and drain the kidney.

Heat the oil in a medium skillet. When the oil is hot, add the onions and cook for several minutes. Add the kidney and cook, uncovered, over a medium heat until it is lightly browned on both sides. Add the garlic, parsley, and salt and pepper, but be careful not to oversalt the kidney. Add the rosemary, mushrooms, and wine; cover and simmer over low to moderate heat for 20 minutes, turning the kidney over occasionally.

Remove the kidney from the skillet and with a sharp knife slice it on the bias.

Garnish the kidney slices with the sauce and serve hot.

═══════ LAMB ═══════

Grilled Butterflied Leg of Lamb

I have changed my mother's simple Easter roast leg of baby lamb to a butterflied leg that I grill. I prefer grilled lamb to roasted. It's tastier and there seems to be less fat.

Unless you are experienced with a knife, I would suggest having the butcher butterfly the leg for you.

Serves 10 to 12.

1 leg of spring lamb (about 8 pounds), boned and butterflied	4 fat cloves garlic, sliced
	2 tablespoons chopped fresh or dried rosemary
1½ cups wine vinegar, preferably aged or homemade (page 314)	Freshly ground black pepper to taste

Place the leg of lamb in a shallow, noncorrodible (such as stainless steel or glass) roasting pan. Pour the vinegar over it, then scatter the garlic and rosemary on top. Grind a generous amount of pepper over, cover with wax paper, and refrigerate overnight, basting the lamb occasionally with the marinade.

Start your fire well in advance and have about 50 to 55 hot coals—really gray ones—ready before you start grilling. Grill the lamb about 5 inches away from the heat for 10 minutes on each side for medium-rare meat (140° internal temperature), or longer, depending upon your taste. Let the lamb stand on a cutting board for 10 minutes, then slice thinly on the diagonal and serve with the Fresh Mint Sauce that follows or with one of the pestos on page 228.

Fresh Mint Sauce

Fresh mint is popular in Italian cooking and is used with fish, meats, and vegetables, and is especially good with lamb and grilled fish. I use it often because it is perhaps one of the hardiest of herbs. Mint can tolerate a hard frost and is available from early spring on. In the fall we dry it for tea and winter foods. I am especially partial to wild spearmint.

Makes ¾ cup.

2 cups fresh mint, stems
   removed
2 teaspoons finely chopped
   flat-leaved parsley
¼ cup pine nuts
4 cloves garlic, finely chopped

¼ cup extra virgin olive oil
¼ cup chicken broth, or more
   as needed, preferably
   homemade (page 194)
Salt and freshly ground black
   pepper to taste

Combine all the ingredients in a food processor and blend until the sauce achieves the consistency of heavy cream, adding more broth as needed.

Burnt Fingers

This Roman specialty is prepared only in the spring. The secret to its success is to serve the lamb as soon as it is cooked. You must eat the pieces with your fingers, and they must be so hot that your fingers burn while holding them.

Serves 2.

1 pound lamb, from the breast
   or shoulder, cut into 3- by
   1-inch pieces

Salt and freshly ground black
   pepper to taste
Garnish: Lemon wedges

Broil the lamb pieces over hot coals on a grill for about 2 minutes on each side. Sprinkle with salt and pepper and serve on heated plates with the lemon wedges. Eat at once, with your fingers.

Lamb Shanks with Turnips

I make this dish in the spring with turnips I have put in the previous fall specifically for a spring harvest. They are another example of what we call "found" vegetables (page 8). If you have never bought lamb shanks—veal shanks being more usual—you will find that they are smaller than veal. I like to serve this dish with crusty French or Italian bread and boiled potatoes or rice.

Serves 2.

2 lamb shanks
Salt and freshly ground black
    pepper to taste
2 tablespoons vegetable oil
2 tablespoons olive oil
1 medium onion, finely
    chopped
⅓ cup finely chopped carrots
1 tablespoon crushed dried
    rosemary
Hot pepper flakes to taste
    (optional)

3 cups peeled, seeded, and
    chopped tomatoes
1½ cups chicken or beef broth,
    preferably homemade (for
    chicken broth, see page 194)
2 medium carrots, cut into
    2-inch pieces
4 medium-to-small white
    turnips (about ¾ pound), cut
    in half crosswise

Preheat the oven to 400°.

Season the lamb shanks with salt and pepper. In a medium skillet heat the vegetable oil until hot, add the lamb shanks, and sauté them until light brown. Discard the oil and fat in the skillet, then add the olive oil to the skillet along with the onion, chopped carrots, rosemary, and hot pepper flakes, if using. Cook, uncovered, over moderate heat until the onion begins to brown. Add the tomatoes and broth and bring to a boil.

Transfer the mixture to a baking dish, cover, and bake, stirring occasionally, for 30 minutes. Add the carrot pieces and the turnips and bake 35 to 40 minutes, or until the vegetables are cooked.

Lamb with Peas and Potatoes

Serves 4.

2 tablespoons olive oil
2 pounds lamb, from shoulder
    or leg, cut for stewing
4 tablespoons dried rosemary
Salt and freshly ground black
    pepper to taste
2 whole cloves garlic, unpeeled
1 pound small white onions,
    peeled (page 59)
¼ cup wine vinegar

3 tablespoons coarsely chopped
    fresh mint
2 cups chopped tomatoes
3 medium carrots, cut into
    1-inch pieces
¼ cup hot water
2 potatoes, peeled and cut into
    large pieces
1 cup peas, blanched for
    2 minutes and drained

In a medium shallow saucepan heat the oil until hot. Season the lamb with rosemary and salt and pepper to taste and sauté, uncovered, over moderate heat until the meat is brown on both sides. Add the garlic, onions, and vinegar and cook, turning the lamb occasionally, until the vinegar cooks out. Add the mint, tomatoes, carrots, and water. Cover and simmer over low to moderate heat, stirring occasionally, for about 45 minutes. Add the potatoes and peas and cook until the potatoes are tender, about 10 to 15 minutes.

========== GOAT ==

Baby Goat (Kid)

When I was a boy, my father would go out to a farm in Connecticut a week or two before Easter and buy a live baby goat or lamb. We would bring it home and I would feed and play with it, but I was made to understand that this was an animal we were going to eat. I personally like kid better than lamb and purchase it whenever I can. Spring lamb can be used in place of goat in the following recipes.

Baked Baby Goat with Potatoes and Olives

Serves 12 to 15.

1 baby goat (12 to 15 pounds), dressed and cut into serving pieces, with liver, heart, sweetbreads, and kidneys reserved for Sufritto (recipe follows)

Salt and freshly ground black pepper to taste

6 potatoes, peeled and quartered lengthwise

½ cup fresh lemon juice

½ cup olive oil

2 tablespoons chopped fresh or dried rosemary

36 large cured green olives, pitted and sliced*

1 cup dry white wine

⅓ cup coarsely chopped garlic

Preheat the oven to 500°.

Sprinkle the meat with salt and pepper and put into a large shallow baking pan in one layer. Arrange the potato pieces around the meat, add the lemon juice, oil, and rosemary, and scatter the olives over the mixture. Bake, uncovered, for about 10 minutes. When the meat begins to brown, add the wine and garlic. Continue baking, turning the meat occasionally, for about 25 minutes. Let rest for 10 minutes and serve on warm plates.

VARIATION WITH GRILLED BABY GOAT: Instead of roasting, grill the goat over hot coals (page 243), basting with the **lemon juice, oil,** and **rosemary,** turning from time to time. It will take about 45 minutes.

* I use my own cured olives (page 316) for this recipe. If you use olives packed in brine, soak the slices in cold water for 15 minutes before using.

Baby Goat Stew

Serves 2 or 3.

1½ pounds baby goat shoulder or leg, cut into serving pieces

Salt and freshly ground black pepper to taste

2 tablespoons olive oil

1 medium onion, coarsely chopped

2 whole cloves garlic, unpeeled

½ cup dry white wine

1 teaspoon chopped fresh or dried rosemary

2 cups peeled, seeded, and chopped tomatoes

1 ounce dried Italian mushrooms, soaked in warm water for 20 minutes, drained, with soaking liquid strained and reserved

Sprinkle the meat with salt and pepper. In a medium skillet heat the oil until hot, then add the onion, garlic, and goat meat and sauté, uncovered, over moderate heat until the onion begins to brown. Add the wine and rosemary, cover, and simmer, stirring occasionally, until the wine cooks out. Add the tomatoes and the mushrooms and their strained liquid, cover, and simmer over low to moderate heat for 1¾ to 2 hours. Remove the garlic clove and eat it yourself on a little bread, or squeeze it back into the sauce. Serve the stew on heated plates with rice or steamed potatoes.

Sufritto

The innards of a milk-fed baby goat or lamb are regarded by many, including myself, with such esteem that it is almost worth buying the kid or lamb just for its innards!

This recipe is very good served over polenta (page 141).

Serves 4 to 6.

2 tablespoons olive oil
1 tablespoon safflower oil
1 medium onion, coarsely
   chopped
2 cups sliced fresh mushrooms,
   or 1 ounce dried Italian
   mushrooms, soaking liquid
   reserved (page 86)
2 cloves garlic, finely chopped
Salt and hot pepper flakes to
   taste
Heart, liver, sweetbreads, and
   kidneys of a baby goat or
   lamb, rinsed, dried, and cut
   into bite-sized pieces

½ cup dry white wine
1 teaspoon crushed dried
   rosemary
1 tablespoon finely chopped
   flat-leaved parsley
1 cup peeled, seeded, and
   chopped tomatoes
1½ cups peas, blanched and
   drained

In a medium skillet heat the oils until hot, then add the onion and mushrooms and cook, uncovered, until the onion becomes translucent. Add the garlic, salt and hot pepper flakes, heart, liver, sweetbreads, and kidneys and cook over moderate heat, stirring often, until the onion begins to brown and the innards begin to color. Add the wine, rosemary, and parsley. Cover and simmer over low to moderate heat until the wine is almost cooked out. Add the reserved soaking liquid (if using dried mushrooms), the tomatoes, peas, and more salt, cover, and simmer for about 45 minutes.

Rabbits

There is a natural rhythm to gardening and
raising animals. Fresh manure—full of nitrogen—
is wonderful for the garden, and the weeds you pull can be fed
to the animals. It is a full cycle that keeps everything going.

Of course, it is no fun killing domestic animals, but if you are
not a vegetarian, someone has to kill and dress the meat you eat.
We do not eat meat often, and I prefer to eat rabbits and
chickens that we raise rather than those sold in the markets.
Our animals are better cared for, and better tasting, and,
of course, the flesh is free of chemicals.

So if you raise domestic animals for food,
then you have to know how to kill and dress them.

To kill a rabbit: Rabbits are easy to kill painlessly and quickly.
Hold the rabbit by its hind legs so that the rest of the body is
hanging down. When the rabbit calms down, strike it with one
strong stroke behind the ears with a sturdy stick. A 2-foot section of
broom handle will work well.

To skin and clean a rabbit: With a sharp knife, cut a 1-inch slit
behind its back foot between the hamstring and the bone. Repeat the
process on the other back foot. Drive two large nails about 6 inches
apart into a timber at about your height. Hang the rabbit by forcing
the nail heads through the slits in the back legs. The rabbit is now
hanging head down. (If you wish you can lash the legs with heavy cord
instead.) With a small sharp knife, carefully cut the fur and outer skin
through to the meat around each leg close to the foot, then cut through
the fur and skin between the back legs. Cut off the tailbone and pull
the skin down through the forelegs, then cut off the front paws. At this
point, you can either cut off the head, or skin it close to the bone as you
work down.

Carefully slit the thin skin covering the stomach all the way to the
rib cage. Remove the insides and discard everything except the liver,
kidneys, and lungs. Carefully remove and discard the small green sac
attached to the liver—this is the gallbladder. Be careful not to break it.

If it is a cold day, let the rabbit hang for several hours. If it is warm,
put the dressed rabbit in a pot and cover with cold water. Let it rest for
several hours.

Never refrigerate freshly killed meat while it is still warm.

Once you get the knack of skinning a rabbit, you can do it in a few minutes. The ideal age for a tender rabbit is 12 weeks; the older the rabbit, the more difficult to skin.

No, it isn't fun to kill and dress a rabbit or chicken, but someone has to do it. I have always felt it was my obligation to present my family with the healthiest and tastiest food possible by gardening, making wine, canning, and making prosciutto and sausages, so I prefer to do my own dirty work instead of delegating it to someone else. This information is for those who feel the same.

To cut up a rabbit: Cut up a rabbit the same way you would a chicken except the back pieces should be cut into 3 or 4 sections across. Don't cut through the kidneys; leave them intact and cook them with the meat.

Rabbit Soup

If you like a clear, delicate soup, you will find this recipe unique. The tougher, older rabbits make the best soup, although a young 3-pound rabbit will do nicely, too.

Serves 6.

1 rabbit (3½ to 4 pounds)	1 large leek, cut into large
4 quarts water	pieces (page 59)
2 large carrots	Salt and freshly ground black
2 ribs celery	pepper to taste
2 bay leaves	

Put all the ingredients in a large soup pot and boil gently for about 2½ to 3 hours. Strain broth, discard vegetables, but reserve rabbit. Serve as boiled meat or grind and make croquettes (see patties, page 203).

Since there is no fat on rabbit there is no need to defat the broth.

Serve the broth with rice, capellini, or nests (nidi) pasta cooked in it or, if you prefer, have it plain.

Domestic Animals

Most farm children know right from the start that the animals that are raised for food are going to be slaughtered, and they accept that fact.

We have always raised domestic animals for food, and I think we did a pretty good job of helping our children understand that although the animals were to be killed, they were to be taken care of, fed properly, and treated with kindness. It is not a good idea to give them names if they are going to be eaten, although some children will do it regardless. It helps if they know that all meat, fowl, and fish they eat were once living creatures.

Incidentally, I think it is a dreadful practice to give young children small animals such as rabbits, chickens, and ducklings—sometimes dyed pastel colors—and allow the children to maul them. I do not believe living creatures are toys, and they should not be used as such.

Fried Rabbit

I like this recipe with an interesting salad like Fennel with Rucola (page 77).

Serves 3 or 4, depending on size of rabbit.

1 young, freshly killed rabbit (not more than 3 months old), dressed and cut into serving sections (page 250)
1 cup milk
Vegetable oil

Salt and freshly ground black pepper to taste
Flour for dredging
Garnish: Lemon wedges or Tomato Horseradish Sauce (page 53)

Soak the rabbit in cold water for several hours and then rinse it. Place the rabbit sections in a small bowl with the milk. Heat approximately ½ inch of oil in a medium skillet. While the oil is heating, remove the rabbit from the milk, salt and pepper it, and then dust it lightly with the flour.

When the oil is hot, but not smoking, gently place some of the rabbit sections (uncrowded) into the oil with tongs and fry over a moderate heat, turning the sections often until they are golden brown, about 8 minutes. Blot with a paper towel and keep warm; repeat this process until all of the pieces are cooked. Serve with lemon wedges or Tomato Horseradish Sauce.

Braised Rabbit with Tomatoes and Mushrooms

This is a recipe my father often made, and no one did a better job at it. It can be made with wild or domestic rabbit. I like to serve this recipe with risotto (page 134) or polenta (page 141).

Serves 4.

1 rabbit (about 3 to 3½ pounds), dressed and cut into serving pieces (page 250), with liver set aside
Salt and freshly ground black pepper to taste
1 tablespoon chopped fresh or dried rosemary
3 tablespoons olive oil
3 whole cloves garlic, unpeeled
3 cups sliced mushrooms (I prefer wild)
1 cup dry white wine
2 cups peeled, seeded, and chopped tomatoes

Season all the rabbit pieces and liver with salt and pepper and set liver aside. Put rabbit pieces in a large heavy skillet. Sprinkle with rosemary and cook, uncovered, over medium heat, turning the pieces often, until they begin to brown. The purpose is to sear the rabbit immediately and keep the moisture in; the pieces won't stick. Now add the olive oil and garlic and continue cooking, uncovered, until the rabbit is golden brown. Add the liver and cook it for several minutes. Remove the liver and reserve. Add the mushrooms and wine, cover, and lower the heat. Simmer gently until the wine cooks out. Add the tomatoes, cover, and simmer for about 45 minutes. The cook may eat the garlic spread on a piece of bread or squeeze it back into the sauce. Let the rabbit stand for 15 minutes before serving.

Rabbit with Polenta

Serves 6.

2 tablespoons vegetable oil
1 pound pork neck bones (ribs
    or a split pig's foot will do)
1 rabbit (about 3½ to 4
    pounds), dressed and cut
    into serving pieces (page 250)*
3 whole cloves garlic, unpeeled
1 large onion stuck with
    4 cloves
1 cup dry white wine
1 teaspoon chopped fresh or
    dried rosemary
Salt and freshly ground black
    pepper to taste
2 tablespoons chopped fresh
    basil, or 1 tablespoon dried

2 quarts seeded and chopped
    tomatoes
2 carrots, cut into 1½-inch
    pieces
1 thick rib celery, cut into
    1-inch pieces
4 cups sliced wild mushrooms,
    or 4 cups cultivated
    mushrooms plus 1 ounce
    dried Italian mushrooms,
    soaked in warm water for
    15 minutes, drained
Polenta made with 2 cups
    cornmeal (page 141)
Garnish: Freshly grated
    Parmesan

Heat the oil in a shallow pot that is large enough to hold the bones and rabbit sections without overlapping, then add the bones and sauté, uncovered, over a moderate heat until they begin to brown. Add the rabbit (including the liver) and brown on all sides over high heat. Lower the heat, push the rabbit to one side and add the garlic and onion and brown lightly. Remove the liver and set it aside. Add the wine, rosemary, salt, pepper, and basil, cover, lower the heat, and simmer until the wine cooks out. Add the tomatoes, carrots, and celery and boil gently, covered, for 1½ hours, stirring occasionally. Toss in the mushrooms, taste for salt, and simmer the rabbit and sauce for an additional hour, adding the liver the last 15 minutes. Remove the garlic and eat it yourself on a little bread, or squeeze it back into the sauce. Remove the bones from the sauce, cool, remove the meat, discard the fat and bones, and return the meat to the sauce. Slice the liver and add to the dish.

Ladle the polenta onto hot plates and add a serving of sauce and a piece of rabbit on top of each. Serve immediately, garnished with grated Parmesan.

* An older rabbit can be used in this recipe.

Game

About Game

My father loved game and only he cooked the game in our kitchen. He did not hunt but hunters from all over town would bring game to our house.

As a cook my father had an uncanny sensitivity about game. He would look at game he had never eaten and he would know how to cook it. Simply by studying the flesh, he knew if it should be marinated first, stewed or broiled, or cooked in a tight sauce or a loose sauce, and he was rarely wrong.

One day while he was visiting us in Katonah, I killed a large snapping turtle, which weighed about 35 pounds, near our house. I'd been concerned about the snapping turtle because we had three small children running around, and a big turtle can snap the hand or foot off a child. When my father saw the turtle, he said, "You know, I heard they are good to eat." I was enthusiastic so we cut out the legs, and after my father investigated the meat, he decided how he would cook it. He stewed it in a very light tomato sauce with onions, garlic, flat-leaved parsley, white wine, and a touch of hot peppers, and it was delightful.

In retrospect I think that my father was so fond of game because he liked the idea of eating a creature (or plant) that lived in its natural environment, and he understood the logic of eating off the land. It was a form of self-proclaimed independence; he was turning his back on the system and proclaiming his independence by saying, "I can survive with more dignity without you or perhaps in spite of you."

Grilled Venison

There's a lot of venison now because there are too many deer and the population needs thinning. It is a naturally healthful meat. (See also Venison Sausage, page 271.) I like to serve this recipe with grilled polenta (page 141).

Serves 4.

  1 pound venison (I use the
      rump), sliced ¼-inch thick

The marinade:

  ½ cup dry white wine   2 tablespoons olive oil
  2 cloves garlic, finely chopped   Freshly ground black pepper to
  1 teaspoon chopped fresh or   taste
      dried rosemary

  Salt to taste   *Garnish:* Lemon wedges

Place the venison slices in a shallow noncorrodible baking pan (such as stainless steel or glass).

For the marinade: Mix the marinade ingredients and pour over the meat. Marinate in the refrigerator overnight.

Remove the venison from the marinade and sprinkle it to taste with salt. Grill close to hot coals for about 1 minute, turning constantly. Cook for 1 minute longer if you prefer it well-done. Serve immediately, garnished with the lemon wedges.

Smoked Venison

Smoking venison is one way of preserving it. It also tastes delicious. Serve at room temperature with a sauce, if you wish, such as Horseradish Tomato Sauce, page 53.

Serves 6.

The brine:

Salt
About 8 quarts water
6 bay leaves
¼ cup whole peppercorns
½ cup sugar

¼ cup fresh or dried rosemary
1 tablespoon whole cloves
1 teaspoon saltpeter
¼ cup crushed garlic
¼ cup allspice

2 venison shoulders (about 3
    pounds each)—I use meat
    from a young doe

Make the brine: Gradually add salt to the water until a fresh egg will float in it, then add the rest of the brine ingredients. Pour over the venison and marinate for 10 days in a cool place (under 45°) or in the refrigerator.

Now the venison is ready for smoking. Smoke in a smoker in medium heat (about 300 to 350° inside the smoker) until the center of the meat reaches about 150°, approximately 2 to 2½ hours. Since all smokers are different, the best way to know when the meat is ready is to use an instant meat thermometer to check internal temperature.

The Ultimate Revenge

Many people think that raccoons make fine pets, but anyone who owns birds and rabbits knows the other side of the raccoon. They are vicious killers and can easily kill even a dog. I used to believe that raccoons only killed when they were hungry, but that is not true. One evening I lost about 30 rabbits—they were torn apart and most of the meat not eaten. The rabbits were destroyed by a family of raccoons that lived in the attic of the pen. I have lost many chickens and rabbits to coons, and the following story is another episode.

In the late sixties, we bought a beautiful bantam rooster and hen for our daughter Gena. She named them Sampson and Delilah and she adored them. Every morning before going to school, Gena fed those chickens and brought one small egg that Delilah had laid back to the house and had it for breakfast.

One morning Gena came back from the pen in tears. She said a racoon had killed Sampson and Delilah. I went to the chicken coop and saw the hole in the wire that the coon had made to get into the coop. Delilah was gone and only half of Sampson remained. I was furious and frustrated.

Raccoons are very intelligent and difficult to trap, but I baited a large Have-A-Heart trap with Sampson's remains. I never expected to trap the coon, but I had to do something to ease my frustration. The next morning, to my surprise, I found a coon—so large that he seemed stuffed into the trap. He looked at me with intelligent eyes that seemed to say, "I goofed." I looked him straight in the eye and said, "That's right, you goofed and I am going to eat you."

I killed and skinned him and made the best coon alla cacciatora (that is, hunter's style) you ever tasted.

Coon alla Cacciatora

A good-sized coon serves 6.

  1 freshly killed adult raccoon
  1 cup kosher salt or ½ cup
    table salt

The marinade:

1 cup wine vinegar

2 bay leaves

4 cloves garlic, crushed

6 tablespoons vegetable oil

Salt and freshly ground black
  pepper to taste

1 large onion, finely chopped

3 cloves garlic, finely chopped

1 tablespoon chopped fresh or
  dried rosemary

1 cup dry white wine

2 tablespoons chopped fresh
  basil, or 1 tablespoon dried

4 cups chopped tomatoes

4 cups sliced wild mushrooms
  (honey mushrooms would
  do fine) or cultivated
  mushrooms

Chicken or beef broth if
  needed for thinning

To prepare the coon for cooking, skin and dress it the same way you would a rabbit (page 250). Remove and discard all of the fat from the inside and outside of the raccoon. Remove and discard the single gland under each foreleg and on each side of the spine in the small of the back. Cover the coon with cold water and the salt. Soak for 12 hours. Remove the coon from the salt water, wash with cold water, and put into a pot.

For the marinade: Cover the coon with fresh cold water, vinegar, bay leaves, and garlic and marinate overnight. When you are ready to cook the coon, remove it from the marinade, pat it dry, and cut it into serving pieces.

To cook, heat 4 tablespoons of the oil in a large skillet. Sprinkle the coon sections with salt and pepper and add them to the hot oil. Brown the meat over a medium heat, turning the pieces often. When the meat is brown, remove it, discard the oil, and wash the skillet.

Heat the remaining 2 tablespoons of oil in the clean skillet, add the coon sections along with the onion, and cook over moderate heat, uncovered, until the onion browns, then add the garlic and cook for a minute more. Add the rosemary along with the wine and basil; cover and cook over a low heat until the wine cooks out. Toss in the tomatoes and mushrooms and gently simmer, covered, over moderate to low heat for 2 to 2½ hours. Add some broth if the sauce becomes too thick.

Squirrel with Mushrooms

I ate squirrel when I was a child because my father used to cook it.

Serves 2.

2 young squirrels,* skinned
and cleaned (see instructions
for rabbit, page 250)
Salt and freshly ground black
pepper to taste
4 tablespoons olive oil
1 teaspoon chopped fresh or
dried rosemary
2 whole cloves garlic, unpeeled
½ cup dry white wine

1 medium onion, finely
chopped
1½ cups coarsely chopped
tomatoes
2 tablespoons chopped fresh
basil, or 1 tablespoon dried
4 cups chopped wild
mushrooms, cut into large
pieces †

After the squirrels are skinned and washed, let them soak in cold water to cover for several hours. Rinse and pat dry, then cut each squirrel into serving pieces—4 legs, torso in 3 pieces.

Salt and pepper the squirrel pieces. Heat 3 tablespoons of the olive oil in a medium skillet, add the squirrel pieces, sprinkle with rosemary, and sauté, uncovered, over moderate heat, turning to brown the squirrel evenly. When the squirrel begins to brown, add the garlic along with the wine, cover, and cook until the wine cooks out.

Meanwhile, in a small skillet, heat the remaining 1 tablespoon oil, add the onion, and cook until it becomes translucent. Add the tomatoes, basil, and mushrooms and cook for 5 minutes, then combine the tomato mixture with the squirrel; cover, and continue to cook for 30 minutes more. Serve with polenta wedges (page 141).

* You can tell if a squirrel is young when you skin it; if the skin doesn't come off easily, discard the squirrel—it's old and tough.

† I use honey mushrooms, but any good-tasting mushroom, such as hen-of-the-woods, oyster, or boletus, can be substituted.

Curing Pork,
Canning Tuna,
and
Making Sausages

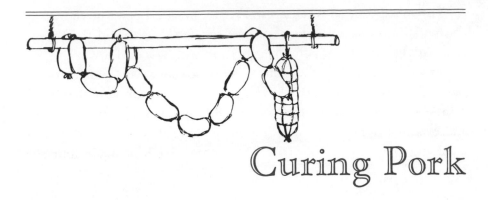

Curing Pork

My grandfather, who raised pigs on his farm in Centobuchi in the Italian Marches, always made his own prosciutto (cured ham), lonza (cured pork tenderloin), and several kinds of sausages. He knew exactly how to cure pork because he would adapt his timetable in accordance with the weather. He understood that the quality of the pork is directly related to what is fed the pigs. All his pigs were well fed with corn and garden vegetables in the summer and a mixture of warm cooked vegetables and grain in the winter. The pigs were kept clean, their stalls washed down every day.

The prosciutto he made was more robust than the famous prosciutto of Parma, and he liked it that way. What I make at home now is very similar to his prosciutto. Mine may not be quite as tasty because I can't get those large pigs that were so well fed, but I buy the biggest fresh ham that I can find, and I must admit the results are pretty good.

I had never tasted a cured tenderloin of pork before I went to Italy, where it is called lonza. The pork is cured like prosciutto, then rubbed with chopped orange skins and stuffed into a casing and tied up like salami. It is delightful and my grandfather became a master at making it.

My grandfather's pork liver sausages were particularly magnificent. He would cut the liver into cube-sized pieces, mix it with caul fat, chopped orange skins, garlic, salt, and pepper, then stuff it into pork casings. When I was an art student living in Italy I would visit my grandfather every Christmas and he would send me back to Florence with a suitcase filled with liver sausages, lonza, and prosciutto. Now I make them all myself, as well as a sweet Italian sausage, cotechino, and lamb, venison, and even tuna sausages.

Why make your own sausages? From a practical point of view, it is cheaper. But more important, you control the quality and the flavor. And sausages combine with other foods in such wonderful ways.

Remember that all of these meats are seasoning meats, and you don't eat them in great quantity. A lot of people today are afraid of preserved meats—justifiably so because they are full of chemicals, preservatives, and even hormones. But what you make yourself is pure. And it is so satisfying to present to your friends something you have made yourself.

Prosciutto

The best time to make prosciutto is in December or early January. The ham must be fairly well cured before the warm weather sets in or it will spoil.

1 whole fresh ham, with bone in (at least 15 pounds, preferably heavier)
Approximately ½ cup kosher salt or coarse salt

2 to 3 tablespoons coarsely ground black pepper

To prepare the ham, remove the pelvic bone fragment with a sharp pointed knife at the joint where it joins with the femur (thighbone). The knob of the femur must be clear of flesh and the pelvic bone. (This will ensure that bacterial growth will not form in the joint and eventually spoil the ham.) Rub a good amount of salt and pepper in and around the femur knob.

Remove the bone fragment of the foot that is still attached to the lower knob of the femur by slowly working a small sharp knife point into the joint, cutting away the cartilage until the bone fragment is free from the knob. Rub salt and pepper around the knob.

The next step is to cut away the skin from the part of the ham that was attached to the leg—that is, the inner thigh. (Salt and save the skin for soups, etc.) Remove the fat, but be careful not to cut the meat. The fat can be salted and preserved for future use. Cut off the loose ends of meat and fat (save for sausages) and fashion the ham into a neat form.

Massage the meat with your fingers near the bone so as to force out the remaining blood from the main artery. Leave the outside skin of the ham intact and rub the entire ham with a generous amount of salt and black pepper.

Put some salt in the bottom of a noncorrodible tray (wood is all right) and place the ham on top, skin side down; check to be sure that the entire surface of the ham has been rubbed with salt and pepper. In France they pour some cognac on the femur knob, and I have heard of grappa being used in the same way in some parts of Italy.

Place the ham in a cool dry place, somewhere between 30° to 40°, where air circulates, but you don't need a fan, just an open door and a breeze. Sprinkle more salt on the ham as it is absorbed, being especially careful to salt near the exposed knobs.

After a week, arrange three small sticks under the ham to keep it out of the moisture. After 3 more weeks, hang the ham in a cool, well-ventilated place for approximately 10 days.

Now rub salt on the skin side of the ham and place it skin down on the tray. Place a heavy weight on the ham—30 to 50 pounds should do it—in order to force out the remaining moisture. Keep the ham under the weight for about 10 days, during which time remove the weight every 2 days and rub the ham down with salt if it becomes too moist. After 10 days, wrap the ham in cheesecloth and tie the cloth around the ham so that it is secure. The reason for the cheesecloth is to keep insects off the ham, especially flies; if they lay their eggs on the ham, it can spoil. Continue to hang the ham in a well-ventilated place through the spring, summer, and autumn. The ham should hang for at least 9 months; 12 months is even better.

Before eating the prosciutto, trim off about 1 inch of skin, fat, and outer dried flesh from one side of the ham. The skin and fat from a cured prosciutto is excellent in soups and stews, so save it. Cut paper-thin slices of prosciutto with a sharp knife and serve them as a first course. Keep the prosciutto in a cool place. It is not necessary to refrigerate the ham except in hot weather.

Tagliatelle with Prosciutto

Serves 6 to 8.

¼ cup olive oil
12 ounces cultivated
  mushrooms, sliced, or
  1 ounce dried Italian
  mushrooms covered with
  warm water and soaked for
  at least 15 minutes, then
  drained, or 1 pound wild
  mushrooms, such as honey,
  boletus, or oyster
  mushrooms, sliced
1 medium onion, finely
  chopped
¼ pound sliced prosciutto,
  chopped

3 tablespoons sweet vermouth
4 cups chopped tomatoes
2 tablespoons chopped fresh
  basil, or 1 tablespoon dried
Salt and freshly ground black
  pepper to taste
1 cup fresh peas, blanched and
  drained, or 1 cup frozen
  peas, thawed
1½ pounds tagliatelle or other
  pasta
Garnish: Finely chopped flat-
  leaved parsley or freshly
  grated Parmesan

Heat the oil in a medium saucepan, add the mushrooms and sauté until the liquid cooks out, then add the onion and cook, uncovered, until the onion begins to brown. Add the prosciutto, continuing to sauté for several minutes more. Pour in the vermouth, cover, lower the heat, and simmer for several minutes. Add the tomatoes, along with the basil and salt and pepper, and simmer, covered, for 1 hour. Add the blanched or thawed peas and simmer for another 10 minutes.

Cook the pasta in rapidly boiling salted water until it is done al dente. Drain, place in a serving dish, ladle the sauce on top, and garnish with finely chopped flat-leaved parsley or grated Parmesan.

Lonza

Lonza is pork loin cured in a casing. It is easier to make than prosciutto because weevils and flies can't penetrate the casing. I have never seen a recipe for it written down, and these instructions are based on the way my grandfather made it. He would use the whole loin, but I use a piece about 3½ pounds. It is best to start curing the meat in January, and then you can eat it in May or June. If you are worried about trichinosis, take the precaution of freezing the meat overnight before you cure it. Lonza is served as a cold meat the way prosciutto is, and you can also use pieces of it as a seasoning meat.

1 boneless pork loin
   (about 3½ pounds)
1½ tablespoons kosher salt
About 3 tablespoons coarsely
   ground black pepper
2 cups dry white wine
¼ cup chopped orange zest,
   cut into slivers about
   ¾ by ⅛ inch
Hog casing, about 18 inches
   long, and 2 inches in
   diameter

Rub the loin all over with the salt and 1½ tablespoons of the coarsely ground pepper. Place the loin on a rack and keep it in a cool place (between about 30° and 40°), turning occasionally and sprinkling with more salt as needed; be sure to salt the ends of the loin, too.

After the loin has been cured for 3 days, wash it thoroughly in the wine. Rub it with more black pepper and with orange zest, slipping the zest into the crevices wherever possible.

Soak the casing in warm water for 15 minutes. Rinse under a running faucet, then slip the casing over the loin; it will take some patience, but with effort it can be done. Bind the stuffed loin with string as you would a roast, tying it at 1-inch intervals. Prick the casing with a clean pin in a number of places to remove air bubbles.

At this point you can hang the meat the way my grandfather did, for a few hours each day hanging it near the fireplace with a fire going; watch it and when the skin starts to dry after one week (squeeze it—it should still give a little), remove it to a cool place where there is a flow of fresh air. Or you can skip this step and simply leave it hanging in the cool place; make sure it does not freeze. It will be ready to eat in 5 to 6 months.

Serve in thin slices, as you would prosciutto.

Canning Tuna

Italian-Style Canned Tuna

It is absolutely necessary to can tuna under pressure using a canning pressure cooker—this will assure a botulism-free product.

Makes 72 half-pints.

About 14 pounds fresh tuna, skinned and boned	Kosher salt
	Olive oil

Equipment needed:

72 half-pint glass jars, sterilized in boiling water
72 canning rings and lids, sterilized in boiling water

Large canning pressure cooker

Cut the tuna into large pieces and pack it into the sterilized jars. Add 2 teaspoons kosher salt to each jar of tuna, then pour in enough olive oil so that the fish is covered. Using a fork, try to work the oil into the air pockets between the tuna sections. Screw the lids on and place in the pressure cooker. Follow the standard precautions and guidelines for your pressure cooker.

Process at 15 pounds pressure for 1 hour and 20 minutes. Allow the pressure cooker to cool according to standard precautions in your owner's manual, remove the jars, tighten the lids, and store in a cool place. Age for at least 3 months (preferably 6 months) before using. Serve garnished with some extra virgin olive oil, freshly ground black pepper, and thinly sliced onions.

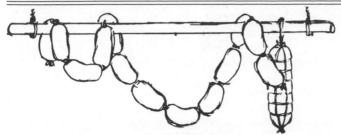

Making Sausages

I cannot think of any food easier to prepare than homemade sausages. You can stuff a sausage casing with pork, liver, chicken, fish, game, vegetables—any combination you wish. Sausages are ideal for people who raise chicken and rabbits, because they are bound to have some old creatures that are too tough for eating but are fine and flavorful when ground into sausage meat. The secret to a juicy sausage is for the meat to be coarsely ground (this way you do not need to use as much fat). Actually I prefer to use coarsely chopped meat rather than ground because the ground meats tend to be drier. I do not use a mechanical sausage stuffer. I think it's just another gadget to clean and store, and it isn't necessary unless you make large quantities of sausages. All you need is a simple funnel with a wide spout, and hog casings. You can buy both in stores in Italian neighborhoods.

Italian Sweet Sausage

These sausages can be broiled, grilled, sautéed, or stewed.

Makes about 2½ pounds sausage.

About 3 feet of hog casing,
  cut into 2 to 4 equal
  lengths
3 pounds pork butt
2 teaspoons table salt, or
  2½ teaspoons kosher salt

2 tablespoons freshly ground
  black pepper
2 teaspoons crushed fennel
  seeds (optional)
Hot pepper flakes to taste
  (optional)

Soak the casings in cold water at least 1 hour. Slip an inch or so of the casing over your faucet and run cold water through the casing, allowing the water to run out the other end.

Remove most of the fat from the pork butt and discard. Place the meat on a flat surface, slice it thinly, then chop it coarsely. Or you can put it through a meat grinder, using the blade with the largest holes. Mix the salt, pepper, and optional fennel and hot pepper flakes to taste with the meat. To adjust seasonings, fry a little bit of the sausage meat until brown and then taste critically and correct seasonings if necessary.

Now stuff one casing at a time. Slip one end of the casing over the mouth of the sausage funnel, using your fingers to push the casing over the spout. Tie the end of the casing with a string. Place the funnel in an upright position, holding the spout in one hand while you feed meat into the funnel with your other, pushing the meat through the spout into the casing with your thumb and allowing the stuffed casing to gradually slip away as it is filled. Tie the sausage-filled casings every 3 inches to make links, or twist the sausage completely around to form the links. If there are any air bubbles or pockets of air, prick the sausage with a clean needle to let the air escape.

VARIATION:

Venison Sausage

Use venison that has hung for several days.

Makes 6½ to 7 pounds sausage.

The sausage:

5½ to 6 pounds coarsely ground venison, preferably from the leg of a young doe

1 pound coarsely ground pork fat

5 tablespoons finely chopped garlic

¼ cup chopped fresh or dried rosemary

1 cup dry white wine

2 tablespoons kosher salt

¼ cup freshly ground black pepper

Hog casing, about 9 feet long, prepared as instructed on page 270

Mix the sausage stuffing ingredients together and stuff the casing as instructed on page 270.

VARIATION:

Rabbit or Chicken Sausage

Serves 10 to 12.

The sausage:

2 medium rabbits or 2 chickens (about 3½ pounds each)

1 pound coarsely ground pork

2 tablespoons chopped fresh sage, or 1 tablespoon dried

1 cup finely chopped orange zest

3 tablespoons finely chopped flat-leaved parsley

1 tablespoon finely chopped garlic

½ cup dry red wine

1½ tablespoons kosher salt

1½ tablespoons coarsely ground black pepper

Hog casing, about 4 feet long, prepared as instructed on page 270

With a very sharp knife, bone the rabbits (or chickens). Start with the back and work down close to the bone. Remove all of the meat. Reserve the two fillets on the top of the back along both sides of the spine. Cut the fillets, hearts, and livers into ½-inch pieces. Coarsely grind the rest of the meat.

Mix the sausage stuffing of the rabbit meat along with the rest of the sausage ingredients. Stuff the casing as instructed on page 270.

VARIATION:

Lamb Sausage

If you combine the ground lamb in this recipe with ground pork, you will have a more flavorful sausage and one only slightly higher in fat. Also, if you are making these around mid-May, try incorporating spearmint for the fresh mint. The aroma is superb.

Makes 3 pounds sausage.

The sausage:

3 pounds coarsely ground lean lamb, or 2 pounds ground lamb plus 1 pound coarsely ground lean pork

¼ cup finely chopped fresh mint or spearmint

3 tablespoons finely chopped flat-leaved parsley

2 tablespoons kosher salt

2 tablespoons finely chopped garlic

¾ tablespoon coarsely ground black pepper

½ cup dry white wine

Hog casing, about 3½ feet long, prepared as instructed on page 270

Mix the sausage stuffing and fill the casing as for cotechino (page 278) for a larger sausage or as instructed for Italian Sweet Sausage (page 270).

VARIATION:
Pork Liver Sausage

A sausage that tastes best when grilled over hot coals. It is very filling and a small amount goes a long way, but I do enjoy this recipe several times a year. If you prefer a milder liver sausage, mix 1 pound liver with 1 pound of coarsely ground pork.

Serves 6.

The sausage:

2 pounds very fresh pork liver, cut into ½-inch cubes (tough membranes discarded)

¾ cup coarsely chopped pork caul or pork fat

¾ cup finely chopped orange zest

3 fat cloves garlic, finely chopped

1 to 2 teaspoons kosher salt

Freshly ground black pepper to taste

Hog casing, about 3 feet long, prepared as instructed on page 270

Mix the sausage ingredients together and stuff the casing as instructed on page 270.

Casserole of Sausage and Eggplant

We enjoy this recipe with a fresh tomato and fennel salad.

Serves 4.

5 tablespoons olive oil

1 small eggplant, cut into ½-inch cubes (about 4 cups)

1 large onion, coarsely chopped

1 bell pepper, preferably red, coarsely chopped

3 tablespoons wine vinegar

4 medium potatoes, unpeeled

¼ cup freshly grated Pecorino Romano or Parmesan

Salt and freshly ground black pepper to taste

Freshly grated nutmeg to taste

1 pound Italian Sweet Sausage (page 270)

Preheat the oven to 400°.

Heat 3 tablespoons of the oil in a medium skillet, add the eggplant, onion, and bell pepper and sauté, uncovered, over medium heat, stirring often, until the onion begins to brown. Add the vinegar, cover, and cook for 10 minutes. Remove the pan from the heat and reserve the mixture.

Boil the potatoes in salted water until tender but still firm, drain, peel, and put through a ricer. Stir in the grated cheese and salt, pepper, and nutmeg to taste, and set aside.

Meanwhile, heat the remaining 2 tablespoons oil in a skillet, prick the sausage and brown, turning occasionally. Remove the sausage and slice into ½-inch pieces.

Spread the vegetable mixture over the bottom of a 10-inch-square casserole, and arrange the sausage slices on top. Spread the potato-cheese mixture over the sausages, cover, and bake in the oven for 20 minutes. Remove the cover and lightly brown the potatoes under the broiler.

Sausage with Beans and Cabbage

Serve this dish with crusty bread or Bruschetta (page 294).

Serves 6.

1 cup dried cannellini or Great Northern beans, soaked overnight in 3 cups water and drained	Salt and freshly ground black pepper or hot pepper flakes to taste
3 cups chicken broth, preferably homemade (page 194), or water	1 pound fresh Italian-style sausage
2 whole cloves garlic, peeled	1 medium onion, finely chopped
1 teaspoon chopped fresh or dried rosemary	12 cups (about 1 head) shredded savoy cabbage leaves, blanched and drained
	1 tablespoon finely chopped flat-leaved parsley

Put the soaked beans in a medium pot, and add the broth or water, garlic, rosemary, and salt and pepper or hot pepper flakes. Cover tightly, and boil gently for 1¼ hours or until the beans are tender but firm, stirring them from the bottom of the pot occasionally.

Prick the sausage and brown it on all sides in a skillet over a low heat for about 20 minutes. Remove from the skillet and discard the fat, then cut the sausage into 2-inch sections and return to the skillet. Add the onion and cook, uncovered, over medium heat until the onion begins to brown. Add the beans and drained cabbage. Toss in the parsley and adjust the salt and pepper; cover and cook over low heat for approximately 20 minutes. Serve hot.

VARIATION:

Sausage with Brussels Sprouts

This dish goes well with boiled potatoes.

Serves 6.

1½ pounds fresh Italian-style sausage

1½ medium onions, thinly sliced

6 tablespoons wine vinegar

3 cups brussels sprouts, blanched

1½ cups chopped tomatoes

3 tablespoons chopped fresh basil, or 1½ tablespoons dried

Salt and freshly ground black pepper to taste

Prick the sausage and slowly brown on all sides. Drain and discard the fat, then add the onions and cook until they begin to brown. Lower the heat, pour in the vinegar, and cook, covered, for 5 minutes. Add the brussels sprouts along with the tomatoes, basil, and salt and pepper to taste and cook, covered, until the sprouts are tender, about 10 minutes.

VARIATION:

Sausage with Peppers and Potatoes

Serves 6.

3 large potatoes, unpeeled

1⅓ pounds fresh Italian-style sausage

2 tablespoons olive oil

1⅓ pounds sweet red or green peppers, cut into ½-inch slices

2 onions, thinly sliced

½ cup wine vinegar

1 tablespoon chopped fresh oregano, or ½ teaspoon dried

Salt and freshly ground black pepper to taste

Cover the potatoes with salted water and cook until done but firm; drain and cool. Peel and cut into ½-inch-thick slices; set aside. Prick the sausage and brown in a large skillet, remove the sausage and discard the fat. Add olive oil and sauté the peppers over medium heat, stirring often, for approximately 5 minutes. Add the onions and continue cooking until the onions begin to brown. Then return the sausage to the skillet along with the sliced potatoes and the vinegar, oregano, and salt and pepper to taste. Cover and cook over medium heat, stirring occasionally, for approximately 15 minutes. Serve hot.

VARIATION:

Sausage with Broccoli and Brussels Sprouts

Serves 6.

3 cups broccoli flowerets
1 pound brussels sprouts
1½ pound homemade sausage
   (page 270)
3 tablespoons olive oil
3 cloves garlic, sliced

Hot pepper flakes to taste
5 tablespoons white wine
   vinegar
5 tablespoons water
Salt to taste

Cook the broccoli and brussels sprouts together in boiling salted water, uncovered, for about 3 minutes, drain, and set aside. Prick the sausage and brown lightly on both sides, then drain and discard the fat, but leave the sausage in the skillet. Add the olive oil, and cook the garlic and hot pepper flakes over moderate heat until the garlic begins to color. Add the broccoli and brussels sprouts and pour the vinegar and water over all. Season with salt and cook, covered, over moderate heat for about 5 minutes, until the sprouts are tender. Serve hot.

VARIATION WITH CAULIFLOWER: Instead of broccoli and brussels sprouts, use about **4 to 5 cups cauliflower flowerets,** blanched for 1 minute.

VARIATION:
Sausage with Beans and Rape

This recipe is especially good with broiled squares of polenta (page 141).

Serves 6.

1 pound fresh Italian-style
sausage
2 tablespoons olive oil
3 cloves garlic, finely chopped
2 cups cooked white beans and
their liquid (page 73), or
20-ounce can cannellini
beans, drained

8 cups chopped rape, blanched
2 minutes and drained (page
61)
Salt and freshly ground black
pepper to taste

Prick the sausage and brown, uncovered, in a medium skillet. Remove the sausage from the skillet and cut into 2-inch sections; discard the fat that cooked out. Heat the olive oil in the same skillet the sausage cooked in and sauté the garlic for a few seconds, then return the sausage to the skillet along with the beans and cook, covered, over medium-low heat for about 10 minutes, then add the rape and simmer, covered, for 40 minutes. Taste and adjust for salt and pepper halfway through the cooking process.

Lamb Sausages with Artichoke Hearts

This combination is particularly good served over plain polenta (page 141).

Serves 4.

4 tablespoons olive oil
2 pounds lamb sausages
(8 sausages, about 4
inches long, page 272)
1 large onion, thinly sliced
1 cup chopped Italian plum
tomatoes

Hot pepper flakes to taste
9 ounces frozen artichoke
hearts, thawed
Salt to taste
Garnish: Minced fresh
coriander (cilantro)

*Lamb
Sausages
with
Artichoke
Hearts
(continued)*

In a skillet heat 2 tablespoons of the olive oil and prick the sausages and brown on all sides; remove from the skillet and keep warm. Discard the oil from the skillet, add 2 more tablespoons olive oil and sauté the onion until it becomes translucent; then stir in the tomatoes and hot pepper flakes to taste and cook, covered, for 5 minutes. Add the artichoke hearts and sausages and simmer, covered, stirring occasionally, for 30 minutes. Add salt to taste, garnish with minced coriander and serve at once on heated plates.

VARIATION WITH PEAS: In a skillet brown the sausages as in recipe above but do not remove the sausages from the skillet. Pour off the oil and fat in the skillet and add **2 tablespoons olive oil** and **1 medium onion, sliced,** to the sausages in the skillet; sauté until the onion begins to brown. Add **1½ cups peas, blanched and drained,** and **½ cup warm water,** cover, and cook over moderate heat for about 7 minutes. Serve at once.

Cotechino Sausage

To make cotechino you need a special kind of sausage casing—one that is about 2 inches in diameter. You should be able to find this in better pork stores.

The basic ingredients in cotechino are coarsely ground pork, salt, and freshly ground black pepper. Sometimes a little saltpeter is added to preserve the color of the meat, but I prefer to avoid nitrates. A variety of herbs can be added to the cotechino; I have included sage and a few spices that I particularly like in the following recipes. A dash of grappa or brandy also goes well in cotechino—I suggest brandy, as most people are not familiar with grappa.

By the way, it is best to cook the cotechino intact and then slice it once it is cooked.

Makes two 1½-pound sausages.

The sausage:

3 pounds coarsely ground pork butt, with most of the fat trimmed off	1½ teaspoons kosher salt
	1 tablespoon finely chopped garlic
¾ tablespoon freshly ground black pepper	½ teaspoon freshly grated nutmeg
	½ teaspoon saltpeter (optional)

Pork gut for casing, 2 inches in
    diameter and about 2 feet long

Soak the pork casing for several hours in salted water. Wash very
well by running cold water through the casing for several minutes. Tie
one end of the casing with kitchen twine.

Mix all of the sausage ingredients and stuff the casing with the
sausage (see page 270 for technique), forcing the meat so that it becomes
about 2 inches in diameter. After about 9 inches of casing are stuffed,
tie it off and repeat the process with the second half of the casing.

The cotechino is now ready either for cooking or drying for later use
(follow directions for drying lonza, page 267). Prick the cotechino with
a clean needle all over before cooking or drying.

VARIATION WITH SAGE AND BRANDY OR GRAPPA: Prepare
and stuff the cotechino casing as instructed in the basic recipe, using
the following mixture: **3 pounds coarsely ground pork butt,** with most
of the fat trimmed off; **3 tablespoons dried sage; 1½ teaspoons freshly
ground black pepper;** and **3 tablespoons brandy or grappa.**

Lentils with Cotechino

Serves 4 to 6.

3 tablespoons olive oil
1 medium onion, finely chopped
1 large carrot, finely chopped
1 rib celery, finely chopped
3 whole cloves garlic, unpeeled
1½ cups lentils
4 cups water
Salt and freshly ground black
    pepper or hot pepper flakes
    to taste

1 teaspoon chopped fresh or
    dried rosemary
1 cotechino (about 1½ pounds)
    (opposite page)
1 pound rape, stems peeled, cut
    into bite-sized pieces*
4 to 6 medium potatoes,
    unpeeled
Garnish: Extra virgin olive oil
Chopped flat-leaved parsley

Heat the olive oil in a medium soup pot, add the onion, carrot, celery,
and garlic and sauté over medium heat, uncovered, stirring often, for
40 minutes. Add the lentils, water, salt and pepper or hot pepper flakes

*An equivalent amount of dandelion greens, spinach, or escarole may be used instead of the rape.

to taste, rosemary, and cotechino, pricked all over with a clean needle. Cover and simmer gently, stirring often, for about 50 minutes. Add the rape and cook an additional 30 minutes. The cook may eat the garlic on a little bread or squeeze it back into the lentils.

While the soup is simmering, cook the potatoes in boiling salted water to cover until tender. When cool enough to handle, peel and set aside.

Serve each portion of the lentils with 2 slices of the cotechino, sliced about ¾ inch thick, and a boiled potato. Serve hot. I like to garnish each serving with a drizzling of extra virgin olive oil and flat-leaved parsley.

Cotechino with Onions and Wine

I like this recipe with boiled potatoes or other vegetables such as carrots sprinkled with a little extra virgin olive oil.

Serves 3.

2 tablespoons vegetable oil
2 medium onions, thinly sliced
  (about 2 cups)
1 cotechino, about 1½ pounds
  (page 278)
2 cups dry white wine or
  chicken or beef broth,
  preferably homemade (for
  chicken broth, see page 194)

1 tablespoon chopped fresh or
  dried rosemary
Freshly ground black pepper to
  taste

Heat the oil in a medium saucepot and sauté the onions until they are translucent, then add the cotechino. Cover and cook for 10 minutes, then pour in the wine or broth along with the rosemary and black pepper. Cover and cook over medium heat for 20 minutes. Remove the cotechino and cut on the bias in slices ¾ inch thick. Serve with the onion sauce.

Cotechino with Rape

Serves 4.

1 cotechino, about 1½ pounds
  (page 278)
12 cups rape, stems peeled
  (page 61)

3 tablespoons olive oil
3 cloves garlic, finely chopped
Salt and hot pepper flakes to
  taste (optional)

Preheat the oven to 400°.

Prick the cotechino with a clean needle and place it in a baking dish with about 1½ inches of water. Bake, uncovered, for about 45 minutes. Let it cool slightly and cut into 1-inch pieces.

Meanwhile, blanch the rape in boiling salted water, uncovered, for several minutes. Drain and spread the rape in a baking dish about 2 inches deep. Add the olive oil, garlic, optional salt and hot pepper flakes, and cotechino slices. Bake, uncovered, for about 20 minutes.

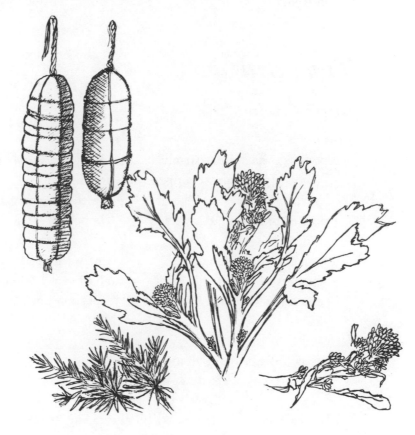

Tuna Sausage

The first time I experimented making fresh tuna sausages, I was working from a very dim but fond memory of a Sicilian combination that incorporated fragrant orange zest and herbs into the sausage filling. I began by grinding fresh tuna steaks and quickly discovered that the sausage, when cooked, was much too dry. Then my friend Butch Conte, owner of Conte's Fish Market in Mount Kisco, New York, suggested I mix in some tuna belly because it contains more fat. (It's usually thrown away because no one wants it.) Following Butch's lead, I made a mixture using ⅔ ground tuna belly to ⅓ ground tuna steak. The result, which follows, was lovely, particularly when served with simple boiled potatoes, roasted red peppers, or baked asparagus. The simplest way to serve these sausages is to place them on a rack or grill over a shallow baking tray. Prick the sausages, then pour about ½ inch water into the tray and bake in a preheated 500° oven for 15 minutes. Serve with lemon wedges.

Tuna Sausage

Makes 8 sausages.

The sausage:

2 pounds tuna belly, coarsely ground (preferably chopped by hand)

1 pound tuna steak, coarsely ground

¼ cup dry white wine

¼ cup olive oil

¼ cup finely chopped flat-leaved parsley

2 tablespoons finely chopped fresh mint

4 to 6 cloves garlic, finely chopped

Zest of 1 medium orange, finely chopped

1 tablespoon kosher salt

¾ teaspoon hot pepper flakes

Sausage casing, about 30 inches long (prepared as instructed on page 270)

Mix the sausage stuffing and fill the casing as instructed for Italian Sweet Sausage (page 270).

Tuna Sausage with Cheese and Red Wine

Serves 6.

½ pound tuna belly, coarsely chopped

½ pound tuna steaks (remove all dark areas), coarsely chopped

4 to 6 cloves garlic, crushed

4 cloves garlic, finely chopped

3 tablespoons finely chopped flat-leaved parsley

3 tablespoons of grated Pecorino cheese

1 cup of bread crumbs, preferably homemade

¼ cup of extra virgin olive oil

½ teaspoon hot pepper flakes

Salt and freshly ground black pepper

1 cup of dry red wine

Lemon wedges for garnish

1 pork casing about 56" long (prepared as instructed for Italian Sweet Sausage on page 270)

Mix all ingredients together except the pork casing and stuff casing as directed for Italian Sweet Sausage (page 270). Serve with lemon wedges for garnish. It is best broiled, and excellent sauteed with vegetables such as broccoli.

VARIATION WITH ORANGE RIND: (This recipe makes 8 sausages.) Prepare a **30-inch-long sausage casing** as instructed for Italian Sweet Sausage (page 270). Mix the sausage stuffing of **2 pounds tuna belly,** coarsely ground (preferably chopped by hand), plus **1 pound tuna steak,** coarsely ground, **¼ cup dry white wine, ¼ cup olive oil, ¼ cup finely chopped flat-leaved parsley, 2 tablespoons finely chopped fresh mint, 4 to 6 cloves garlic, finely chopped, zest of 1 medium orange, finely chopped, 1 tablespoon kosher salt, ¾ teaspoon hot pepper flakes.** Stuff the casing as instructed for Italian Sweet Sausage (page 270).

Tuna Sausage with Potatoes and Broccoli

Serves 4 to 6.

1 pound tuna sausage (page 282)

3 large potatoes, boiled until almost cooked, peeled, and cut into 1-inch-thick pieces

1 bunch broccoli, separated into large flowerets, blanched for 1 minute and drained

¼ cup olive oil

1 large onion, coarsely chopped

3 tablespoons finely chopped flat-leaved parsley

2 tablespoons coarsely chopped fresh mint

½ cup dry white wine

Salt and freshly ground black pepper to taste

Preheat the oven to 450°.

In a baking dish just large enough to hold them in one layer, arrange the sausage, potatoes, and broccoli. Top with the remaining ingredients, cover, and bake for 15 minutes. Remove cover and bake for 5 minutes more. Serve at once.

Breads
and
a Few Desserts

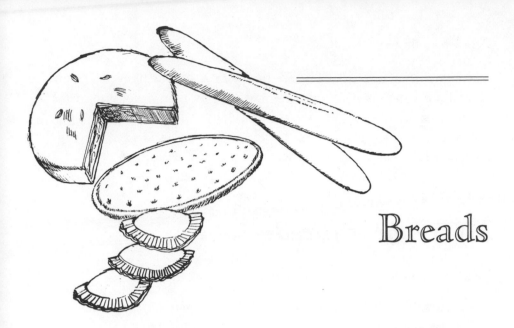

Breads

We have been making the same traditional breads in our household for a long time, so many of the recipes in this section have appeared in my earlier books. The same is true of the desserts, which in our family are generally reserved for holidays. Ordinarily we finish a meal simply with fresh fruit. You will find an excellent naturally sweetened fresh fruit sorbet (page 298), which can be varied with whatever seasonal fruits and berries are at hand, and this makes a lovely, light ending to a meal.

About Bread

My mother used to make bread every week. She made very large loaves. After she formed the loaves, she would put them in a big low tub with two handles and cover them with a light blanket. My sister, Mary, and I would then take hold of one handle each and carry the tub of bread to a commercial bakery about a block away. We would leave the bread and return the next day to pick up the tub filled with large, thick-crusted bread. I'll always remember how wonderful the warm bread smelled as we carried it home. On cold days we would put the tub down and warm our hands on the bread.

Now my wife makes fresh bread all year round. The smell of baking bread during winter seems especially nice, perháps because it all started in our home on a snowy winter day. It was in the sixties and we experienced the worst snowstorm in my memory. The drifts were 5 feet high and it was 3 days before the main road was plowed. It took several more days to clear our driveway. My mother was visiting us at the time, so needless to say, we ate well. It was during that week that she taught my wife how to bake bread and Pizza Caccia a Nanza (page 292), and Ellie has been baking wonderful bread ever since.

My Mother's Bread

Makes 2 small loaves or 1 large loaf.

5 cups unbleached flour   1½ tablespoons corn oil
1½ teaspoons dry yeast   2 cups warm water
1 tablespoon salt

Put the flour in a bowl, and mix in the yeast, salt, and corn oil. Make a well in the center, then add the warm water and work until well mixed. Turn the dough out onto a work surface and knead until velvety smooth—about 5 minutes or more. Clean the bowl and place the dough in it. Cover with a cloth and put in a warm spot. Allow to rise until double in size, then punch down and knead for 5 minutes. Return to the bowl, cover with the cloth, and allow to rise until double in size a second time. Punch the dough down and knead for 5 minutes. Shape dough into 2 loaves and place in 2 floured 8-inch bread pans, or shape into 1 loaf and place in a larger pan, about 10 inches long. Cover with the cloth and allow to rise again until double its bulk.

Preheat the oven to 450°.

Bake the bread for 25 minutes or until brown. During the first 10 minutes of baking, throw an occasional ice cube onto the oven floor to create steam. Reduce the heat to 350°, take the bread out of the bread pan(s), and bake on the rack in the oven for 45 minutes.

Fried Pizzas

When my mother made bread she always put some dough aside to make fried pizzas. It was a breakfast treat we looked forward to.

Use either My Mother's Bread (opposite) or Ellie's Italian-Style Bread (below), and after the dough has risen twice, form pizzas by breaking off a piece of dough about 2 inches in diameter for each person. With your hands form the dough into rounds about 4 inches in diameter and about ¼ inch thick.

Pour about ¾ inch of olive oil in a small skillet just large enough to hold one pizza. Heat the oil and when it is very hot, but not smoking, add the pizza. Turn it over to brown it lightly on both sides, blot with paper towels, and keep warm. When all of the pizzas are fried, serve one pizza to a plate, then add sugar, jam, or fruit sauce.

Ellie's Italian-Style Bread

The grain that my wife, Ellie, uses for this bread comes from her grandfather's farm in Arkansas near the banks of the Mississippi River. They send us the whole grain, and Ellie grinds the wheat into flour with an electrically powered kitchen-sized stone mill.

Makes about 8 loaves, 20 inches long and 3 inches wide.

2 tablespoons active dry yeast	2 tablespoons kosher salt, or
8 cups warm water	1¼ teaspoons table salt
About 16 cups flour*	

Mix the yeast and water together and let sit about 5 minutes.

Pour most of the flour along with the salt into a large bowl. Add the yeast water to the flour gradually, mixing as you pour. Work the dough

* All-purpose, unbleached flour or whole wheat flour, or whole wheat and all-purpose flours combined, can be used in this recipe. We like ⅔ whole wheat mixed with ⅓ all-purpose flour.

with your hands into a manageable ball. Remove it to a lightly floured pastry board or countertop and knead it until the ball of dough has an elastic consistency, adding more flour as needed—about 10 minutes.

Wash and dry the mixing bowl and pour in a little vegetable oil. Roll the ball of dough in the oiled bowl until it is lightly covered with oil. Cover with a damp cloth or sheet of plastic wrap and place the bowl in a warm place. (We put the bowl near our stove.) Allow the dough to double its bulk—about 2 hours.

Turn the dough out and punch it down. Cut the ball into 8 equal pieces and form into long loaves—about 18 inches long and 2 inches wide. You can place formed loaves on oiled baking sheets or use lightly oiled French bread baking forms. Allow the loaves to double their bulk— about 1 hour.

Preheat the oven to 425°.

Place the baking sheets or baking forms in the oven and bake about 30 minutes. During the first few minutes of baking, occasionally throw several ice cubes onto the oven floor to create steam, which will make the crust crisp. Turn the loaves over (if using baking forms, take the loaves out of the pans and place directly on the oven racks), lower the heat to 350°, and bake about 20 minutes more or until the bread is a golden brown. Cool on racks.

About Pizzas

There are many different ways to make pizza, and in my opinion the least interesting pizzas are the ones that are soggy with tomatoes and cheese. For a filled pizza I prefer the Sicilian-style pielike pizza with the filling enclosed between a bottom and a top crust.

Pizza with Ground Meat

Serves 6.

The dough:

1 teaspoon active dry yeast	1 teaspoon salt
1 cup warm water	3½ cups flour

The filling:

1½ pounds lean ground pork
1 tablespoon oil
6 cups thinly sliced onions
½ cup wine vinegar
1 tablespoon finely chopped
   flat-leaved parsley

½ cup chopped tomatoes
2 teaspoons chopped fresh
   oregano, or 1 teaspoon dried
Salt and freshly ground black
   pepper or hot pepper flakes
   to taste

For the dough: Stir the yeast into the warm water and let it sit 5 to 10 minutes. Add the salt.

Put the flour on a working surface and make a well in the center. Pour the dissolved yeast into the well slowly, mixing in the flour as you pour. When well mixed, knead the dough, adding a little more flour if necessary, until it is smooth and elastic. Put it in a large bowl, cover with a damp towel, and let rise in a warm spot until it has doubled in volume, about 1 hour.

Preheat oven to 400°.

To make the filling: Brown the meat in the oil until the moisture cooks out. Add the onions and cook until they become transparent, and add the vinegar. Cook for several minutes over a high heat, then add the rest of the ingredients and cook 5 minutes.

Lightly oil a round baking dish about 9 inches in diameter and 1½ inches deep. Turn the dough out onto a floured work surface, punch it down, and cut it in 2 pieces, one portion slightly larger than the other. Roll out the larger piece to a circle about 11 inches in diameter and transfer to the baking dish, tucking the dough into the sides. Fill with the pork mixture. Roll out the second piece of dough and place it on top of the filling. Pinch the edges to seal them and trim off excess dough if necessary.

Bake for 15 minutes, then lower the oven heat to 350° and bake about 30 minutes more until golden on top. Serve at room temperature or warm.

VARIATION WITH TUNA, BROCCOLI, AND BLACK OLIVES: Instead of ground meat, use **1 7-ounce can of tuna packed in olive oil, 4 cups blanched broccoli** cut in pieces, **15 black olives, 4 tablespoons olive oil, 1 teaspoon oregano,** and **salt and pepper** to taste.

Pizza Caccia a Nanza

The literal translation of caccia a nanza *is "take out before." When bread was made at home in the area where my mother lives, a piece of dough was reserved to make pizza. The pizza was placed in the oven with the bread, and since it cooked more quickly, it was taken out before the bread, hence the name. Pizza Caccia a Nanza is a specialty of a medieval town in the Marches called Castel di Lama. This recipe first appeared in my book* Italian Family Cooking, *published in 1971 by Random House, long before white pizzas were written about in America. Focaccia is the name for the toma-toless pizza served in Tuscany. White pizzas make wonderful sandwiches. Cut a wedge from this puffy round of bread and slice it in half horizontally. Fill the halves with thin slices of prosciutto (page 264), or lonza (page 267), or cooked vegetables such as rape or broccoli for a delightful sandwich.*

Serves 6 to 8.

The dough:

2½ cups flour	¾ teaspoon active dry yeast
½ teaspoon salt	1 cup warm water

2 to 4 cloves garlic, cut into slivers	3 tablespoons olive oil
2 tablespoons rosemary, preferably fresh	Salt and freshly ground black pepper to taste

For the dough: Combine the flour, salt, yeast, and water in a mixing bowl. Blend well, then turn the dough onto a lightly floured board. Knead well, about 15 minutes, and shape the dough into a ball. Place the dough in a lightly oiled bowl, cover with a towel, and let rise in a warm place until double in bulk, about 1½ hours.

Preheat the oven to 400°.

Turn the dough onto the board and knead again. On a lightly floured surface, roll it out to a ½-inch thickness. Rub a baking sheet with oil, transfer the round of dough to the baking sheet, and make indentations over the surface of the dough. Insert a sliver of garlic and a leaf or two of rosemary in each indentation. Put the dough in a warm place and let the dough rise a second time to twice its volume—about 30–40 minutes. Pour the olive oil over the pizza, sprinkle the dough with salt and pepper, and bake until golden brown, about 15 minutes, occasionally spraying the pizza with water as it is cooking. The steam will assure crispness.

Ricotta Pie with Prosciutto

This pizza—in fact, a covered pie—is one of my mother's recipes. She always prepared it in our house during the Easter season. It was the perfect snack, which we would nibble around four in the afternoon and always standing on our feet. You would never have thought to sit down to eat it. She made it in the spring because of the availability of fresh ricotta. I now make it as well with my own homemade prosciutto (page 264).

Should there be leftovers, which is not likely, don't refrigerate them. None of these ingredients improve in flavor or texture chilled.

Serves 6.

The filling:

¾ pound prosciutto, cut into
⅛-inch slices and diced
1 link dried sweet sausage,
diced

½ pound mozzarella, diced
1½ pounds fresh ricotta
1 cup freshly grated Pecorino
Romano

The dough:

2 cups all-purpose flour
2 eggs
3 tablespoons milk

3 tablespoons unsalted butter,
melted

Preheat the oven to 350°.

Prepare the filling: In a bowl combine well all the filling ingredients.

Make the dough: On a work surface, mound the flour, make a well in the center of it, and add the eggs, milk, and butter. Mix lightly with a fork to blend. Working from the inside with a fork and stirring only in one direction, gradually incorporate the flour into the liquids. Continue until all the flour has been absorbed into a ball of dough. Knead the dough on the work surface until it is a shiny, elastic ball. With a sharp knife divide the ball in half and cover one half while you roll the other out on a floured surface into a round about ⅛ inch thick.

Fit the dough into a 10-inch pie pan or baking dish and spread the filling evenly over it. Roll the remaining dough into a round slightly larger than the pie plate and cover the filling with it, sealing the edges together firmly. Bake the pie in the middle of the oven for about 1 hour, until the top crust is brown. Let the pizza come to room temperature before serving to let the texture set.

Bruschetta

This garlic bread, a staple of my childhood, can be prepared in one of two ways. The bread can be drizzled with oil, then toasted and rubbed with garlic, as it is below, or it can be toasted first, then drizzled with oil and rubbed with garlic. Either way, it is delicious with any number of dishes, but it is particularly good with bean soup and salad. Bruschetta can also be served as an appetizer, a wonderful one, particularly with tomatoes (see variation below).

Serves 4.

Extra virgin olive oil
4 slices Italian or French bread, cut into ½-inch-thick slices

Garlic cloves, peeled and cut in half

Preheat the broiler.

Sprinkle about 1 teaspoon olive oil on each slice of bread and then toast the slices until golden on both sides. Rub generously with the cut garlic on one side.

VARIATION WITH TOMATOES: After rubbing the garlic on the toast, cover the slices with about **1 cup peeled and coarsely chopped, fully ripened tomatoes,** season with **salt and pepper,** and broil close to the heat until the tomatoes are heated through.

A Few Desserts

Almond Cake

This is one of the Christmas cakes my mother made when I was a child.

Serves 6 to 8.

The cake:

- ¼ pound butter, at room temperature
- 1 cup sugar
- 1 teaspoon vanilla extract
- 2½ cups flour
- 2 tablespoons grated lemon zest
- ¾ cup milk
- 1 tablespoon baking powder

The topping:

- 1¼ cups almonds, shelled but not skinned
- 2 egg whites
- 1 teaspoon vanilla extract
- 1 cup sugar
- 2 tablespoons grated lemon zest

For the cake: Cream the butter and sugar together, stir in the vanilla extract, and then add the flour along with the lemon zest and mix well. Pour in the milk and baking powder, thoroughly mix, and set aside.

Preheat the oven to 400°.

For the topping: Blanch the almonds in boiling water, drain, cool, and remove the skins. Place in a single layer on a baking tray and toast in the oven until light brown, approximately 10 minutes. Shake the almonds from time to time to prevent burning; let cool. Chop the almonds by hand or in a food processor.

Turn the oven to 350°. Mix the egg whites and vanilla extract, then add the sugar, almonds, and lemon zest and mix well.

To assemble, butter and flour a 13- by 9- by 2½-inch baking pan. Pour in the batter and spread the topping over all. Bake for 40 minutes or until golden brown.

Ultra Plus Mousse

Years ago Pierre Franey dictated this recipe off the top of his head for me and I made it for a New Year's Day feast with some of our friends. It was such a hit that we all agreed that it was the best chocolate mousse creation we ever whipped up.

Serves 12.

½ pound sweet chocolate
6 eggs, separated
½ cup sugar
¼ cup Marsala or sweet
   liqueur, such as Grand
   Marnier or Amaretto

2 cups heavy cream, very cold
Garnish: Grated chocolate

Cut the chocolate into small pieces and melt in a saucepan over low heat.

Place the yolks, 6 tablespoons of the sugar, and the liqueur in a saucepan or a stainless steel bowl that fits over one of your other saucepans. Place over simmering but not boiling water, and with a wire wisk, vigorously and constantly beat the egg yolk until the mixture thickens to the consistency of zabaglione or hollandaise sauce. If the water is boiling, you may cook the yolks too rapidly and the mixture will curdle or "break." Remove from the heat at once, fold in the melted chocolate, and let cool. Beat egg whites until peaks start to form, then gently fold the whites into the mousse.

Have the cream very cold. Whip the cream until it begins to thicken, add the 2 remaining tablespoons of sugar, and continue to beat until stiff peaks form. Fold into the mousse.

Spoon the mousse into a serving bowl and garnish with grated chocolate. Refrigerate until ready to serve. May be prepared a day in advance.

Note: Chopped nuts may be added to the mousse when the chocolate is added or as a garnish.

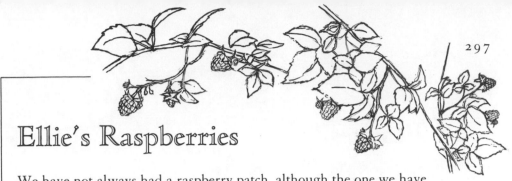

Ellie's Raspberries

We have not always had a raspberry patch, although the one we have right now is flourishing. It is the first thing you see as you approach the upper garden, and today you could justifiably describe it as unruly. Ellie got the patch going by exchanging with a friend down the road our strawberry plants for raspberry ones—a unique variation of barter. Raspberries multiply unless pruned, and we have picked as many as 50 pounds of berries, with plenty still left on the bushes for the birds.

Poached Peaches with Raspberry Sauce

Serves 6.

6 medium ripe but firm
  peaches
2¾ cups water
1½ tablespoons vanilla extract
6 whole cloves

1 cup plus 1 tablespoon sugar
1½ cups raspberries
1 teaspoon plum brandy or
  kirsch

Blanch the peaches in boiling water for about 30 seconds, drain, and let cool. Peel the peaches, cut them in half, and remove the pits.

Mix the water, vanilla, cloves, and 1 cup of sugar in a saucepan and boil, uncovered, over high heat for 5 minutes. Add the peaches, lower the heat, and simmer for 15 minutes. Pour the peaches and syrup into a bowl and refrigerate.

While the peaches are chilling, puree the raspberries by pushing them with the back of a spoon through a fine sieve into a bowl. Discard the seeds. You should have 1 cup of puree. Stir in the remaining tablespoon sugar and the liqueur, blend well, and refrigerate.

To serve, use a slotted spoon and transfer the peach halves to individual bowls or to a serving bowl and pour the raspberry puree over them.

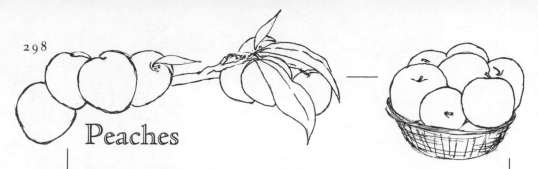

Peaches

My father adored peaches, and we always had peach trees in the backyard in Waterbury, Connecticut, where I grew up. My father would simply plant the pits. Within a year the sapling would be about 2 feet high. He would then transplant it, and we would be eating peaches in 3 to 4 years. Peach trees do not last long, on the average about 7 to 10 years, so we would always have a young one growing to replace the old. I have followed the same tradition. My father never sprayed his peaches, but I have a problem with bugs that attack the blossoms, so I spray with a mixture of vegetable soap, such as Palmolive (shave the soap into water to mix) and sweet garden lime (2 cups to 1 gallon of soapy water). Try the mixture on a few leaves just as they're coming out, and if your solution tends to burn the leaves, reduce the amount of soap. If the bark is infested, a paste of wood ash and sweet lime is helpful.

Peach and Orange Sorbet

I make fresh fruit sorbet with freshly squeezed orange juice instead of sugar syrups, which adds a natural sweetness so you don't need sugar. Here is a basic recipe that may be varied with whatever fruits and/or berries are in season. The peach trees on our place yield a wonderful amount of fruit, and when they do, there are two desserts I make immediately—this one and Poached Peaches with Raspberry Sauce (page 297).

Serves 4.

  4 medium ripe peaches
  2 cups fresh squeezed orange
    juice

Blanch the peaches in boiling water for about 30 seconds, drain, and let cool. Peel, remove the pits, and cut into pieces. Place the peaches in a food processor and puree, then stir together with the orange juice and pour into an ice cream freezer. Freeze following the instructions of your ice cream maker.

Figs Stuffed with Almonds

I first tasted figs with almonds in my grandfather's home in Italy. It is important that you use a fine-quality, moist dried fig for this recipe. I prefer to buy almonds in their skins and blanch and skin them myself; they're fresher and less expensive that way.

I think of this recipe as a wintertime treat, and I like to serve it along with fresh fruits on a large platter.

Serves 6.

12 almonds, shelled but not skinned	12 dried figs

Preheat oven to 400°.

Blanch the almonds in boiling water, drain, cool, and remove the skins. Place on a pie plate or baking tray and toast in the oven until light brown, approximately 10 minutes. Shake the almonds from time to time to prevent burning; let cool.

Cut a slit in each fig and slip a toasted almond inside.

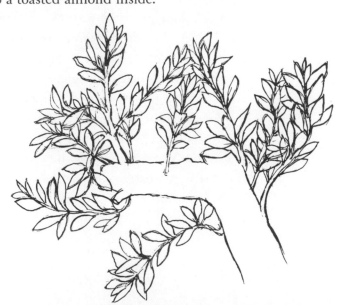

Ricotta Pie with Rice

I am especially fond of the desserts my mother made with ricotta, this ricotta pie being my favorite.

Serves 6 to 8.

The filling:

½ cup rice
1½ cups milk
1½ pounds ricotta
½ cup sugar

Grated zest of 1 lemon
¼ teaspoon cinnamon
3 eggs

The dough:

2 cups flour
2 tablespoons sugar
½ teaspoon baking powder
Grated zest of ½ lemon

2 eggs
3 tablespoons unsalted butter,
   melted

Preheat the oven to 400°.

Make the filling: In a saucepan cook the rice in the milk until tender, about 10 to 15 minutes; cool. Combine with the rest of the filling ingredients.

Prepare the dough: Put the flour on a work surface and mix in the sugar, baking powder, and zest. Make a well and crack the eggs into the center, then pour in the melted butter. Fork lightly to mix, then incorporate the liquid ingredients with the dry. Knead into a smooth dough, adding a little warm water, if needed, to achieve a smooth consistency. The dough can be mixed in a food processor.

Cut off about ⅓ of the dough, and on a floured surface, roll it out into a 6- by 10-inch rectangle, ¼ inch thick. With a sharp knife cut 6 strips about 1 inch wide and 10 inches long.

Flour the surface again and roll out the remaining dough into a round about 12½ inches in diameter. Fit the dough into a 10-inch pie plate. Pour in the filling, lay the reserved strips of dough over the filling in a crisscross pattern, then press and crimp the ends firmly into the edge. Bake for 30 minutes, reduce the oven temperature to 350°, and bake for another 30 minutes. Let the pie cool before serving.

Ricotta Balls

Another one of my mother's wonderful Easter desserts, which I included in my first book, Italian Family Cooking.

Makes about 48 balls.

3 eggs
2 tablespoons sugar
1 pound ricotta
1 cup flour
5 teaspoons baking powder
¼ teaspoon salt
3 teaspoons brandy or sweet liqueur (Marsala is also good)

Vegetable or corn oil for frying (I prefer corn as it has a higher burning temperature)
Powdered sugar for dusting

In a bowl combine all the ingredients except the vegetable or corn oil and the powdered sugar for dusting. Cover and let stand for 1 hour.

Pour about 1½ to 2 inches oil into a medium skillet and heat until hot but not smoking. Drop 1 teaspoon of the batter at a time into the skillet, up to a total of 12. (The oil should boil violently when the batter is added.) Cook until the balls are golden brown. Remove with a slotted spoon, blot on paper towels, and dust with the powdered sugar.

Note: Instead of dusting the balls with sugar, you can serve them with a sweet sauce, such as jam or a puree of fresh fruit.

Grape Turnovers

In the fall when we made wine, my parents would always set aside some of the grapes to make a concentrate that would be used during the Christmas holidays to make various sweets, particularly a pastry turnover called calgionetti, *which we loved. We still maintain the tradition in our family.*

About 60 calgionetti.

The dough:

3 cups flour	½ cup water
Pinch of salt	½ cup olive oil
½ cup dry white wine	

The filling:

Zest of 1 orange, finely chopped	1 cup grape concentrate*
12 walnuts, shelled and finely chopped	

Corn or peanut oil for frying	Powdered sugar for sprinkling

For the dough: Put the flour and salt in a bowl, make a well in the center, then pour the remaining ingredients into the well. Using a fork, work the flour into the liquid ingredients until the dough thickens. Continue to work the dough with your hands, then turn it out onto a floured work surface and knead until well blended. Roll into a ball and cut in half. Roll out one half on a floured surface until you have a circle about ⅟₁₆ inch thick.

Mix all ingredients for the filling together. Starting about 2 inches from the top of the dough circle spoon 1 teaspoon of the filling onto the dough, leaving 2 inches between each mound. Now roll the 2-inch strip over this first row of filling and seal the bottom edge. With a sharp knife or pastry wheel cut out half circles (as you would ravioli), sealing

* To make the concentrate: Boil crushed wine grapes, stems removed, for about 10 minutes. Let cool, then force the pulp through a sieve, pressing out as much juice as possible. Boil down the juice to reduce it by half or two-thirds, depending on how thick the syrup is—you want to have it the consistency of loose jelly. Store the concentrate in a crock or glass jar in the refrigerator. If mold forms on the syrup, simply remove it and boil the syrup slowly for about 10 minutes.

the edges with a fork. Repeat this procedure with subsequent rows until the circle is used up. Then roll the remaining dough into a ¹⁄₁₆-inch-thick circle, and repeat the procedure.

Heat about 1 inch of oil in a large skillet. When it is very hot, slip in 5 or 6 turnovers, one at a time, and fry, turning once, until they are golden on both sides. Remove from the oil, drain on paper towels, and repeat, adding more oil as necessary, until all the turnovers are fried. Sprinkle sugar over them when done.

VARIATION WITH HONEY AND CHICK-PEA FILLING: Instead of using the filling above, mix together **¾ cup blanched, shelled, and toasted almonds, 1½ cups cooked chick-peas pureed, 2 tablespoons grated orange peel, ¼ teaspoon cinnamon,** and **¼ cup honey.** Fill the pastry with this mixture and proceed as directed above.

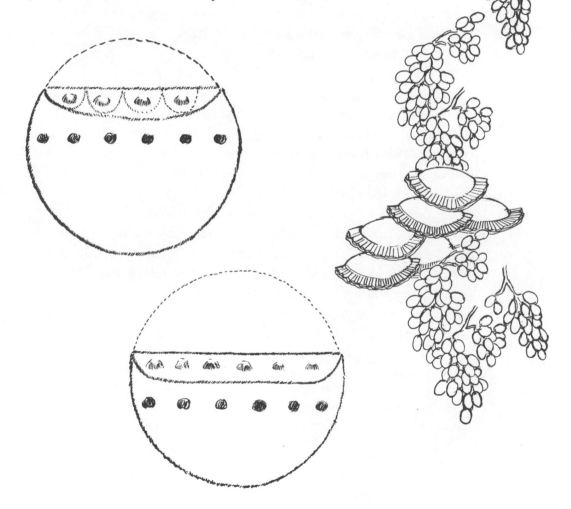

Biscotti (Almond Cookies)

I first tasted these biscotti in the home of Jo and Roberto Bettoja in Rome while visiting them with Craig Claiborne and Pierre Franey. In Tuscany they are served with a sweet wine called Vin Santo so that the dry biscuit can be dipped into the wine to flavor and soften it. A port or sherry would be fine instead. Today in America biscotti have become quite popular served with coffee.

Makes about 36 cookies.

2 cups flour

1⅓ cups sugar

2 large eggs

1 tablespoon grated lemon rind

¼ cup anise-flavored liqueur
    such as Sambuca or anisette

¼ cup rum, light or dark

1½ cups blanched, peeled
    whole almonds, toasted

2 teaspoons baking powder

Mix together the flour, sugar, eggs, lemon rind, liqueur and rum in a mixing bowl and beat with a wooden spoon until thoroughly blended. Beat in the almonds and baking powder. Pick up half the dough in your hands and form it into a long sausage shape. Arrange it on one half of a baking pan that you have oiled and dusted lightly with flour; don't place it too close to the edge of the pan. Arrange the other half alongside but not too close because the dough will spread as it bakes.

Bake in a preheated 350° oven for 1 hour. Remove and let cool for about 20 minutes. Carefully and gently run a spatula under the pieces of baked dough. Let stand until almost at room temperature. Using a serrated bread knife, cut each mound on the bias into crosswise slices, each about 1 inch thick. Arrange the slices in one layer on a baking sheet and return them to the oven to dry out, about 10 minutes. Let cool, then store. The biscotti are improved if a little anisette or other anise-flavored liqueur is brushed over them just before serving.

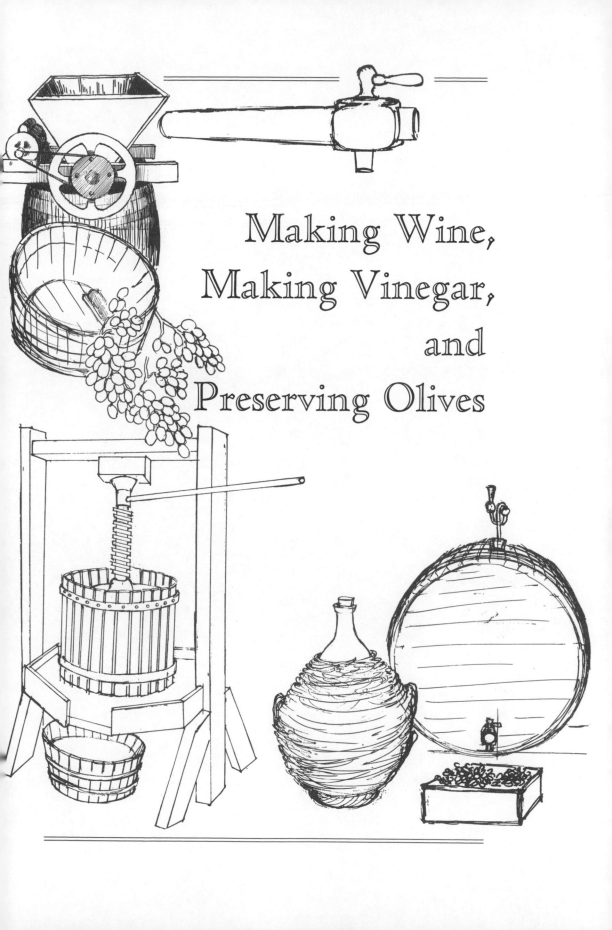

Making Wine,
Making Vinegar,
and
Preserving Olives

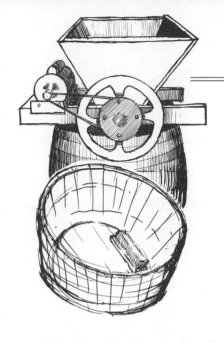

Making Wine

My father always managed to make at least one 50-gallon barrel of wine a year; often, much more. The idea of a meal without wine was inconceivable to him, and even during the height of the Depression, he managed to make a barrel. In Italy the poorest Italian has wine—maybe not meat, but bread and wine (one can practically live off bread and wine). My father used to look at me with disdain when, as a boy, I drank milk at the table. He could not understand why a fourteen-year-old boy would prefer milk.

I used to help my father make wine when I was a child. I remember going with him to the railroad yards in Waterbury, Connecticut, to buy the grapes that had arrived by freight car. He would inspect them all studiously and tell me that the drier the grape, the better the wine. He also stressed that it was best if the stems were brown rather than green, and he would squeeze a grape between his thumb and forefinger and work it around until a certain amount of juice had evaporated. He could tell by the stickiness of the juice between his fingers what the sugar content was; he didn't even have to taste the grapes. (Years later as an art student in Florence, I was taught to test the strength of rabbit skin glue in the same way.)

Then there was the soaking and swelling of the barrels and the crushing of the grapes. It was festive— like harvesttime—and I can still recall the sweet, divine taste of the grapes as I would nibble a few from each crate and later the wonderful smell of the fermenting wine. As I grew older, I was strong enough to hand my father the 38-pound crates as he crushed the grapes in them.

Late in the spring each year my father would taste his new wine with three or four of his friends. I would go down in the cellar with them and watch this ritual with fascination. First, they would lift their glasses up to the light bulb that was hanging from the ceiling and gaze intently at the wine. Then they would nod approvingly. Next, they would sniff the wine and very gently lift the glasses to their lips for a mere sip. It seemed that the wine remained in their mouths for ages before they would swallow, and after swallowing, they made comfortable noises—gentle grunts, sometimes a kind of moan. Then the men would look at my father and say *"è buon."* I was always amazed that their large, rough and calloused hands could hold a fragile glass with such gentleness.

In 1966 my father died, and when the winemaking season arrived, I was faced with a dilemma. I did not think I would be able to make wine. Furthermore, it was much easier to buy it. But what about the wine-making tradition that had existed in our family for centuries? God only knows how many centuries! The thought of that tradition dying out because of me gave me pause. Finally I decided that I didn't have the right to deprive my children of that tradition, that it was up to me to carry it on and pass it along to them. I began by appropriating some of my father's equipment and barrels. My wife bought me a wonderful secondhand winepress. And luckily I had a friend, Nick Mastropietro, who was from Abruzzi and knew how to do everything, so I could call on him often for help. He would answer all my questions, and, to my amazement, I made a very decent wine that first year. Since then each year my wine has become progressively better.

About Wine Making

There is nothing more basic than making wine—
with the exception of making bread. You
mash grapes, then the grape juice mixes with
the yeast on the grape skins, and that causes
the sugar in the juice to ferment, transforming
it into alcohol. Allowed to settle and clarify
during the winter, the wine is drained in the
spring from the sediment and left to age. It is
that simple. Some experience and knowledge is
required, such as knowing the quality of the
grapes, the state of the barrels, the temperature
of the cellar, and so on, but the beginner should
approach wine making without trepidation.

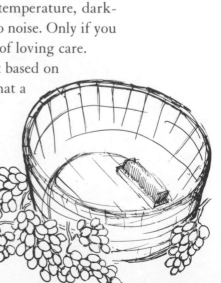

I should add, however, that most descriptions of wine
making that I have read, for the most part, would suppress
any desire you might ever have to make wine. According to such instructions you have to be a biochemist to make wine—and, believe me, bio-
chemists do not make good wine. I believe that the beginning wine
maker should concern himself less with the chemistry and more with
the simple logic of wine making, the natural process.

When you consider the abuses that commercial wines undergo, it is
no wonder that commercial wine makers are involved with the chemistry. Sulfides, preservatives, and so on are all, alas, necessary to protect
the wines from the treatment they get in overlit stores and overheated,
noisy environments. A pure, unadulterated wine would not last a week
under such conditions. Wines like a cool, constant temperature, dark-
ness, a certain amount of humidity, no movement, no noise. Only if you
produce them yourself can you give them that kind of loving care.

So I offer you instructions that I have worked out based on
the way my father made his wine. I am convinced that a
beginner may follow them and have surprisingly
good results.

Incidentally, the garden will benefit from
spreading the pressed grapes—the lees
which would ordinarily be discarded—
over the soil in the fall.

To Make 50 Gallons of Wine

The equipment: All of the equipment described below can be purchased in a store specializing in wine-making equipment. You'll find
such shops in California and in Little Italys in cities all over the country,
and the equipment can also be purchased through mail order. The
grapes you must get through wholesalers. Ask in the fall in Italian
neighborhoods when the grapes will be on the market.

Grape crusher
Winepress
Two 50-gallon oak barrels with one end removed
   (used barrels will do)
One 50-gallon white-oak or chestnut barrel in good condition
   (I strongly urge you to buy a new one)
Twenty 38-pound crates of wine grapes

The grapes: Needless to say, the sugar content of the grapes (ideally
21 percent to 25 percent sugar) and the proper amount of acid (0.7 to
0.9 per 100 cubic centimeters acidity) will influence what proportions
you use of the combinations of the grapes suggested below. There are
instruments that can measure the sugar and acid content, but a good
wholesaler will know and will tell you. This sugar and acidity count
will produce wine that contains from 11 percent to 13 percent alcohol.
It is the sugar that ensures the proper alcohol content, and it is the acid
that creates a better taste. A wine with low acidity is flat, and the proper
acidity guarantees a longer life. A superior grape will have the ideal
amount of sugar and acid. I use California grapes.

Some suggested grapes for *red wine* are:

10 crates of Cabernet and 10 crates of Merlot
13 crates of Zinfandel and 7 crates of Grenache

Some suggested grapes for *white wine* are:

20 crates of Chenin Blanc
20 crates of Sauvignon Blanc
13 crates of Muscat and 7 crates of Thompson seedless

Red wine, the first stage: Place the grape crusher over one of the empty open 50-gallon barrels. Crush 10 crates of grapes over the barrel, then do the same over the other barrel. There should be about 10 inches of space between the tops of the barrels and the grape mixture, which will include the skins, stems, and juice. This space is needed because as the juice ferments it expands. The unfermented grape juice and crushed solids that you now have are called the must.

Cover the barrels loosely with the ends that were removed or with planks and a piece of burlap. After a day or two the must will begin to ferment, and as it does, the solids will rise above the juice. Push the solids back down into the juice with a forked stick every morning and every evening, and as you do so, pull out and discard some of the larger grape stems. Too many stems— because of the tannin they contain—will give the wine a slight bitterness, although a little tannin adds to the taste of the wine.

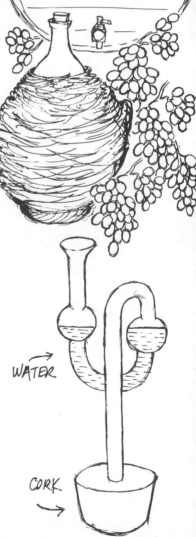

As fermentation becomes more active, the must will rise higher each day. Then after a week or so, the must will start to decline, which means that the fermentation has now reached its peak.

Place the clean barrel with the bunghole about 12 inches off the floor and set it in the coolest part of the cellar. The ideal temperature is about 45° to 50°. I use a former root cellar with a dirt floor as my wine cellar. There the temperature ranges from 38° to 60°, and it seems to be an ideal climate.

Now siphon or drain off the wine from the two full barrels into the empty one with the bunghole. It will not take all the wine and you want to leave room for the solids; press these through your winepress and add them. When the barrel is full, you will have several gallons of wine left over. Be sure to reserve them. Place an air lock (see illustration) in the bunghole to allow the gases to escape as the wine continues to ferment. Air—the mortal enemy of wine—should never enter the barrel. Every week or so, as the barrel absorbs some of the wine in it, add some of the reserved wine to keep it full. This is known as topping off. (More of the reserve will be needed later in the spring when you change the wine.)

WATER →

CORK →

Later, toward winter, when there is no more fermentation activity, put a cork in the bunghole and allow the wine to settle down over the winter.

White wine, the first stage: Crush the grapes over the open barrels the same way as above, only instead of letting the wine ferment, press the solids now and add them, then pour the wine right away into the clean barrel and allow it to ferment there. After the fermentation slows down, place the air lock in the bunghole. Again, you will need about 3 gallons of reserved wine to top off the barrel as it absorbs some of the wine. Again, toward winter, cork the bunghole.

The second stage: For both red and white wine the second stage takes place in the spring. Now you must siphon or drain off the wine into a clean temporary barrel, being careful not to stir up any sediment. The purpose is to remove the wine from the sediment before the weather warms up because then it will start its final fermentation. Do this chore on a calm sunny day when the moon is on the wane. All of the old timers I know who make excellent wine follow this timetable. They maintain that the sediment rises with the moon and with climatic agitation so the wine would not be clear. Last year I changed a barrel of white wine at the wrong time and it *was* cloudy; it never cleared up. Old wives' tale? Perhaps so, but farmers plant according to the phases of the moon, fishermen fish according to the phases of the moon, so why not the wine maker? I have to admit that I believe many things that I do not understand.

After you have removed the wine from the sediment, wash out the barrel and drain it well. Then return the wine to the clean barrel. Top it off with some of your reserved wine and replace the air lock because at this point you will most likely get a second fermentation that will turn the remaining sugar in the wine into alcohol. So be certain that you keep the barrel full.

You should be able to drink the wine, be it red or white, that June. If the red wine, after you have tasted it, seems particularly good, you might consider aging some of it in bottles for several years (see below for bottling instructions). I like my own white wine best drawn from the barrel as I need it. However, you should not draw from the barrel for more than 2 or 3 weeks or you will create an air pocket. At that point bottle the remaining wine right away.

Bottled white wine will last several years. A good red wine will last many years.

The final stage: Now is the time for cleaning up and getting ready for next year's wine making. After you have bottled the wine, do not wash out the barrel. Instead, simply burn a sulfur stick (obtained at a wine supply store) in the barrel by suspending the stick from a wire about 1 foot long. Light the stick, and as soon as it flames, carefully hang it through the bunghole down into the barrel, leaving about 2 inches of wire outside. Seal the bunghole with the cork so that no smoke can escape. The next day remove the wire and charred sulfur stick and tightly cork the barrel. Repeat this process again in 6 months.

When the barrel is ready for new wine the next fall, wash it out. Should the barrel leak, swell the wood by leaving water in it for several days. After that the barrel will be ready for use. Smoking the barrel with a sulfur stick is the best way to prevent mold from forming when the barrel is empty. Mold will kill the wine. A moldy barrel can be used for fermenting the must but should never be used for storing the wine.

Bottling instructions: Soak new corks for several hours. Wash the bottles. I use 1-quart and 2-quart bottles (I do not buy them, I save them). Place the bottles in 300° oven and leave them there for 1 hour. Open the oven door and allow the bottles to cool, then remove them from the oven. Fill the bottles with wine and cork them with a hand corking machine (available in wine equipment stores). Store the corked wine bottles on their sides for future use.

Making Vinegar

About Wine Vinegar

As with wine, there is good vinegar and bad vinegar. It is imperative to have good vinegar in the kitchen. Every Italian wine maker I know makes his own vinegar, and he takes as much pride in making it as he does in making his wine.

Contrary to common belief, vinegar is not spoiled wine. Spoiled wine goes dead; it is tasteless and has a lifeless, muddy color. You don't get vinegar by simply letting leftover wine sit in a bottle. Vinegar is produced when bacteria in wine turns the alcohol to acetic acid.

First, you need to start with a wine that is alive—that is, not a pasteurized wine (usually cheap domestic wines are pasteurized). Your own homemade wine is ideal. Second, you need a starter. The starter is called a mother, and most likely you will have to get it from friends who make their own vinegar. It will look like a slimy skin that first floats on the surface of the vinegar and eventually gets heavier and sinks to the bottom. Sometimes it resembles a piece of soft liver; sometimes it is in layers, like a stack of pancakes. Once it is combined with live wine, it will start turning the wine into vinegar in a matter of days. Never touch the mother or the vinegar with your fingers; the bacteria on your hands can kill it. If the mother dies, the vinegar will become tasteless and turn a muddy color. The vinegar in which olives and pickles are preserved will also cloud up if you stick your fingers in the jar.

Good homemade vinegar, which in my opinion is much better than anything you can buy, has a pungent aroma and is excellent for cooking. The acetic acid cooks out and what remains is a very pleasant taste.

Wine vinegar is not to be confused with the balsamic vinegar made in Northern Italy that has become so popular here in recent years and is now available in finer food stores. Balsamic vinegar is made with the must of unfermented grapes that is boiled down for 4 to 6 hours, depending on the type of grape used, to produce a sweet, overpowering syruplike concentrate. (My grandfather used to boil weak must to make a sweet wine called *vino cotto.*) The concentrate is put into vinegar barrels—in some cases a little vinegar is added to the barrel—and aged, Balsamic vinegar is good for marinating certain foods, but it is often too overpowering for cooking.

White wine vinegar is often used in fish dishes, and as a rule I prefer it to red wine vinegar.

To make vinegar: Put the mother into a 1- to 5-gallon crock and pour some wine over it. You can start with just a cup or two and keep adding more. The wine must have air, so cover with only a loose wooden cover or with several layers of cheesecloth. The vinegar will be ready in 4 to 8 weeks. You will know when it is ready by tasting it. Draw the vinegar off as you need it. You can continue to add more wine, giving each new addition a few weeks before drawing off the vinegar.

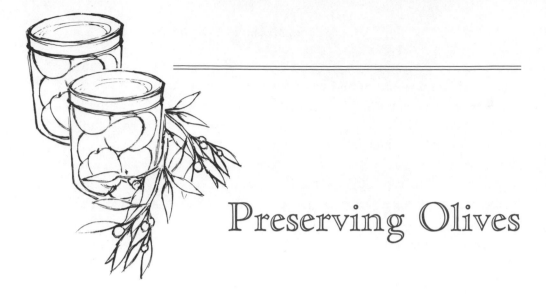

Preserving Olives

Preserved Olives

I got this recipe from a Sicilian butcher, and it's simple because you don't have to brine the olives. Shasta olives are available in the fall in markets, usually in Italian sections. Serve these olives as an appetizer or use them in cooking (see index).

Makes 1 pint.

20 to 22 fresh green shasta
    olives
2 cloves garlic, peeled
½ teaspoon dried oregano
⅓ cup chopped celery, cut into
    ½-inch rounds
⅓ cup chopped carrots, cut
    into 3-inch sections

⅓ cup olive oil
⅓ cup good wine vinegar,
    preferably white, boiled for
    30 seconds
Hot pepper flakes to taste
    (optional)

Scald a 1-pint jar. Put the olives, garlic, oregano, celery, and carrots in the jar so that the olives are tightly packed. Add the olive oil, vinegar, and optional hot pepper flakes and cover the jar loosely so that air can escape. After 2 weeks, tighten the cap. Allow the olives to rest for approximately 4 to 5 weeks until the bitterness is gone. They will keep for 4 to 5 months; after that they lose their crispness, but are still excellent for cooking.

Index

A NOTE ABOUT THE AUTHOR

Edward Giobbi was born in Waterbury, Connecticut, of Italian immigrant parents. A well-known artist, he has always been interested in good food and is recognized by Craig Claiborne and others in the food community as one of the most talented cooks around today. His first cookbook, *Italian Family Cooking,* was published in 1971, and his second, *Eat Right, Eat Well—The Italian Way,* was published in 1985. He and his wife live in Katonah, New York.

A NOTE ON THE TYPE

This book was set in Granjon, a type named in compliment to Robert Granjon, but neither a copy of a classic face nor an entirely original creation. George W. Jones based his designs for this type on that used by Claude Garamond (1510–61) in his beautiful French books, and Granjon more closely resembles Garamond's own type than does any of the various modern types that bear his name.

Composed by Dix Type Inc., Syracuse, New York

Printed and bound by Courier Book Companies, Westford, Massachusetts

Designed by Mia Vander Els